ISRAELITE PROPHECY AND
THE DEUTERONOMISTIC HISTORY

Society of Biblical Literature

Ancient Israel and Its Literature

Thomas C. Römer, General Editor

Editorial Board

Suzanne Boorer
Marc Brettler
Victor H. Matthews
Benjamin D. Sommer
Gale Yee

Number 14

ISRAELITE PROPHECY AND THE DEUTERONOMISTIC HISTORY

PORTRAIT, REALITY, AND THE FORMATION OF A HISTORY

Edited by

Mignon R. Jacobs and Raymond F. Person Jr.

Society of Biblical Literature
Atlanta

Copyright © 2013 by the Society of Biblical Literature

All rights reserved. No part of this work may be reproduced or transmitted in any form or by any means, electronic or mechanical, including photocopying and recording, or by means of any information storage or retrieval system, except as may be expressly permitted by the 1976 Copyright Act or in writing from the publisher. Requests for permission should be addressed in writing to the Rights and Permissions Office, Society of Biblical Literature, 825 Houston Mill Road, Atlanta, GA 30329 USA.

Library of Congress Cataloging-in-Publication Data

Israelite prophecy and the Deuteronomistic history : portrait, reality, and the formation of a history / edited by Mignon R. Jacobs and Raymond F. Person, Jr..
   p. cm. — (Society of Biblical Literature ancient Israel and its literature ; number 14)
   Includes bibliographical references and index.
   ISBN 978-1-58983-749-2 (paper binding : alk. paper) — ISBN 978-1-58983-750-8 (electronic format) — ISBN 978-1-58983-885-7 (hardcover binding : alk. paper)
   1. Prophecy—Judaism. 2. Bible. Deuteronomy—Criticism, interpretation, etc. I. Jacobs, Mignon R. II. Person, Raymond F., Jr., 1961–.
   BM645.P67I87 2013
   222'.095—dc23   2013030904

Printed on acid-free, recycled paper conforming to
ANSI/NISO Z39.48-1992 (R1997) and ISO 9706:1994
standards for paper permanence.

Contents

Abbreviations vii

Introduction
    Mignon R. Jacobs and Raymond F. Person Jr. 1

Reflections of Ancient Israelite Divination in the Former Prophets
    Rannfrid Thelle 7

Prophets and Priests in the Deuteronomistic History: Elijah
and Elisha
    Marvin A. Sweeney 35

Court Prophets during the Monarchy and Literary Prophets in
the So-Called Deuteronomistic History
    Diana Edelman 51

Prophetic Memories in the Deuteronomistic Historical and the
Prophetic Collections of Books
    Ehud Ben Zvi 75

Prophets and Prophecy in Joshua–Kings: A Near Eastern
Perspective
    Martti Nissinen 103

Moses, Israel's First Prophet, and the Formation of the
Deuteronomistic and Prophetic Libraries
    Thomas C. Römer 129

Samuel: A Prophet Like Moses or a Priest Like Moses?
    Mark Leuchter 147

Prophetic Stories Making a Story of Prophecy
   Mark O'Brien 169

Prophets in the Deuteronomic History and the Book of Chronicles:
   A Reassessment
   Raymond F. Person Jr. 187

Bibliography 201
Contributors 225
Scripture Index 227
Author Index 238

Abbreviations

AB	Anchor Bible
ANET	Ancient Near Eastern Texts Relating to the Old Testament. Edited by James B. Pritchard. 3rd ed. Princeton: Princeton University Press, 1969.
AOAT	Alter Orient und Altes Testament
ARM	Archives royales de Mari
ATANT	Abhandlungen zur Theologie des Alten und Neuen Testaments
AusBR	Australian Biblical Review
BASOR	Bulletin of the American Schools of Oriental Research
BBB	Bonner biblische Beiträge
BBET	Beiträge zur biblischen Exegese und Theologie
BEATAJ	Beiträge zur Erforschung des Alten Testaments und des antiken Judentum
BETL	Bibliotheca ephemeridum theologicarum lovaniensium
BEvT	Beiträge zur evangelischen Theologie
Bib	Biblica
BJS	Brown Judaic Studies
BLS	Bible and Literature Series
BWANT	Beiträge zur Wissenschaft vom Alten und Neuen Testament
BZABR	Beihefte zur Zeitschrift für Altorientalische und Biblische Rechtsgeschichte
BZAW	Beihefte zur Zeitschrift für die alttestamentliche Wissenschaft
Cahiers de l'IPOA	Cahiers de l'Institut du Proche-Orient Ancien du College de France
CBET	Contributions to Biblical Exegesis and Theology
CBQMS	Catholic Biblical Quarterly Monograph Series

CHANE	Culture and History of the Ancient Near East
CSJCA	Center for the Study of Judaism and Christianity in Antiquity
EABS	European Seminar in Historical Methodology
FAT	Forschungen zum Alten Testament
FGrH	Felix Jacoby, *Die fragmente der griechischen historiker*. 3 vols. in 14. Berlin: Weidmann, 1923–1958.
FOTL	Forms of the Old Testament Literature
FRLANT	Forschungen zur Religion und Literatur des Alten und Neuen Testaments
HCOT	Historical Commentary on the Old Testament
HKAT	Handkommentar zum Alten Testament
HSM	Harvard Semitic Monographs
HTKAT	Herders theologischer Kommentar zum Alten Testament
HUCA	*Hebrew Union College Annual*
Int	*Interpretation*
IRT	Issues in Religion and Theology
JBL	*Journal of Biblical Literature*
JR	*Journal of Religion*
JSOT	*Journal for the Study of the Old Testament*
JSOTSup	Journal for the Study of the Old Testament Supplement Series
KHC	Kurzer Hand-Commentar zum Alten Testament
LHBOTS	Library of Hebrew Bible/Old Testament Studies
NABU	Nouvelles assyriologiques breves et utilitaires
NCBC	New Century Biblical Commentary
NovTSup	Novum Testamentum Supplements
OBO	Orbis biblicus et orientalis
OIS	Oriental Institute Seminars
OTE	*Old Testament Essays*
OTL	Old Testament Library
OTM	Oxford Theological Monographs
OTS	Old Testament Studies
PFES	Publications of the Finnish Exegetical Society
PHSC	Perspectives on Hebrew Scriptures and Its Contexts
POS	Pretoria Oriental Series
RB	*Revue biblique*
RevQ	*Revue de Qumran*

SAA	State Archives of Assyria
SBLAIL	Society of Biblical Literature Ancient Israelite Literature
SBLANEM	Society of Biblical Literature Ancient Near East Monographs
SBLMS	Society of Biblical Literature Monograph Series
SBLSBL	Society of Biblical Literature Studies in Biblical Literature
SBLSCS	Society of Biblical Literature Septuagint and Cognate Studies
SBLSP	Society of Biblical Literature Seminar Papers
SBLSymS	Society of Biblical Literature Symposium Series
SBLWAW	Society of Biblical Literature Writings from the Ancient World
SDSRL	Studies in the Dead Sea Scrolls and Related Literature
SEÅ	Svensk Exegetisk Årsbok
SFEG	Schriften der Finnischen Exegetischen Gesellschaft
SHCANE	Studies in the History and Culture of the Ancient Near East
SJOT	*Scandinavian Journal of the Old Testament*
TB	Theologische Bücherei: Neudrucke und Berichte aus dem 20. Jahrhundert
TDOT	*Theological Dictionary of the Old Testament.* Edited by G. J. Botterweck and H. Ringgren. Translated by J. T. Willis, G. W. Bromiley, and D. E. Green. 17 vols. Grand Rapids: Eerdmans, 1974–
THAT	*Theologisches Handwörterbuch zum Alten Testament.* Edited by Ernst Jenni, with assistance from Claus Westermann. 2 vols. Stuttgart: Theologischer Verlag, 1971–1976
USQR	*Union Seminary Quarterly Review*
UTB	Uni-Taschenbücher
VT	*Vetus Testamentum*
VTSup	Supplements to Vetus Testamentum
WMANT	Wissenschaftliche Monographien zum Alten und Neuen Testament
WUNT	Wissenschaftliche Untersuchungen zum Neuen Testament
ZAW	*Zeitschrift für die alttestamentliche Wissenschaft*

ZTK   *Zeitschrift für Theologie und Kirche*

Introduction

Mignon R. Jacobs and Raymond F. Person Jr.

At the 2010 Annual Meeting of the Society of Biblical Literature, the Deuteronomistic History section and the Israelite Prophetic Literature section held a joint session devoted to the exploration of the Deuteronomistic History as prophetic literature. The steering committees of these two sections understood that the changing discussions concerning prophecy and concerning the Deuteronomistic History required our coming together to explore the areas of common interest, and invited four distinguished scholars with different backgrounds and approaches to give substantive papers on the topic. Revisions of these four papers—the chapters by Marvin Sweeney, Diana Edelman, Ehud Ben Zvi, and Thomas Römer—are included in this volume, as well as other essays solicited by the editors. Together these essays provide a wide and varied survey of current scholarship on prophecy as a phenomenon behind the literature and the literary portrayal of prophecy in Deuteronomy–Kings.

Earlier scholarship on prophecy drew sharp lines between various cultic functionaries (for example, priest versus prophet) and focused on the Latter Prophets, thereby often ignoring the Former Prophets, or Deuteronomistic History.[1] Although they too showed evidence of redactional histories, the Latter Prophets were understood to be closer to prophetic speech, since they consisted primarily of prophetic oracles, in contrast to the prophetic narratives in the Former Prophets. However, the privileged position of the Latter Prophets as more reliable for historical research has now been undermined by its sharp contrast with the portrayal of prophecy in other ancient Near Eastern literature.[2] The prophetic books

---

1. For a lengthier review of this literature, see the contribution below by Rannfrid I. Thelle, 7–33.
2. See the essays in Martti Nissinen, ed., *Prophecy in Its Ancient Near Eastern*

of the Hebrew Bible are unique in comparison to other contemporary prophetic literatures, because of their long complex redactional histories and their generic variance. That is, most references to prophetic activity in ancient Near Eastern sources occur in nonprophetic genres which did not undergo further copying or revision (such as the Mari letters). In those few instances in which they were incorporated into another genre (as in the Neo-Assyrian collections), even these genres did not continue to be copied and preserved for new situations in later generations. Thus, the prophetic literature of the Hebrew Bible remains unique generically in relation to other ancient Near Eastern literature on divination. This uniqueness raises questions concerning its utility for historical reconstruction relative to these other genres. Together, these trends undermine the validity of using both the Deuteronomistic History and the Latter Prophets for a reconstruction of the historical phenomenon of prophecy in ancient Israel and Judah. Nevertheless, these remain our only sources for ancient Israelite and Judean prophecy. Therefore, even though biblical prophetic literature brings with it even more difficulties for such historical reconstruction than other ancient literature, scholars interested in prophecy in ancient Israel nevertheless must find ways to approach this literature for historical research.

Although Martin Noth's hypothesis of the Deuteronomistic History continues to have a tremendous influence on the study of Deuteronomy and the Former Prophets, the notion of a "Deuteronomistic History" has itself come under attack more recently.[3] Noth's notion of a single Deuteronomistic redaction was quickly challenged by scholars postulating additional redactions, but even the American consensus of two redactions

---

Context: Mesopotamian, Biblical, Arabian Perspectives (SBLSymS 13; Atlanta: Society of Biblical Literature, 2000). See also Martti Nissinen, "Spoken, Written, Quoted, and Invented: Orality and Writtenness in Ancient Near Eastern Prophecy," in *Writings and Speech in Israelite and Ancient Near Eastern Prophecy* (ed. Ehud Ben Zvi and Michael H. Floyd; SBLSymS 10; Atlanta: Society of Biblical Literature, 2000), 235–71; and Martti Nissinen, "How Prophecy Became Literature," *SJOT* 19 (2005): 153–72.

3. For recent reviews of scholarship on the Deuteronomistic History, see Albert de Pury, Thomas Römer, and Jean-Daniel Macchi, eds., *Israel Constructs Its History: Deuteronomistic Historiography in Recent Research* (JSOTSup 306; Sheffield: Sheffield Academic Press, 2000); Thomas Römer, *The So-Called Deuteronomistic History: A Sociological, Historical, and Literary Introduction* (London: T&T Clark, 2005); and Raymond F. Person Jr., *The Deuteronomic School: History, Social Setting, and Literature* (SBLSBL 2; Atlanta: Society of Biblical Literature, 2002).

and the European consensus of three redactions have come under serious challenge, so that it is unclear what the scholarly consensus concerning the Deuteronomistic History is. Increasingly, scholars are emphasizing the diversity within the Deuteronomistic History, especially in the differences among the individual books. Furthermore, the redaction history of the Deuteronomistic History is being pushed beyond the earlier assumptions of an exilic setting into the Persian period. Despite this growing diversity of approaches to its redactional history, the vast majority of scholars assume that this literature underwent multiple redactions in different historical periods. However, there remains little consensus on which literary passages should be assigned to what historical periods. Nevertheless, no matter which particular redactional model one accepts, such a complex redactional history suggests a significant span of time between the earlier sources in which the portrayal of the various prophetic figures occurs and the latter redactional stages, undermining the possible value of the prophetic material in the Deuteronomistic History for historical reconstruction.

This collection of essays concerns the relationship of prophecy to the Deuteronomistic History, including the historical reality of prophecy behind the literature and the portrayal of prophecy in the literature (often with the assumption that it probably does not accurately reflect the historical reality of prophecy behind the Deuteronomistic History). Although not all of the essays are concerned with reconstructing the historical reality of prophecy, all of the contributors start with the assumption that the portrayal of prophecy in the literature reflects the ideology of the Deuteronomists, so that any historical reconstruction must draw from the careful comparison of this portrayal with other literature—for example, Pentateuchal traditions, pre-Deuteronomistic sources, and other ancient Near Eastern literature. Thus, it is not surprising that those contributors interested in reconstructing the historical reality of ancient Israelite prophecy find greater diversity of intermediaries, as is found in other ancient Near Eastern cultures. For example, Rannfried Thelle, Diana Edelman, and Martti Nissinen emphasize a broader range of specialists in divination in ancient Israel similar to that found in Mari and Nineveh. Marvin Sweeney identifies differences between Israelite and Judean prophets and their roles as cultic functionaries, both of which fit well into the larger cultural context and the ancient Near East. Furthermore, some of the contributors emphasize that for ideological reasons the portrayal of prophecy and some of the characters in the Deuteronomistic History strongly privileges one function over another or one group of cultic specialists over another. For example, Diana Edelman suggests that כהן (*kōhēn*) may best be translated "diviner" or "oracle-giver" rather than "priest," and Thomas Römer and Mark Leuchter argue that Moses and Samuel, respectively, are redefined by the Deuteronomists as being more prophetic than the earlier sources and redactions show them to be.

Despite the general agreement among all of the contributors that intermediation in ancient Israel was more varied than Deuteronomistic literature portrays, we must not overlook the fact that the portrayal of prophecy in the Deuteronomistic History nevertheless remains within the purview of its large cultural context. Therefore, three contributors examine the complementary relationship of the Deuteronomistic History with other literary portrayals of prophecy. Ehud Ben Zvi compares the Deuteronomistic History with the Latter Prophets; Martti Nissinen with literature from Mari and Assyria; and Raymond Person with the book of Chronicles. Although differences may occur between the portrayal of prophecy in the Deuteronomistic History and in these other works, we must be careful not to privilege one perspective over the other as we strive to reconstruct the historical phenomenon of prophecy behind the literature.

In "Reflections of Ancient Israelite Divination in the Former Prophets," Rannfrid Thelle provides an excellent survey of the secondary literature concerning the use of the Deuteronomistic History for understanding the phenomenon and history of prophecy in ancient Israel, and concludes on the basis of her reading of the primary sources that Israelite prophets were the religious experts to whom kings and royal officials turned for divine consultation. Thus, in contrast to older understandings that often distinguished divine inquiry from proclamation, Thelle argues that we should view the variety of perspectives on divination within the Former Prophets and between the Former Prophets and the Latter Prophets "as reflections of a larger phenomenon of divination."[4]

In "Prophets and Priests in the Deuteronomistic History: Elijah and Elisha," Marvin Sweeney focuses on northern prophetic figures and the ways they are contrasted with southern prophetic figures, especially in relation to priestly functions. He concludes that in the northern kingdom prophets functioned more as priestly figures than their southern counter-

---

4. Thelle, p. 24.

parts did, and that this distinction has important consequences for understanding the religious differences between Israel and Judah.

In "Court Prophets during the Monarchy and Literary Prophets in the So-Called Deuteronomistic History," Diana Edelman argues that the ecstatic prophet was simply one of many and various practitioners of divination available to the royal courts in ancient Israel, but the Deuteronomists favored the ecstatic prophets over the others in their portrayals of the kings' always having access to divine consultation.

In "Prophetic Memories in the Deuteronomistic Historical and the Prophetic Collections of Books," Ehud Ben Zvi examines the understanding of prophecy by the literati of Persian Yehud in the Deuteronomistic History and the Latter Prophets. He concludes that both collections of prophetic literature "balanced and informed each other" within the "*Sitz im Diskurs* in which they were read."[5]

In "Prophets and Prophecy in Joshua–Kings: A Near Eastern Perspective," Martti Nissinen argues that, despite some differences, the portrayal of prophets in Joshua–Kings compares favorably with what we know of prophecy in Mari and Assyria, concluding that "the socioreligious foundation of prophecy in Joshua–Kings consists of the institutions of divination, kingship, and worship."[6]

In "Moses, Israel's First Prophet, and the Formation of the Deuteronomistic and Prophetic Libraries," Thomas Römer examines the relationship between Deut 18:15-20 and other pentateuchal sources, on the one hand, and other deuteronomistic books (especially Kings and Jeremiah), on the other hand. He concludes that Moses as Israel's first prophet was a deuteronomistic construction in Deuteronomy that influenced the portrayal of deuteronomistic prophets in Kings and Jeremiah. This central image of prophecy was transformed when Deuteronomy became a book in the Torah, and when the Elisha and Elijah narratives were inserted in Kings.

In "Samuel: A Prophet Like Moses or a Priest Like Moses?" Mark Leuchter reconstructs the portrayal of Samuel as a pivotal figure in Israel's history paralleling Moses in pre-Deuteronomistic sources and in the Deuteronomistic redactional material. He argues that the Deuteronomists transformed the more priestly Samuel of their sources into a more prophetic Samuel in their reworking of the tradition.

---

5. Ben Zvi, "Prophetic Memories in the Deuteronomistic Historical and the Prophetic Collections of Books," p. 102.

6. Nissinen, p. 127.

In "Prophetic Stories Making a Story of Prophecy," Mark O'Brien uses the stories from the books of Samuel and Kings to discuss the ways in which the ancient authors reused literary resources. Defining "story" as having two senses—characters and their interaction, and author/redactor—he proposes that both senses may be found in the story of prophecy in Samuel and Kings, as is evident in the recurrent prophecy-fulfillment schema. O'Brien notes that many of the stories in the Deuteronomistic History depicted the encounter between prophets and kings and became integral to the story of the monarchy. The essay therefore looks at two central aspects of the prophetic stories: (1) the creativity in the composition and use of prophetic stories and (2) the limitations of prophetic stories leading to another stage in the story of prophecy.

In "Prophets in the Deuteronomic History and the Book of Chronicles: A Reassessment," Raymond Person argues against the consensus model that suggests that the portrayal of prophecy in the Deuteronom(ist)ic History represents an exilic understanding of prophecy that differs significantly from that of the book of Chronicles, which represents the postexilic understanding. Rather both portrayals can be understood as similar, faithful representations of the ideology of prophecy within the broader tradition among the ancient Israelite elite of the Persian period.

Together these essays strongly suggest that the ancient Israelite prophets were not isolated charismatic individuals, but intermediaries who functioned within larger cultic settings. However, the contributors generally agree that within the portrayal of prophecy in the Deuternomistic History, the Deuteronomists strove to limit which intermediaries were considered authoritative and to delineate more carefully the prophetic role from those of other cultic figures. Thus, this collection of essays contributes to the ongoing discussion concerning the tension between the historical reality of prophecy behind the Deuteronomistic History and prophetic literature in general, as well as the ideological portrayal of prophecy in biblical literature, especially in the Deuteronomistic History.[7]

---

7. Two recent collections of essays reach similar conclusions: Lester L. Grabbe and Martti Nissinen, eds., *Constructs of Prophecy in the Former and Latter Prophets and Other Texts* (SBLANEM 4; Atlanta: Society of Biblical Literature, 2011); Mark J. Boda and Lissa M. Wray Beal, eds., *Prophets, Prophecy, and Ancient Israelite Historiography* (Winona Lake, Ind.: Eisenbrauns, 2013). Unfortunately, the timing of the publication of these volumes meant that the contributors to this volume did not have access to these collections.

Reflections of Ancient Israelite Divination in the Former Prophets

Rannfrid Thelle

The words and acts of figures called prophets are described both in passing and in some detail in Joshua–2 Kings. Even after a very superficial glance at some of the narratives of the Former Prophets,[1] one might be forgiven for thinking that texts that speak of prophetic figures should provide a rich source of knowledge about ancient Israelite prophecy. The debates of the last several decades show, however, that the situation is not that simple. Descriptions and systematic presentations of prophets and prophecy in the literature of the Former Prophets are numerous. Yet, as the history of research on prophets amply illustrates, we face serious challenges both from the nature of the texts and the history of reading practices.

The Study of Ancient Israelite Prophecy

The time may be long past when scholars—usually Protestant Christians—who wrote about ancient Israelite prophecy began with Amos as the first "true" prophet and continued with each of the great writing prophets.[2]

---

1. I prefer the term "Former Prophets" to designate Joshua, Judges, 1–2 Samuel, and 1–2 Kings, because of the ideological nature of the term "Deuteronomistic History." Although "Former Prophets" also indicates a specific tradition—the Jewish canonical tradition—I feel that it is the most appropriate term for designating these books collectively. When I do on occasion use the term "Deuteronomistic History" (DH) for the sake of familiarity, I am using it to designate the books Joshua–Kings as a collection without implying anything about authorship or redaction. I avoid the term "Historical Books," because it implicates the books of Ruth, Chronicles, Ezra and Nehemiah.

2. Considered by past scholarly consensus as the true substance of ancient Israelite prophecy, the "classical prophets" were accorded enormous significance: as reform-

However, even though the prophets of classical historical-critical scholarship are no longer hegemonic, they still cast their guiding light—or murky shadows—on approaches taken, and also on many "givens" in present scholarship. The privileging of the "classical prophets" resulted in an overemphasis on the Prophetic Books[3] as a source for the study of Israelite prophecy, and a corresponding disregard for the material from the Former Prophets. The "pre-prophetic prophets"[4] were seen simply as a stage in the development of prophecy toward its peak, and were often termed "primitive," "pre-literate" or just "early" prophets.[5] Even material that was clearly

---

ers of Israelite religion, as harbingers of a new ethical revelation, as forerunners of Christ, and even as instigators of world history. From Bernhard Duhm's *Die Theologie der Propheten als Grundlage für die innere Entwicklungsgeschichte der israelitischen Religion* (Bonn: Adolph Marcus, 1875), and for the next one hundred years, the role of the "classical" prophets in the history and religion of Israel was seen as crucial. Duhm considered the Assyrian Empire and the Israelite prophets of the eighth century B.C.E. to be the two "movements" responsible for the initiation of *Weltgeschichte* (see *Israels Propheten* [Tübingen: Mohr Siebeck, 1916], 1–3). This type of analysis can be found repeated all the way to 1976, when Siegfried Herrmann refers to the Israelite prophetic movement as a decisive event in world history (*Ursprung und Funktion der Prophetie im alten Israel* [Rheinische-Westfälische Akademie der Wissenschaften 208; Opladen: Westdeutscher, 1976], 1–2). Wellhausen's work on the religion of Israel had a significant influence on this privileged view of prophecy, which has been well documented; see, e.g., Peter H. A. Neumann, ed., *Das Prophetenverständnis in der deutschsprachigen Forschung seit Heinrich Ewald* (Wege der Forschung 307; Darmstadt: Wissenschaftliche Buchgesellschaft, 1979); and John W. Rogerson, *Old Testament Criticism in the Nineteenth Century: England and Germany* (London: SPCK, 1984), 268; and, most recently, the useful essay by Martin J. Buss, "The Place of Israelite Prophecy in Human History," in *Israel's Prophets and Israel's Past: Essays on the Relationship of Prophetic Texts and Israelite History in Honor of John H. Hayes* (ed. Brad E. Kelle and Megan Bishop Moore; LHBOTS 446; New York: T&T Clark, 2006), 325–41.

3. I use the term "Prophetic Books" to designate the fifteen books that are named after prophets and alternate with the label "Latter Prophets."

4. This term was used by Rudolph Kittel in *Das Volk in Kanaan: Geschichte der Zeit bis zum babylonischen Exil* (vol. 2 of *Geschichte des Volkes Israel*; 6th ed.; Gotha: Friedrich Andreas Perthes, 1925), 317.

5. Joseph Blenkinsopp (*A History of Prophecy in Israel* [rev. ed.; Louisville: Westminster John Knox, 1996], 2–3, 23, 73) criticizes how this division and tradition of seeing Amos as the first of the "classical" prophets has led to a tendency not to see continuity with the past. Nevertheless, he still uses the same layout in his history. Blenkinsopp sees the international, historical situation of the expanding Neo-Assyrian Empire as the explanation for a new type of literary form—the prophetic book—in which the prophet speaks to the whole nation. This is, in part, what has led scholars to

understood as depicting prophecy was often not incorporated into comprehensive presentations of prophecy.[6]

In spite of major challenges, the emphasis on the classical, writing prophets in biblical scholarship cannot be underestimated. This legacy can be felt as an obstacle to a fair assessment of the material on prophecy in the books of the Former Prophets. Specifically, the privileging of the "classical" prophets brings with it an understanding of prophecy exclusively as unsolicited, divinely inspired speech, spoken by free spirits without institutional connections.[7] This understanding isolates what should be seen as one *type* of prophetic activity from the larger context to which it belongs.

While the biblical writers' own agendas of polemicizing against particular modes of divination and prohibiting certain types of divinatory activity contributed to this way of viewing prophecy, its roots were in nineteenth-century historicism and idealism and the Protestant privileging of the "Word" over what was thought of as "empty" ritual. Claus Westermann's classic *Grundformen der prophetischen Rede* represents the epitome of this view of prophecy.[8]

Admittedly, I might be in danger of overstating and caricaturing this heritage of biblical scholarship. The debate has certainly moved on. From the late 1980s onward, a number of major studies of prophecy have applied a much broader approach, highlighting the social setting of prophecy[9] and

---

see a complete break with Amos, according to Blenkinsopp (73). In the last decade or so, the historical situation that is applied in order to understand the genre of the prophetic book has shifted to the Persian period. See, e.g., Ehud Ben Zvi, "The Prophetic Book: A Key Form of Prophetic Literature," in *The Changing Face of Form Criticism for the Twenty-First Century* (ed. Marvin A. Sweeney and Ehud Ben Zvi; Grand Rapids: Eerdmans, 2003), 276–97.

6. For example, in Gillis Gerleman and Eberhard Ruprecht, "דרש, *drš*, fragen nach," in *THAT* 1:460–67, a whole range of texts is listed in which this verb is used in a situation of prophets inquiring of YHWH. However, this significant information is hardly ever discussed as a unified phenomenon in general presentations of prophecy. Claus Westermann ("Die Begriffe für Fragen und Suchen im Alten Testament," *Kerygma und Dogma* [1960]: 2–30, here 21) provides one example of how these texts are marginalized or disregarded in comprehensive descriptions of prophecy.

7. On the influence of the endeavor to define and describe a prophetic "office," see William McKane, "Prophet and Institution," *ZAW* 94 (1982): 251–66.

8. Claus Westermann, *Grundformen der prophetischer Rede* (4th ed.; BEvT 31; Munich: Chr. Kaiser, 1971).

9. Robert R. Wilson, *Prophecy and Society in Ancient Israel* (Philadelphia: Fortress, 1980); David L. Petersen, *The Roles of Israel's Prophets* (JSOTSup 17; Sheffield:

its divinatory function within the broader ancient Near Eastern practice.[10] At the same time, the "great" prophets came under serious challenge as historical figures.[11] From representing the geniuses of ancient Israelite religious development, the prophets have been rendered inaccessible as figures in space and time. Through these challenges, the prophets have become recognized as characters in a text, literary figures that represent the imaginations of the writers of the texts.

Perhaps the most recent approach to gain acceptance is the response to the challenge of the "writtenness" of the biblical texts.[12] Since what is

---

JSOT, 1981); Thomas W. Overholt, *Channels of Prophecy: The Social Dynamics of Prophetic Activity* (Minneapolis: Fortress, 1989); Lester L. Grabbe, *Priests, Prophets, Diviners, Sages: A Socio-historical Study of Religious Specialists in Ancient Israel* (Valley Forge, Pa.: Trinity Press International, 1995).

10. E.g., William L. Moran, "New Evidence from Mari on the History of Prophecy," *Bib* 50 (1969): 15–56; Eduard Noort, *Untersuchungen zum Gottesbescheid in Mari: Die "Mari-prophetie" in der alttestamentlichen Forschung* (AOAT 202; Kevelaer: Butzon & Bercker, 1977); Abraham Malamat, *Mari and the Bible* (SHCANE 12; Leiden: Brill, 1998); Frederick H. Cryer, *Divination in Ancient Israel and Its Near Eastern Environment: A Socio-historical Investigation* (JSOTSup 142; Sheffield: Sheffield Academic Press, 1994); Ann Jeffers, *Magic and Divination in Ancient Palestine and Syria* (SHCANE 8; Leiden: Brill, 1996); Martti Nissinen, "Die Relevanz der neuassyrischen Prophetie für die alttestamentliche Forschung," in *Mesopotamica-Ugaritica-Biblica* (ed. M. Dietrich and O. Loretz; AOAT 232; Kevelaer: Butzon & Bercker, 1993), 217–58; Hans M. Barstad, "*Comparere necesse est?* Ancient Israelite and Ancient Near Eastern Prophecy in a Comparative Perspective," in *Prophecy in Its Ancient Near Eastern Context: Mesopotamian, Biblical, Arabian Perspectives* (ed. Martti Nissinen; SBLSymS 13; Atlanta: Society of Biblical Literature, 2000), 3–11, and other essays in that volume. A great source book for comparative study has also been made available with the publication of Martti Nissinen (with contributions by Choon-Leong Seow and Robert K. Ritner), *Prophets and Prophecy in the Ancient Near East* (SBLWAW 12; Atlanta: Society of Biblical Literature, 2003).

11. James M. Ward, "The Eclipse of the Prophet in Contemporary Prophetic Studies," *USQR* 42 (1988): 97–104. The most significant literature and the debate are summarized nicely in Martti Nissinen's "The Historical Dilemma of Biblical Prophetic Studies," in *Prophecy in the Book of Jeremiah* (ed. Hans M. Barstad and Reinhard G. Kratz; BZAW 388; Berlin: de Gruyter, 2009), 103–20. Nissinen focuses on the Prophetic Books and discusses the difficult but unavoidable questions involved when using the biblical prophetic books in order to reconstruct ancient Israelite prophecy; see esp. pp. 106–8 for an up-to-date perspective and relevant literature.

12. Ehud Ben Zvi and Michael H. Floyd, eds., *Writings and Speech in Israelite and Ancient Near Eastern Prophecy* (SBLSymS 10; Atlanta: Society of Biblical Literature, 2000); Ben Zvi, "Prophetic Book."

reflected in the biblical texts is *literary prophecy*, it may in its present form have little to do with prophecy as a social, historical phenomenon. Instead, texts recording prophetic oracles come to constitute a body of literature that can be interpreted, reinterpreted, and also rewritten to generate new literature. In a recent essay, Martti Nissinen argues that in being a written phenomenon, biblical prophecy in the Prophetic Books actually comes closer to being an object of divination rather than representing prophecy as a social, historical phenomenon. According to this approach, the Prophetic Books function as a body or corpus of signs for future interpretation, in ways similar to Mesopotamian collections of omens.[13]

The Former Prophets as Written Text

If we accept that the Latter Prophets can be thus viewed as a body of divinatory signs for interpretation and the creation of "new" prophecy by virtue of constituting a written, scribal phenomenon, we may ask about the nature of the Former Prophets. How may we view the status and character of the stories about prophets in the Deuteronomistic History as written text?

The books of the Former Prophets cannot so obviously be characterized as "literary prophecy" as the collections of oracles in the Latter Prophets, and are harder to characterize or categorize on the whole. We are dealing with a very composite type of literature, which incorporates numerous genres, with many sections not about prophets. One of the books of the collection, Joshua, does not even mention prophets.[14] The books of the

---

13. Martti Nissinen, "Prophecy and Omen Divination: Two Sides of the Same Coin," in *Divination and Interpretation of Signs in the Ancient World* (ed. Amar Annus; OIS 6; Chicago: The Oriental Institute of the University of Chicago, 2010), 341–51; idem, "Pesharim as Divination: Qumran Exegesis, Omen Interpretation, and Literary Prophecy," in *Prophecy after the Prophets? The Contribution of the Dead Sea Scrolls to the Understanding of Biblical and Extra-biblical Prophecy* (ed. Kristin De Troyer and Armin Lange with the assistance of Lucas L. Schulte; CBET 52; Leuven: Peeters, 2009), 43–60.

14. There is a reference to Moses as a איש האלהים in Josh 14:6, but this reference is likely a synonym for the designation commonly used of Moses in the DH, "servant of YHWH"—עבד יהוה. This is discussed in Hans M. Barstad, "Some Remarks on Prophets and Prophecy in the 'Deuteronomistic History,'" in *Houses Full of All Good Things: Essays in Memory of Timo Veijola* (ed. Juha Pakkala and Martti Nissinen; PFES 95; Helsinki, 2008), 300–315.

so-called Deuteronomistic History have been characterized as history or as "history-like"; the Jewish canonical tradition has included them under the rubric of *nevi'im*.[15] Some scholars have determined that the Deuteronomistic History is designed on a scheme of prophecy and fulfillment.[16] Stories about prophets are significant and may perhaps have contributed to the shaping of specific literary patterns in the prophetic narratives.[17] The narratives concerning prophets have often been considered individually, or have in other ways been separated from the overall narrative context.[18]

To throw in another complication, one could further ask: If the "classical prophets" have faded from view as individual historical figures, what might have happened to the prophets of the narratives in the Deuteronomistic History? The same theoretical problems that affect the Latter Prophets regarding the connection between the literature and "historical reality" apply to the Former Prophets also. However, these prophets do not have the same legacy of privilege as the "classical prophets." Further, as literary collections the Former and Latter Prophets are quite different,

---

15. This reflects the Jewish tradition of ascribing authorship of these books to "prophets," thereby giving the books authority: Joshua wrote Joshua, Samuel wrote Judges and Samuel, and Jeremiah wrote Kings.

16. Argued by, e.g., Gerhard von Rad, *Studies in Deuteronomy* (London: SCM, 1953), 78–82; and most often implemented by proponents of the DH hypothesis in its various forms, e.g., Richard D. Nelson, *The Double Redaction of the Deuteronomistic History* (Sheffield: JSOT, 1991), 13; Mark O'Brien, *The Deuteronomistic History Hypothesis: A Reassessment* (Freiburg: Universitätsverlag, 1989), 12, 17, 225.

17. In three short articles, Burke O. Long suggested that specific literary patterns derived from prophetic genres had shaped many narratives involving prophets in the "historical" books. See his "Two Question and Answer Schemata in the Prophets," *JBL* 90 (1971): 129–39; "2 Kings III and Genres of Prophetic Narrative," *VT* 23 (1973): 337–48; and "The Effect of Divination upon Israelite Literature," *JBL* 92 (1973): 489–97.

18. Alexander Rofé, for example, attempted to classify the "prophetic stories," and developed descriptions of various categories in his *The Prophetical Stories: The Narratives about the Prophets in the Hebrew Bible, their Literary Types and History* (trans. D. Levy et al.; Jerusalem: Magnes, 1988). There are also those who think the prophetic stories are among the latest additions to the DH, and therefore represent perhaps only a late stage in the history of composition. These include, for example, John Van Seters, *In Search of History: Historiography in the Ancient World and the Origins of Biblical History* (New Haven: Yale University Press, 1983); Stephen L. McKenzie, *The Trouble with Kings: The Composition of the Books of Kings in the Deuteronomistic History* (VTSup 42; Leiden: Brill, 1991).

though there are overlapping passages (2 Kgs 18–20 and Isa 38–39; 2 Kgs 24–25 and Jer 52).

We might not be able to solve the issue of how to categorize adequately or to understand the Former Prophets as a literary collection, whether we use a diachronic or a synchronic approach. Each individual book is also different from the others in respect to prophets and prophecy. However, the collection does seem to gain its cohesion and rationale from the overarching storyline. It is the story of Israel and its God YHWH, from the time of its conquest of the promised land to its expulsion from that land. As such, it provides an identity-sustaining narrative for those who identify with Israel. However, it is not clear how this narrative complex can compare with the Latter Prophets in providing a written body of revelation for future interpretation in the way suggested above.

What is clear, however, is that figures called prophets appear in this literature and their behavior and words are recorded in various narrative contexts. In addition to the descriptions of the activities of prophets, the Deuteronomistic History also contains descriptions of specific types of divinatory activity in which the religious expert involved is not a prophet, but may be one of several types of figures, such as a king, a priest, the people, or someone else. The same functions performed by these figures are also sometimes performed by prophets.

Moreover, whereas the Prophetic Books often lack information about the character of the prophet—with the exception of Jeremiah and some details about Hosea and Amos—the books of the Former Prophets have narratives about several profiled characters, such as Samuel, Elijah, and Elisha. As a result, these specific, highly individualized characterizations to some extent determine the portrayal of prophecy. A list of some of the prophets in the Deuteronomistic History shows a very wide range of profiles, including the charismatically endowed Deborah, various anonymous figures with the title "man of God," the "Renaissance man" Samuel,[19] the disturbingly ecstatic Saul, the zealous Elijah, the elusive wonderworker Elisha, Ahab and Jezebel's prophets of Baal and alleged prophets of Asherah, court prophets as varied as Gad, Nathan, Zedekiah ben Chenaanah (and the many other prophets with him), Micaiah, and Huldah (who might not be a court prophet, but is consulted by King Josiah), and the one

---

19. Meaning that he wears many hats, not that he has a broadminded creative personality.

prophet who overlaps with the prophetic books, Isaiah.[20] Although each of the characters is intriguing in his or her own right, and though it might go a long way, this variegated material is not enough on which to base a comprehensive picture of prophecy in Israel or its development. It is too sketchy, and deciding what is "typical" and what might simply reflect the eccentricities of specific characters is too difficult.

Divine Inquiry: One Form of Divination Reflected in the Former Prophets

Based on these limitations and challenges, it seems that one way to pursue reflections of prophecy as a social, historical phenomenon in the Former Prophets is by isolating specific situations involving prophets or prophetic functions that are broadly and consistently described. One important prophetic function that is consistently described in the narratives of Samuel–Kings is that of being the religious expert in divine consultation.[21] In situations of distress, such as war, illness, or natural disaster, a prophet is called upon to consult the deity. The inquirer in these stories is almost always the king or a representative of the royal house, in several cases an official delegation. It can also be a private inquiry. The prophet presents the request or need before YHWH and then delivers a favorable or unfavorable divine response to the request. The message is most often delivered in the form of a speech, introduced by the formula "Thus says YHWH." A prophet consults the deity—whether YHWH or another deity—in several narratives in the books of the Former Prophets.[22]

---

20. Jeremiah the prophet is not mentioned in the sections that overlap between Jeremiah and 2 Kings.

21. Texts from Judges will be considered below. Joshua is consistently portrayed as having his mission clarified; he is to fulfill everything "as YHWH had commanded by Moses." There does not seem to be any need to consult the deity to know the right strategy. In fact, Joshua speaks directly with YHWH (e.g., Josh 10:12). See Josh 9, however, for a story about the consequences of the failure to consult YHWH. For a monograph-length survey of divine consultation, see Rannfrid I. Thelle, *Ask God: Divine Consultation in the Literature of the Hebrew Bible* (BBET 30; Frankfurt: Peter Lang, 2002).

22. In 1 Sam 9:9, in 1 Kgs 14:5 and 22, and in 2 Kgs 3, 8, and 22, a prophet consults YHWH, and in 2 Kgs 1 Baal Zebub, god of Ekron, is consulted. In 1 Sam 28, it is ultimately YHWH who is consulted, through conjuring up the prophet Samuel. Even though the means of revelation (necromancy) is considered illicit by the biblical

Two texts will serve as our first examples, 1 Kgs 22:1–28 and 2 Kgs 3:4–27. Both involve the king of Israel facing a battle. In 1 Kgs 22, King Ahab brings out his prophets upon request from the Judean king, his vassal and ally in the upcoming battle. In this specific situation, a simple yes-or-no question is posed to the prophets. Readers are told in a straightforward way that he says: "Shall I go to battle against Ramoth-gilead, or shall I refrain?" (1 Kgs 22:6). The answer is given, "Go up, for YHWH will give it into the hand of the king." The deity has presumably been accessed and the divine response delivered by the prophets to the inquiring kings. They have an answer, a favorable one, with the promise of victory. At this point in the narrative, we have what seems to be a successful divine inquiry with a favorable outcome—we will return to the follow-up shortly.

In 2 Kgs 3 there is also a situation of war involving a campaign under the leadership of the northern king. Now it is Ahab's son Jehoram who is out in the field because of the rebellion of his vassal, the king of Moab. Like Ahab, Jehoram demands the support of the Judean king. Initially, King Jehoram asks King Jehoshaphat for advice on which way to march. The king of Judah suggests they go by way of Edom, having the Edomite king join them as well. At this point they run out of water for their army and animals. In this situation of distress involving lack of water and an impending battle, the Judean king asks for a prophet, as he had in 1 Kgs 22:5, this time adding explicitly, "through whom we may inquire of YHWH." Even though they are out in the wilderness on their campaign, a servant of the Israelite king informs them that Elisha is conveniently nearby.[23] The prophet is not summoned, but the three kings "go down to him."

The encounter between Elisha and the three kings does not initially go smoothly. We assume that they ask him to consult YHWH or that this request is implicit in their seeking him out. Although it is not stated explicitly what they ask of him, Elisha is willing to do whatever it is because of his regard for Jehoshaphat. He has no respect for the northern king. Indicating the role that music may have played in moving the spirit (or hand) of YHWH, Elisha asks for a musician. Elisha delivers the divine response, which is favorable. They will have water and will have what they need. In

---

writers, this is the same type of phenomenon of divine inquiry as we are dealing with elsewhere.

23. It is not clear whether Elisha had gone along as a "battle prophet," or if this was coincidental.

addition, they are promised success in the battle against the Moabites and in future battles as well.

These texts of 1 Kgs 22 and 2 Kgs 3 have points of similarity on the level of motifs and phraseology that go beyond the pattern of divination identified above. In both narratives, there is an impending battle in which the northern king is challenged. In both, he enlists the support of his vassal, the king of Judah, who in almost identical words in each story promises his loyalty. In both cases, the Judean king points out that they should "inquire of YHWH."

In the first text, the Judean king does this twice, the second time asking, "Is there no other prophet of YHWH?" (1 Kgs 22:7). This leads to a further development in the narrative, which will be discussed below. Important for us is that even though this question serves to cast doubt on the truthfulness of the prophets, introducing the theme of lying or false prophecy, the fact that the prophets are prophets of YHWH and that they can inquire about the divine will is not in question.

These two texts illustrate two important prophetic functions. First, in a state of military distress, kings turn to prophets to inquire of YHWH. The kings immediately resort to this idea. Even though it is the southern king who suggests it both times, the northern king does not object in any way; he takes it as the natural thing to do.[24] It is significant that the same function is performed by the prophet regardless of whether he is one of many "court prophets" or is a seemingly independent prophet who is not as obviously tied to a court or sanctuary, such as Elisha. Second, prophets are the ones considered capable of delivering a divine response, in the form of an oracle introduced by the words "thus says YHWH." These two functions, performed by prophets, are clearly illustrated in these texts.

In the extended account of 1 Kgs 22:7–28, even more can be learned about prophets and their behavior when being asked to inquire of the deity. The scene displayed in verses 10–12 is painted with a broad brush and portrays court prophecy as pompous and full of drama. In this case, a well-known type of prophetic or divinatory event is portrayed in a perhaps exaggerated way, as a way of making a social critique or commentary.[25] Of course this serves as a contrast to the second, unfavorable and dark

---

24. There is an underlying theme of a better moral status for the southern king in both of these narratives, which probably drives the narrative comparison of the two kings. This is emphasized by Elisha's objection to King Jehoram.

25. Perhaps we may compare this portrayal to the way in which the "Daily Show"

prophecy of Micaiah, the prophet of whom Ahab says, "I hate him, for he never prophesies anything favorable about me, but only disaster" (v. 8). As the narrative continues, this is also what eventually happens, even though Micaiah's first divine message is positive (v. 15).

A perfect example of the biblical texts' own agenda that shapes the narratives that make up the books of the Former Prophets is 1 Kgs 22:7–28. This text sets the whole phenomenon of prophecy under scrutiny. For example, Micaiah's vision of God asking for a volunteer in heaven to be a lying spirit in the mouths of Ahab's prophets problematizes the dichotomy between true and false prophecy.[26] The book of Jeremiah is another work in which this kind of prophetic critique is very much at the forefront.[27] Prophecy is a contested phenomenon in the Hebrew Bible. Yet, in spite of this, throughout these texts that examine, subvert, and turn prophecy inside out—testing its legitimacy and its legitimate practice—specific types of prophetic behaviors and functions are still described in a recognizable way. In particular, 1 Kgs 22:10–12 shows that there is no essential difference between the type of activity of these prophets, who are traditionally considered "false," and the behavior of "true" prophets. Specific situations and specific expectations expressed toward prophets recur. Based on these, in spite of the thrust of the narratives and the agendas of specific characters, we may draw up a picture of consistently described behavior that underlies the various stories.

As we have seen in both 2 Kgs 3 and 1 Kgs 22, it is explicitly clear that YHWH is consulted through a prophet. Not only is the prophet specifically asked for, but it is made clear in the sentence that YHWH is to be consulted "from him" (מאותו).[28] The prophet is the person the kings can turn to, and the prophet is the one who delivers the divine answer. There

---

reporters make mock "reports" of well-known types of events, thereby exposing or ridiculing them.

26. 1 Kgs 13 is another text that renders such a dichotomy problematic and not straightforward: 1 Kgs 22 shows that true prophets can lie, while 1 Kgs 13 shows that false prophets can both lie and tell the God-sent truth.

27. See my discussion of the negotiations over prophecy in the book of Jeremiah in Rannfrid I. Thelle, "The Book of Jeremiah MT: Reflections of a Discourse on Prophecy in the Persian Period," in *The Production of Prophecy: Constructing Prophets and Prophecy in Yehud* (ed. Diana V. Edelman and Ehud Ben Zvi; BibleWorld; London: Equinox, 2009), 184–207, here 189–95.

28. The same prepositional phrase is found in conjunction with דרש את יהוה also in 1 Kgs 14:5; 2 Kgs 8:8; and 2 Chron 18:7–8.

is in fact no question of asking anyone other than a prophet. These stories underline the function of the prophet as mediator of divine inquiry in particular situations of need. The two stories also provide further details about the means and modes of inquiry, 1 Kgs 22 through the means of YHWH's spirit (רוח) and 2 Kgs 3 through the use of music to move the hand of YHWH (יד יהוה). In both stories an oracular response to the inquiry, a word of YHWH, stands at the center.

The individual stories have different narrative thrusts and various particular characterizations of prophets and other figures. However, even though the stories have their own individual particularities, a recognizably described behavior or "script"[29] emerges from each of the texts that enables us to see a pattern. What we recognize in these and a number of other texts is a "script" of a conventional situation with a highly stereotypic series of events.

Moving on from this finding, we may now expand the investigation to another set of texts. As I have argued extensively elsewhere,[30] a number of texts in the Former Prophets are formally analogous to the inquiry texts just discussed, even though a prophet is not involved. For example, Judg 1 opens with a simple, straightforward narrative in which the Israelites ask YHWH which of the tribes should go first into battle. YHWH answers that Judah should go first, and assures the tribes of victory. Later, in Judg 20, Israelite troops consult God three times at Bethel in the war against their

---

29. The concept of "scripts" comes from cognitive linguistics. Script theory encompasses an understanding of the organization of experience in language that takes the social setting or activity into account. The idea of "scripts" explains why more than what is actually expressed in a text (or in a spoken sentence or series of sentences) is involved when we interpret or understand language. A whole context is invoked by one part of the script when it is recognized as part of a familiar, conventional series of events normally organized in a sequence and framed by experience. A certain amount of competence and knowledge of the culture is required, and misunderstandings might occur on the basis of assumptions made about what is not explicitly expressed. In written texts, these types of misunderstanding can become part of the plot, requiring the reader to recognize the script in order to see the twists and ironies that emerge. See, e.g., W. G. Lehnert, "The Role of Scripts in Understanding," in *Frame Conceptions and Text Understanding* (ed. D. Metzing; Research in Text Theory 5; Berlin: de Gruyter, 1980), 79–95. See also Erving Goffman, *Frame Analysis: An Essay on the Organization of Experience* (New York: Harper & Row, 1974). Form criticism has some points of similarity, but still focuses on genre as a category of classification, whereas the same script can be recognized in more than one distinct genre.

30. Thelle, *Ask God*, 194–97, 199–206.

fellow brother-tribe, the Benjaminites. Their questions again deal with military strategy, and God answers. There is no direct information about whether or not any cultic professionals or prophets are involved. But the third time they inquire, in Judg 20:26–28, the inquiry is fairly formal and is preceded by sacrifices. The readers are told that the ark is at Bethel, and that Phineas officiates there, implying priestly involvement.[31]

In 1 Sam 14:37, Saul inquires of YHWH after being prompted by a priest.[32] As in the previous examples, Saul asks for specific advice on military strategy before a battle, saying, "Should I go down after the Philistines? Will you deliver them into the hand of Israel?" In this case, God does not answer. It is therefore an example of an unsuccessful inquiry. David also asks for advice about specific military maneuvers in 1 Sam 23:1–6, 9–12; 30:8; and 2 Sam 5:19, 22–24. In 1 Sam 30:7, the ephod is mentioned. In all of these examples a similar pattern can be found: in a situation of war, the deity is consulted about matters of strategy, and there is either a favorable or an unfavorable response. The absence of a response can be considered an unfavorable response.[33] In the case of Saul, the fact that he does not receive a response becomes a part of the story of his eventual downfall, and the story of inquiry is built into the larger narrative in a way that prepares for his future judgment. However, this does not detract from the fact that the "script" is fully recognizable in the text about him, just as in the other texts mentioned.[34]

The form in which the question is posed in these texts is completely parallel to the inquiries in the stories involving prophets and kings explored

---

[31]. The divine responses to the first and second inquiry both indicate divine support. However, in both cases, the Israelites suffer defeat, with thousands of casualties. This seems to imply that YHWH is leading them into defeat and that readers are to understand that the Israelites may not have conducted the consultation correctly. On the third occasion, they are promised victory, and this time the battle succeeds, and they defeat the Benjaminites.

[32]. Earlier in the narrative, Saul himself asks the priest Ahijah for the ark, presumably in order to inquire of God (1 Sam 14:18). Although it is unclear what happens exactly, it may be that this consultation is interrupted when Saul asks the priest to withdraw his hand. Even though no divine response is recorded, the battle is successful. But the chaotic inquiry situation prepares the reader for Saul's later frustrations in his frantic attempts to obtain divine sanction for his actions.

[33]. The same form of asking for a divine word also occurs in Jer 37:17; 38:14–18.

[34]. The script is also invoked in texts in which the failure to inquire of YHWH is at issue: Josh 9:14; Isa 30:2; Hos 4:12.

above. In spite of some distinctions, there is no essential difference concerning the phenomenon being described. The verb used to designate the act of inquiry is different in the two sets, with דרש being the verb in the texts involving prophets, and שאל appearing in the second group of texts. Further, in 1 Kgs 22 and 2 Kgs 3, for example, a prophet is explicitly called for, whereas in the texts from Judges and 1–2 Samuel, a priestly context is more or less clearly implied. Both sets of texts describe a phenomenon of divination in a recognizable manner. In a situation of war, help with and reassurance about the outcome is sought through inquiry. Inquiry in a battle context is mediated by a prophet, or without a prophet.

A number of other texts also show prophets and other figures turning to YHWH through prayer or entreaty before a battle, sometimes receiving an oracular response in a way that is entirely comparable to the cases in which they inquire. A prime example of this overlap between intercessory prayer, entreaty, and inquiry is found not in the Former Prophets, but in the book of Jeremiah (Jer 37:1–10 and 42:1–22).[35] Contexts other than a battle, in which divine inquiry is described in the Former Prophets, are royal illness,[36] decisions concerning which road or direction to take,[37] a need for the transfer of authority,[38] the retrieval of lost objects,[39] and others.

The distribution of the examples discussed above is notable. The texts involving prophets and דרש as the verb of inquiry are concentrated in Kings. The texts where שאל is the verb of inquiry and a variety of religious experts perform, several of whom may have a priestly connection, are concentrated in Judges and Samuel. These facts of the distribution and the *distinctions* between the texts have been emphasized in past research. The texts referring to divine inquiry with the verb שאל have been considered to indicate a priestly oracle associated with holy war in the premonarchic

---

35. See also 1 Sam 7:2–12; 13:5–12; 2 Kgs 6:8–23; 13:3–5; 18:13–19:37. On Jer 37, see Rannfrid I. Thelle, "דרש את יהוה: The Prophetic Act of Consulting YHWH in Jer. 21:2 and 37:7," *SJOT* 12 (1998): 249–55.

36. 1 Kgs 14:1–18; 2 Kgs 1:1–16; 8:7–15. This category is special in that it is usually not simply the illness that is the issue; royal illness represents a crisis at the level of the state, in which the fate of the monarch is intimately tied to the fate of the nation.

37. Judg 18:1–6; 1 Sam 21:10, 13, 15 (one could perhaps argue that this case represents a battle context in the struggle between David and Saul); 2 Sam 2:1; Ezek 21:26.

38. Num 27:21; 1 Sam 10:17–24.

39. 1 Sam 9; 2 Kgs 22.

period.⁴⁰ Similarly, an "institution" of inquiry through a prophet was proposed on the basis of the texts involving prophets, although this never received the same attention as the priestly oracle did.⁴¹

Probably without exception, differences between these two groups of texts have been explained as one type of practice having been replaced by the other through time.⁴² This conclusion also reflects the narrative chronology. According to it, YHWH was consulted by priests, kings or Israelites in the "time of the judges" and in the time of the early monarchy. This method of inquiry had a priestly connection. In the "period of the monarchy"—especially the "divided monarchy"—kings and others went to a prophet or "man of God" to consult the deity. Thus, the reconstruction, traditionally featuring the history of religious institutions, conceived of the priestly oracle as being replaced by the "office" of the prophet when the institution of holy war ceased.

---

40. E.g., H. Madl, "Die Gottesbefragung mit dem Verb *ša'al*," in *Bausteine biblischer Theologie* (ed. Heinz-Josef Fabry; BBB 50; Köln: Peter Hanstein, 1977), 37–70. The practice of reconstructing "offices" based on what was understood to be technical terminology is closely associated with form criticism. But it also builds on concepts concerning the distinction between *Beruf* and *Charisma* going back to Max Weber and the ways these categories have been employed in biblical studies. For these texts in particular, the understanding of holy war and the "period of the amphictiony" developed especially by Gerhard von Rad has been central. See his classic *Der Heilige Krieg im alten Israel* (Göttingen: Vandenhoeck & Ruprecht, 1951). His views were also adopted by others. A review and assessment of the concept can be found in Gwilym H. Jones, "The Concept of Holy War," in *The World of Ancient Israel: Sociological, Anthropological, and Political Perspectives* (ed. Ronald E. Clements; Cambridge: Cambridge University Press, 1989), 299–321. A different kind of explanation for the formal features of these texts is offered by Cryer (*Divination*, 295–305), who identified the Mesopotamian omen sacrifice report as the formal background for these texts, though they now stand in a completely different *theological* context.

41. Westermann, "Begriffe." A point of interest is that there is more reluctance among scholars to speak of a prophetic oracle than a priestly one. This reflects the reluctance to associate anything "prophetic" with what would be sensed as resembling divination. Thus, the texts concerning a prophetic "office" of inquiry tend to be associated with discussions involving the early stages of prophecy. For example, Long ("The Effect of Divination," 489) has an explanation that "secularizes" the prophets' role.

42. Gerlemann and Ruprecht, "דרש,"463; Westermann, "Begriffe," 28–30; Madl, "Die Gottesbefragung," 67–70; J. R. Porter, "Ancient Israel," in *Oracles and Divination* (ed. Michael Loewe and Carmen Blacker; Boulder: Shambhala, 1981), 191–214, here 194. More careful about drawing conclusions about a historical development is S. Wagner, "דרש," *THAT* 2:314–29, here 324.

These reconstructions are based on careful observations of texts, and they reflect much of the diversity of the textual material. All of these models and suggestions are derived from important observations about formal characteristics of the texts. However, with the fundamental critique of form-critical methodology and the challenges to the reconstruction of history that scholarship has undergone, many of these conclusions need revision.

We have been forced to admit that it is hard to know specific things about specific religious experts such as priests and prophets and their roles in ancient Israel. The biblical material is spotty, inconsistent, and contradictory. It also likely represents various, even competing interests. It is hard to prove that a priestly oracle associated with the institution of holy war existed, though it most certainly may have. It is likewise hard to prove that such an institution, thought to have been prevalent during the "period of the amphictiony,"[43] was replaced by a prophetic office of "oracle-getting" during the period of the monarchy. However, it is not hard to identify a wide variety of divinatory activities deeply embedded in the worldview reflected in the texts. These texts cumulatively serve to draw a nuanced picture of the functions of religious experts in accessing the divine will in various areas important to society.

The domains of such divination include war, as the examples above illustrate, but also national disaster, royal illness, and divine sanction of the transfer of authority.[44] The biblical texts describing the encounters between prophets and kings and other settings of divine inquiry are fairly straightforward, and clearly reflect a conceptual landscape similar to that of Mesopotamian "prophetic" texts.[45] A case does not need to be made for the historicity of particular episodes described or even of individual pro-

---

43. This concept has become increasingly difficult to uphold in the study of the history of ancient Israel. The structure of the amphictiony as envisaged by scholars based on the biblical account is simply too problematic. The literary world of the "period of the Judges" does not easily translate into a reconstructed historical period.

44. Examples of divination in these particular social settings have been documented in Assyria. Cynthia Jean, in discussing the need for knowledge through divination in Neo-Assyrian texts, lists warfare and the transfer of authority as two areas in which this type of divination was important: "Divination and Oracles at the Neo-Assyrian Palace," in Annus, *Divination and Interpretation of Signs*, 267–75, here 271.

45. Martti Nissinen, "Biblical Prophecy from a Near Eastern Perspective: The Cases of Kingship and Divine Possession," in *Congress Volume: Ljubljana, 2007* (ed. André Lemaire; VTSup 133; Leiden: Brill, 2010), 441–68, here 449–55.

phetic figures. The texts we have discussed—both those with prophets and those without—clearly reflect aspects of the phenomenon of divination.

Prophetic Inquiry and the Divinatory Context of Prophecy

Unfortunately for the study of ancient Israelite prophecy, there has been a reluctance to discuss divination or inquiry of the type described above alongside the concept of prophecy. Rather, divination and prophecy have almost always been set up as distinct from, if not opposed to, each other.[46] When divine inquiry has been discussed in the past, the phenomenon has variously been termed "oracle-getting" (*Orakelerholung*) or "oracular" prophecy, or has been explained as representing a "prophetic institution of inquiry." A distinction was made between this phenomenon and what was understood to be free prophetic proclamation. This distinction follows the customary division of prophecy into "early," "classical," and "late," and also bases itself on the view that unsolicited, direct revelatory messages from God to the prophet represented a higher form of prophecy that was more "authentic," and that was practiced by the "classical Israelite prophets."[47]

This distinction between inquiry and proclamation is arbitrary. It ignores the fact that asking for the divine will and proclaiming the divine response are both parts of the same process. Furthermore, both are contextually tied to the situation that caused the need to inquire of the deity. I am not denying that it is appropriate to distinguish between different methods of obtaining information from the divine realm. It is necessary

---

46. From the classic studies of T. Witton Davies, *Magic, Divination and Demonology among the Hebrews and Their Neighbors* (London: James Clarde, 1898); and Alfred Guillame, *Prophecy and Divination among the Hebrews and Other Semites* (London: Hodder & Stoughton, 1938), to Georg Fohrer, "Prophetie und Magie," ZAW 78 (1966): 25–47; and as recently as Craig Vondergeest, "Prophecy and Divination in the Deuteronomistic History" (Ph.D. diss., Union Theological Seminary and Presbyterian School of Christian Education, 2000). Vondergeest argues for a fundamental difference between prophecy and divination, but does not accept that prophecy simply replaced divination, as Davies and Guillame did. I am grateful to Prof. Vondergeest for providing me with an electronic version of his dissertation.

47. This distinction found increased support after the work of Westermann emphasizing the prophets as messengers of YHWH (Westermann, *Grundformen*). With this function as the core prophetic purpose, any form of prophetic inquiry or solicitation or mediation of a human plea before the deity was severed from the prophetic task of mediating the divine message *to* humans.

and useful to differentiate between solicited and unsolicited oracles, for example, if one is attempting to systematize prophecy and divination in the Hebrew Bible or any other context.[48] However, it is not necessary or useful to isolate phenomenologically the the unsolicited revealed divine "Word" from the divine oracle or message obtained through inquiry or technical means.

Not only has prophetic inquiry as reflected in the Former Prophets been arbitrarily separated from prophecy of the Prophetic Books, but it has also been too strictly separated from its own context: other forms of inquiry and divination in the Former Prophets. In fact, as we have seen, there is a textual basis for viewing prophecy as it is reflected in the Former Prophets *together with* other forms of inquiry.

When one views prophecy as a part of the phenomenon of divination, soliciting a divine oracle by inquiring through a prophet is clearly *analogous* to inquiry through other experts, or through other means of soliciting the divine will. As we have seen, the biblical texts in general, and the Former Prophets in particular, contain a whole range of texts that cumulatively demonstrate a consistently described activity of divine inquiry. The fact that these texts were used to map out the history of institutions or the replacement of one practice by another in itself builds on observations of similarities in function of the religious experts. But instead of concluding that one institution or practice replaced another, or that prophets began to replace priests, I am suggesting that we see all of these texts as reflections of a larger phenomenon of divination.[49]

---

48. One of the problems when using biblical or other texts is that a selection process has already taken place. It could very well be that some of the oracles now presented in collections as oracles that specific prophets *saw* or that *came to* them had in fact required some form of solicitation, or that these collections of oracles are modeled on the type of oracles received after solicitation. So any form of systematization will have to take into account that the sociohistorical phenomenon that the texts reflect is already, in being written, selectively represented. This, again, is where the idea of scripts gives a conceptual aid for taking into account the fact that biblical (and other) texts may be missing parts of the script.

49. Naturally I am not the first to argue this. As far as I know, the only monograph that uses this approach is Jeffers, *Magic and Divination*. Cryer (*Divination*, 264) assumes that prophecy was "a means of socially-sanctioned divination," but chooses not to treat it, instead pointing the reader to the studies of Wilson, Petersen, and Noort, whose work is on Mari (see references to these scholars in nn. 9 and 10, above). These works do not treat prophecy as a part of divination.

A further complication is that scholars have often conflated the distinctions between "asking"—whatever that may have entailed exactly—and more clearly technical means such as lots, arrows, or *urim* and *thummim*, and set all of these apart from "unsolicited" reception (seeing or hearing) of the word of YHWH. Sometimes these more "primitive" methods have also been lumped together with methods that the Bible prohibits, so as to set them clearly apart from the privileged type of prophecy. I believe it is more productive to see all of these various channels as part of one continuum, and as representing different modes of the same basic phenomenon. Such a view also allows for the use of the material on prohibited methods in a new way. Once this is recognized, the next step is to view the phenomenon of inquiry with the help of a prophet together with other textual reflections of situations in which the deity is sought through an expert or by other means, finally placing the prophets of Joshua–Kings in context.

Finally, similar patterns are also recognizable in ancient Near Eastern material. In fact, we come to realize that we are dealing with a broad, basic category of divination. With this approach, a wider textual basis in the biblical literature for the basic situation of divination is rendered available. It provides for a larger context within which to make sense of more of the data. At the same time, it also places the biblical reflections of the social, historical phenomenon of prophecy in ancient Israel more readily within its ancient Near Eastern context.

At its very basis, divination is concerned with accessing and interpreting the divine realm as it relates to the earthly realm. It reflects an understanding of a basic correspondence between these realms, and the idea that "signs" correspond to something in a larger whole. The biblical material reflects this activity in an overwhelming way; there is no need to argue for this. Where we may have trouble making headway is in using the material to reconstruct the exact role of prophet, for example. At the level of the texts, what a prophet was or should be is contested, as the biblical material corroborates. This is yet another reason that reconstructing historical Israelite prophecy is extremely difficult. We might have to be content with less precise, less contingent knowledge. It may be safer to put together patterns and models, and to use comparative knowledge in order to process the available information from the biblical texts. Though they may be highly spotty and arbitrary, the biblical texts do cumulatively provide information that can be used to draw up a picture of Israelite prophecy.

The Bible's Polemic against Specific Divinatory Methods

The biblical agenda of the polemic against and prohibition of specific divinatory methods has also influenced scholars' pursuit of ancient Israelite prophecy, and throws another variable into the mix of potential confusion. The issue of legitimate and illegitimate means of divination is prominent first and foremost in the book of Deuteronomy. But it is also alluded to elsewhere (such as Isa 8:19–22). The material in Deuteronomy brings out tensions between this book and the books of the Former Prophets on the view of prophecy. In fact, the law on prophets in Deut 18:9–22[50] is the longest and most detailed of the laws explicating various offices, such as those of kings and priests. With the description of the role of the prophets as inquirers so consistently described in the Former Prophets, one might have expected a description of this prophetic role when Deuteronomy thematicizes prophecy, but one finds that this is not the case.

Legislation about illicit divination in Deut 18:10–11 includes a whole list of forbidden methods:

> No one shall be found among you who makes a son or daughter pass through fire, or who practices divination, or is a soothsayer, or an augur, or a sorcerer, or one who casts spells, or who consults ghosts or spirits (שאל אוב וידעני)[51] or who seeks oracles from the dead (דרש אל־המתים).[52]

שאל אוב וידעני, "he who consults a medium," is directly followed by דרש אלהמתים, "he who consults the dead, a consulter of the dead," and is preceded by הבר חבר, "a caster of spells." The designation שאל אוב appears together with ידעני also in other texts, but this does not necessarily ease the task of understanding the meaning behind the terms. The exact references of each of these identifications of divinatory activity have been discussed

---

50. Hans M. Barstad does not think there is a "law" on prophets in Deuteronomy, as there are for the priest and the king, but that Deut 18:9–22 represents three disparate elements. See his "The Understanding of Prophets in Deuteronomy," *SJOT* 8 (1994): 236–51, which points out the negative view of prophecy in Deuteronomy and argues that its authors were the successors of the "prophetic movement" in ancient Israel.

51. Whether אוב is an object or a spirit has been discussed, and is not clearly understood.

52. דרש אלהמתים can be translated literally as "a consulter of the dead," a necromancer.

and are not fully understood. The preceding verse also lists a number of methods of divination that are prohibited in Deuteronomy, including divination, soothsaying, and omen-interpretation or omen-seeking.[53] In the context of Deut 18:9–14, these practices are condemned as ones that *other* nations follow. In contrast, the Israelites are to "remain completely loyal to YHWH [their] God" (v. 13). In tension with other biblical texts, these techniques and methods of divination are condemned, not as ineffective, but as abhorrent and idolatrous because they are foreign. This text and others like it are partly behind the reluctance of biblical scholars to see prophecy as a part of divination, and also their seeing parallels in the broader ancient Near Eastern environment.

In Deut 18:15–22, the role of the prophet is discussed. First, it is said that YHWH will allow a prophet to stand up, "a prophet like me," Moses says. He reminds the people that this is what they asked for at Horeb, because they could not stand to hear the voice of YHWH directly. Then YHWH speaks directly to Moses, and privately, it seems, assures him that the people are right in this; he will let a prophet succeed Moses, and then he tells him what the prophet will do:

> I will put my words in the mouth of the prophet, who will speak to them everything that I command. Anyone who does not heed the words that the prophet shall speak in my name, I myself will hold accountable. But any prophet who speaks in the name of other gods, or who presumes to speak in my name a word that I have not commanded the prophet to speak—that prophet shall die. (Deut 18:18–20)

Clearly, Deuteronomy is most concerned with whether or not the prophet speaks a message sanctioned by YHWH. The people need a prophet who can function as an intermediator, as Moses has done. But Deuteronomy

---

53. For discussions of necromancy and witchcraft and the practices to which this text may be referring, see the commentaries on these texts and, e.g., Jeffers, *Magic and Divination*, 31–35, 68–70, 78–81. Brian B. Schmidt (*Israel's Beneficent Dead: Ancestor Cult and Necromancy in Ancient Israelite Religion and Tradition* [FAT 11; Tübingen: Mohr Siebeck, 1994], 179–90, 201–20) does a comparative analysis of the texts of 1 Sam 28 and Deut 18:11 with Mesopotamian, Egyptian, and Greek religion. See also Theodore J. Lewis, *Cults of the Dead in Ancient Israel and Ugarit* (HSM 39; Atlanta: Scholars Press, 1989), 102–17. Though on another text, see, for further interest, Karel van der Toorn, "Echoes of Judean Necromancy in Isaiah 28.7–22," *ZAW* 100 (1988): 199–217.

is most interested in preempting the likelihood of false prophets, either prophets who claim to speak in the name of YHWH but do not, or prophets who speak on behalf of other gods. The text adds,

> You may say to yourself, "How can we recognize a word that YHWH has not spoken?" If a prophet speaks in the name of YHWH but the thing does not take place or prove true, it is a word that YHWH has not spoken. The prophet has spoken it presumptuously; do not be frightened by it. (Deut 18:21–22)

Thus, while the text of Deuteronomy is very much concerned with recognizing false prophecy and false revelation, it is not really very interested in prophets and their role otherwise. In fact, it seems from Deut 13:1–5 that prophets are not considered necessary, despite the text we just read in Deut 18. Chapter 13 opens with an exhortation, so common in Deuteronomy, to follow the commandments diligently, and then warns not to add anything or take anything away. Notably, the subsequent remarks on prophecy are framed with this opening, laying emphasis on the finality of revelation. Not only are new messages from YHWH *not necessary*, but they will not have the same status as the already revealed law. With this point of departure, prophets who arise and whose words come true are more likely to be prophets who try to lead people away from YHWH. These prophets are a test from YHWH, and the prophet who preaches apostasy must be put to death. Only the law of YHWH counts. The words on prophets in Deut 13 are placed in the context of other prohibitions and warnings against treachery and against leading people astray.

We see from this that Deuteronomy is preoccupied with the dangers of prophecy. What is widely described as a common practice of prophets in the Former Prophets, the task of consulting the deity in a time of distress, is not even mentioned in Deuteronomy. In fact, when דרש appears in Deuteronomy, it is never used of inquiring from YHWH (דרש את יהוה).[54]

It is significant that Deuteronomy, in its extensive comments on prophecy, fails to acknowledge something that Samuel and Kings document as the well-known practice of consulting prophets in times of dis-

---

54. One case appears in a context that is not really comparable. It deals with consulting judges to make a juridical decision (17:7). The other case is in legal polemics warning against consulting the dead, in the text prohibiting specific forms of divination (18:11).

tress.⁵⁵ Deuteronomy is mostly concerned with ways to expose false prophets and prophets who lead the people astray, and does not describe how one should seek out a prophet and inquire of YHWH from him or her, as might logically be expected. In Deuteronomy's regulations of divination, limiting prophecy was just as important as condemning specific forms of divination as illegitimate. There was a need to emphasize the finality of the law as the codification of divine revelation.

A pertinent text in this connection is the story of King Saul and the woman of En-Dor in 1 Sam 28. Verse 6 shows that there were several legitimate ways to access the divine will: through dreams, by *urim*, or through prophets. Even though its narrative thrust lies elsewhere, this text illustrates perfectly the context of prophecy as it is presented in Samuel: prophecy was one legitimate method of gaining access to YHWH, alongside dreams and *urim*. Prophets were considered to be one type of religious expert who could be counted on for contacting the deity.

In reality, 1 Sam 28:3–19 is a story of divine inquiry. The situation that calls for consultation is a military threat; the Philistines are coming. In 1 Sam 28:3–6, Saul inquires of YHWH in the face of this threat, but he does not receive an answer. He does not give up, however, and when he does not receive an answer from the ordinary channels from which he expects it (dreams, *urim*, or the prophets), he goes to a medium who consults spirits. Even though the method is in a category condemned elsewhere in the Bible—even Saul himself has prohibited it, though he still must believe that it works— it is nevertheless extremely important to note that Samuel responds just as expected. In spite of being grumpy when he is conjured up, he responds in the same way as prophets and others who deliver the divine response. His answer is introduced by the formula כה אמר יהוה, just as in the texts explored above (1 Kgs 22; 2 Kgs 3). The response is unfavorable, an oracle of judgment.

Both 1 Sam 28, its parallel in 1 Chr 10:13–14, and the prohibitions of Deut 18:10–11 illustrate that divine inquiry has a context of divination. We see that several different methods of obtaining divine information or

---

55. Also the law of the king (Deut 17:14–20) stands in tension with the ways kings are actually portrayed in biblical books. For a fuller analysis of this tension, see my *Approaches to the "Chosen Place": Accessing a Biblical Concept* (LHBOTS 564; London: T&T Clark, 2012), 186–203. Perhaps the tensions concerning prophets and the extent of Deuteronomy's material on it highlight the reality that prophecy was the most contested of the expert positions.

sanction or blessing are considered interchangeable. In the story of 1 Sam 28, consulting a medium is considered a last resort, when all other methods have been tried. In 1 Chr 10:13-14, Saul's consultation of the medium is used as an explanation for his death and is equated with idolatry.

It is likely that the biblical tradition reflects a sharpening of the severity of the prohibition, seen in the way that 1 Chr 10:13-14 blames the downfall of Saul on his quest for the divine will through specific, unsanctioned means, and even goes as far as to specify that he did not seek guidance from YHWH, directly contradicting 1 Samuel. The level of detail about Saul's death in Chronicles stands out in this context. Further, Chronicles is somehow more "Deuteronomistic" than Samuel on the judgment of Saul, since according to Deut 18:10-11, consulting the dead is condemned as a forbidden, foreign, practice, punishable by death. Saul's consultation of the medium is not directly blamed for his death in Samuel, as it is in Chronicles.

If we assume that Chronicles is later than Deuteronomy, this development may represent a growing need to control divination as prophecy began to become a written phenomenon. There is strong indication that Deuteronomy tries to seal prophetic revelation, so to say, and we have seen that it is much more restrictive than the Former Prophets. Chronicles seems to follow up on this. The revelations of the past needed to be controlled and past "transgressions" explained.

Perhaps one key to the restrictive view of prophecy in Deuteronomy lies in the figure of Moses himself. In Deut 18:18, YHWH says to Moses that a prophet like Moses will stand forth, and that the people will listen to him. This text already indicates that Moses is considered a prophet in a category of his own. The designation of Moses as prophet in many ways becomes a means of expressing that revelation ended, temporarily, with Moses.[56] When we get to Deut 34:9-10, this way of reading is reinforced. Moses dies, Joshua son of Nun is filled with the spirit of wisdom because Moses had laid his hands on him, and "the Israelites obeyed him, doing as YHWH had commanded Moses." Joshua, the empowered successor of Moses, will carry out the tasks entrusted him through the authority of Moses. Immediately following, we read that there has never since been such a prophet in Israel as Moses.

---

56. Later interpretive traditions have certainly applied this understanding, with this prophet being interpreted as referring to a future, final prophet—Christ, Mohammed, or a future messiah yet to come.

Deuteronomy really only recognizes one prophet: Moses. His role is primarily that of the lawgiver and servant of YHWH. He tells the Israelites how they are to keep the law when they enter the land. His signs and wonders are also mentioned here at the end of Deuteronomy, so these might also be counted as "prophetic" in official Deuteronomistic eyes. Moses also intercedes for the people, and although this prophetic function, seen also widely in the biblical texts, is not mentioned specifically in Deuteronomy, we can claim that it *allows* it.[57] In a sense, by making the mediator of God's revelation to the Israelites a prophet, Deuteronomy is able to control future prophecy and future revelation. In Deuteronomy, Moses is the "seal of the prophets." There was no prophet like him after him (Deut 34:10), and there was to be no adding to or subtracting from the revelation (Deut 13:1).

The biblical writers' agenda of controlling revelation rises to the surface in several other text complexes. In some examples, it seems that only a prophet who speaks the "word of YHWH" is a legitimate prophet, although even prophets who claim that they do, such as Hananiah, are not considered "true" if their prophecy does not come to pass. However, though the dominant view—and the aspect emphasized by Deuteronomy—is that prophets are primarily speakers of the "word of YHWH," this is not the only understanding of legitimate prophecy in the Hebrew Bible. Texts, especially in the books of Samuel, reflect that divination by dreams, *urim* and *thummim*, and other "technical" methods, were also considered perfectly legitimate, and therefore likely represent the widespread use of these methods. These are not explicitly prohibited, but neither are they thematized alongside prophecy in Deuteronomy. Further, those methods that are prohibited in Deut 18:10–11 are considered foolish and for naught in Isa 8:19–22, but not punishable by death, as in Deuteronomy.[58] Whether or not there is a historical development whereby the more technical methods were at first prevalent and later fell out of use is hard to know, and such points of view are likely informed by the biblical agenda more than by what can be known about any "real" practice. It is at least interesting that later biblical writers did not "clean up" the text completely, but left

---

57. Prophets also function as intercessors, for example in 1 Sam 7, 1 Kgs 13, and various stories about Elisha. On the intercessory role of prophets, see Thelle, *Ask God*, 117–19.

58. Prior to bringing up, in rhetorical fashion, the theme of consulting ghosts and spirits, Isaiah's concern in this text has been with "sealing the revelation."

texts, for example those concerning Saul, that reflect more than one point of view (1 Samuel versus 1 Chronicles).

As we have seen, in its intent to prohibit certain types of divination and prophecy, Deuteronomy severely restricts the criteria whereby a prophet is recognized as a legitimate prophet of YHWH, and does not even touch on many of the prophetic functions that are portrayed in the Deuteronomistic History. In fact, several of the prophets who appear in the Former Prophets would not stand the test of these Deuteronomic criteria. Deuteronomy also explicitly singles out Moses as the greatest prophet, and in reality all but prohibits *new* revelation. In this sense, Moses is the "seal of the prophets."

Ultimately, perhaps, the ambiguous figure of Moses as prophet also provided a means to expand tradition while the biblical books were still fluid. With the figure of Moses as the greatest prophet, law could perhaps continuously be attributed to him as the tradition grew and expanded, but in a way that the tradition could control. This mechanism would make the expansion of law, and thus the addition of "new" revelation, possible. In other words, nothing was to be added or subtracted, unless it was attributed to Moses.

Furthermore, the status of the different corpuses also determined how each was, and is, read. Though it is difficult to pin down a canonization process, it is relatively clear that the Torah was more important than the *nevi'im* from an early point in time, leading to the natural authority of the text of Deuteronomy over that of Joshua through Kings. Perhaps this fact also made it less important that the description of prophecy in the Former Prophets did not conform to the concerns of Deuteronomy.

The Former Prophets between Moses and the "Prophets"

The Pentateuch has exerted an influence on the reading and interpretation of material on prophets in Joshua–Kings. Biblical law as recorded in the Torah and as it is presented as final, revealed, prophecy through Moses constitutes a codified body that does not require future revelation. This seems to create some tension with the *nevi'im* as a written body. If we think along the lines of Nissinen's argument about the "codification" of the Latter Prophets as a body of signs, and recognize also the law code of the Torah as a written body for future interpretation, there is certainly some competition between them.

For the pursuit of ancient Israelite prophecy, the literature of the Former Prophets stands in a squeeze between the scholarly legacy of prophetic studies that privileges the "great" prophets, and the canonical presence of Moses and especially the restrictions of Deuteronomy. The former has shaped the academic field and determined to a large extent what is meant by "prophecy." The latter has subtly shaped readers' ideas about what legitimate prophecy is, and has had power over scholars' readings in spite of the Wellhausian "liberation" of prophecy from law. The presence, within prophetic books such as Jeremiah and Kings, of negotiations over correct and "lying" prophetic messages has no doubt reinforced the restrictive view of prophecy shaped by the Pentateuch, though this prophetic struggle is not about means of prophetic mediation. Finally, the prophetic struggles reflected in Samuel and Kings between prophets of YHWH and prophets of other gods (e.g., 1 Kgs 18), and the agenda of condemning specific divinatory practices both in Deuteronomy and, to a lesser extent, in the Former Prophets, have all contributed to making the information on prophecy in the Deuteronomistic History difficult to utilize fully without bias. In spite of these challenges, however, in ways that we have seen and others that we have yet to explore, numerous reflections in the Former Prophets point toward a rich phenomenon of divination in ancient Israel.

Prophets and Priests in the Deuteronomistic History: Elijah and Elisha

Marvin A. Sweeney

1. Introduction

King Jeroboam ben Nebat of Israel is roundly condemned in the Former Prophets, or Deuteronomistic History, for a number of alleged sins, such as his rejection of the Jerusalem Temple, his promotion of the golden calves for worship at Bethel and Dan, his changes to the liturgical calendar of Israel, his appointment of non-Levites to the priesthood, and others. Nevertheless, it is striking that Jeroboam's actions are largely defensible. The Jerusalem temple is the house of David's royal sanctuary; the golden calves function as a mount for YHWH much as the ark of the covenant does in the south; Num 9 allows for the celebration of passover a month later for those who are away from the land at the time of the holiday; and certain recognized priests in the north, such as Samuel ben Elkanah, do not seem to be Levites.[1] Indeed, a number of other northern prophetic figures in the Former Prophets, such as Ahijah, Elijah, Elisha, and others, also appear to act as priests. Samuel serves as a priest at the sanctuary at Shiloh despite his Ephraimite background. Ahijah is consulted on the potential healing of Jeroboam's sick son Abijah. Elijah presides over sacrifice at Mount Carmel although he is never identified as a priest. And Elisha

---

1. For discussion of the Jeroboam narratives, see Marvin A. Sweeney, *I and II Kings: A Commentary* (OTL; Louisville: Westminster John Knox, 2007), 161–86; idem, *Reading the Hebrew Bible after the Shoah: Engaging Holocaust Theology* (Minneapolis: Fortress, 2008), 67–72.

sets his oracles to music much as the later levitical singers would do in the Jerusalem temple.

Past interpreters argued that such features represent later priestly redaction of the narratives concerning these figures, redaction attempting to impose priestly identity and ideology on them.[2] Such a model might pertain, for example, to the Chronicler's presentation of Samuel in 1 Chr 6:13, but evidence for a priestly redaction of 1 Samuel designed to turn the prophet into a priest is lacking. Furthermore, such efforts presuppose inherent conflict between priests and prophets based on the later model of Protestant conflict with the Roman Catholic Church. They also ignore two important dimensions of ancient Israelite and Judean religion. First, the religions of both Israel and Judah were temple-based, and both nations established priesthoods to officiate at their respective temples throughout their respective histories. Second, although Israel and Judah were allied with each other at various points in their histories and shared some common traditions, they were two autonomous kingdoms throughout most of their histories. As such, they employed different perspectives and practices in their religious establishments, as the examples pertaining to Jeroboam ben Nebat noted above indicate. Indeed, one striking difference between northern Israelite and southern Judean practice appears to be their respective constructions of the priesthood. Northern practice identified the firstborn sons of mothers, such as Samuel ben Elkanah and Hannah, as potential priests, whereas southern Judah employed the tribe of Levi to serve as a priestly dynasty.[3]

With such a distinctions in mind, this paper examines the prophetic figures of Elijah and Elisha as presented in the book of Kings in an effort to demonstrate their priestly functions and perhaps identities. Several important aspects of their presentation are treated, including Elijah's role in presiding over sacrifice at Mount Carmel, YHWH's revelation to Elijah in the cave at Mount Horeb, Elijah's reception of the military units sent to fetch him at the time of King Ahaziah ben Ahab's illness; Elijah's ascent

---

2. E.g., Georg Fohrer, *Elia* (ATANT 53; Zurich: Zwingli, 1968); Steven L. McKenzie, *The Trouble with Kings: The Composition of the Books of Kings in the Deuteronomistic History* (VTSup 42. Leiden: Brill, 1991).

3. See Marvin A. Sweeney, "Samuel's Institutional Identity in the Deuteronomistic History," in *Constructs of Prophecy in the Former and Latter Prophets and Other Texts* (ed. Lester L. Grabbe and Martti Nissinen; SBLANEM 4; Atlanta: Society of Biblical Literature, 2011), 165–74.

to heaven in a fiery chariot and his transference of power to Elisha, Elisha's use of music when presenting his oracles, and the motifs of creation, drought, and restored life in both the Elijah and Elisha narratives. On the basis of this examination, this paper argues that Elijah and Elisha appear to function as priests as well as prophets. Such potential priestly function must be considered in any attempt to posit a distinctive construction of priesthood in northern Israel. The implications of this observation for our understanding of the differences between Israelite and Judean religion are considered.

2. 1 Kings 18: Elijah at Carmel

The narrative concerning the contest between Elijah and the 450 prophets of Baal in 1 Kgs 18 is perhaps one of the most celebrated stories in the Elijah tradition.[4] It presupposes a time of drought in northern Israel when no rain had fallen upon the land, as well as a general persecution of the prophets of YHWH by King Ahab ben Omri of Israel and his queen Jezebel bat Ethbaal of Sidon. The narrative is clearly designed for polemical and dramatic purposes, insofar as it pits Elijah alone against 450 prophets of Baal and 400 prophets of Asherah, pointedly identified as eating at the king's table, in an effort to demonstrate that YHWH and not Baal is the true G-d of Israel, capable of bringing rain to the land. This point is particularly important because Baal is the Canaanite storm god whose chief task is to bring rain to the land so that creation and people might thrive. The contest entails the construction of two altars, each prepared with a bull for an offering, firewood, and everything else necessary for an offering to the respective deities to prompt them to bring about rain. Of course, the prophets of Baal are unable to evoke any response from their god, but Elijah is able to prompt a response by calling upon the name of YHWH. The result is a lightning strike that ignites Elijah's altar, consuming the offering in its entirety, followed by a torrent of rain that brings the drought to an end and enables Elijah to execute the 450 prophets of Baal. Obviously, YHWH is the true G-d of Israel in this narrative.

Although the major contestants, Elijah and the prophets of Baal, are identified as prophets and not priests, their respective altar preparations and rituals indicate the professional actions of a priesthood dedicated

---

4. For discussion of 1 Kgs 18, see Sweeney, *I and II Kings*, 216–30.

to carrying out the sacred procedures of a sacrifice. Indeed, the absence of rain and other features of the sacrifice indicate that the offerings here are constructed as offerings required for the observance of Sukkot, which marks the end of the dry summer and the beginning of the rainy season in ancient (and modern) Israel.

Elijah's preparations include several features that mark his sacrifice as a Sukkot *ʿôlâ*, or "whole burnt offering," required to observe the holiday. The offering of one bull is a portion of the required *ʿôlâ*, for the eighth day of the festival which would normally call for one bull, one ram, seven lambs, grain offerings, and libations offerings according to Num 29:35–38. Elijah's digging of a trench around the altar and then pouring water over the offering prior to calling upon YHWH are also features of his offering. Although some have speculated that Elijah was surreptitiously pouring naphtha or some other flammable substance on the altar to facilitate ignition,[5] such a contention completely misses the significance of Elijah's acts. First, the digging of the trench is a required feature of Israelite altars intended to mark the holy boundaries of the altar site and to provide a place for the blood of the sacrifice to drain back into the earth in the manner prescribed by YHWH for the treatment of blood.[6] Second, the pouring of water on the altar is an essential feature of the Sukkot offering, in which libation offerings are made to symbolize the anticipated onset of rain that the offering is meant to symbolize and bring about.[7] Third, Elijah's calling on the name of YHWH emulates the role of the priest who officiates over the sacrifice in Israelite or Judean temples. Indeed, Elijah acts as a priest throughout this narrative.

Much the same might be said of the prophets of Baal, who despite the polemics of the narrative actually function as legitimate priests themselves. They prepare the altar and the bull as prescribed, and call upon their deity's name in much the same manner as Elijah. Their ritual includes two unique features, (1) the "hopping" or "limping" dance; and (2) the gashing and drawing of blood. The so-called "hopping" or "limping" dance, based on the Hebrew verb *pasēaḥ*, would express the halting procession that would accompany the 3/2 beat *qînâ* or lamentation meter that would have been employed at celebrations of Sukkot to mourn for the dead Baal

---

5. E.g., Ferdinand Hitzig, cited in John Gray, *I and II Kings: A Commentary* (OTL; Philadelphia: Westminster, 1970), 401.

6. See Deut 12:16, 23–24; 15:23; Lev 17:12–13; cf. 1 Sam 14:31–35.

7. See m. Sukkah 4:9; 5:1–3; "Sukkot," *EncJud* 15:495–502.

who was about to be brought back to life by Anath or another goddess, thereby ending the dry summer season and inaugurating the fall rainy season.[8] The self-inflicted gashing and drawing of blood would represent a form of sympathetic ritual for mourning in which the prophets would emulate the suffering of both themselves and the dead Baal in an effort to facilitate the return of the dead god to life. Like Elijah, the prophets of Baal are also acting as priests in a presumably Canaanite analog to the Israelite Sukkot festival designed to celebrate and bring about the onset of the fall rainy season.

In both cases, our major actants in the narrative are identified as prophets, but in fact both Elijah and the prophets of Baal are carrying out the sacrificial ritual of Sukkot in the manner expected of priests. Insofar as the priestly features of this narrative are not dependent on P texts from the Pentateuch such as Num 28–29, 1 Kgs 18 can hardly be the product of late priestly composition.

3. 1 Kings 19: Elijah at Horeb

The narrative concerning YHWH's revelation to Elijah in the cave on Mount Horeb in 1 Kgs 19 is perhaps just as well known as the preceding narrative concerning the contest on Mount Carmel.[9] Chapter 19 continues the plot of 1 Kgs 18 by portraying the attempt by Jezebel and Ahab to kill Elijah as a result of his actions at Mount Carmel. Elijah flees to the wilderness with divine assistance and eventually finds himself at Mount Horeb, the alternative name for Mount Sinai in Deuteronomic/Deuteronomistic tradition. As I have shown in an earlier study, 1 Kgs 19 is one of the intertextual foundations for the composition of the golden calf narrative in Exod 32–34, which similarly portrays YHWH's revelation to Moses in a cave on Mount Sinai.[10] Insofar as Exod 32–34 is generally considered an

---

8. See the mythology pertaining to Ishtar's and Inanna's descent to the underworld, in which the goddess descends to recover the dead male fertility god Tammuz, or Dumuzi, in order to restore rain and fertility to the land at the onset of the fall rainy season (*ANET*, 138–41, 106–9, 52–59, 149–55).

9. For discussion, see Sweeney, *I and II Kings*, 230–34.

10. Marvin A. Sweeney, "The Wilderness Traditions of the Pentateuch: A Reassessment of Their Function and Intent in Relation to Exodus 32–34," in *Society of Biblical Literature 1989 Seminar Papers* (Atlanta: Scholars Press, 1989), 291–99.

EJ narrative, even with priestly editing, 1 Kgs 19 predates the P stratum of the Pentateuch.

The ritual features of 1 Kgs 19 are not as apparent as those of the Mount Carmel narrative. Nevertheless, the revelation of YHWH to Elijah in the cave merits attention. Mount Horeb, also known as Mount Sinai, is one of the quintessential sites of revelation in biblical literature. As Jon Levenson has demonstrated, Mount Sinai/Horeb is constructed as an analog to Mount Zion, the site of the Jerusalem temple, in biblical literature. That is to say, Mount Sinai/Horeb becomes a sacred site for the revelation of the divine presence and divine Torah in the wilderness traditions of the Pentateuch in much the same way that the Jerusalem temple serves such a role in the narratives concerning Israel's and Judah's life in the land of Israel.[11] Although the Jerusalem temple is a complex structure with its courts, altar for sacrificial offerings, and the three-room structure of the temple building itself, the focal point for divine revelation lies in the *dĕbîr* or "holy of holies" of the temple where the ark of the covenant resides, symbolizing the divine presence in the temple. The *dĕbîr* functions as the temple's sacred center. It is demarcated by the curtain embroidered with a cherub to symbolize the cherub who prevents Adam and Eve and their descendants from reentering the garden of Eden following their expulsion. Here, YHWH resides in the Araphel or "deep darkness," akin to the theophanic imagery of smoke and cloud over Mount Sinai and other instances of divine manifestation in the world. It is noteworthy, then, that human entry into the *dĕbîr* occurs at only one time during the year, at Yom Kippur, the Day of Atonement, when the high priest of the Jerusalem temple enters the holy of holies to address YHWH by name in a bid for atonement on behalf of the entire nation. According to Lev 16:3, this sacred precinct is where YHWH states, "in the cloud, I appear over the curtain." Having no tangible form, YHWH's appearance as seen by the high priest is left to the imagination. Examples of such visualization appear in Num 24; Isa 6; Ezek 1–3; Dan 7; the Heikhalot literature and other instances in biblical and subsequent Jewish tradition.

The intangible nature of the divine appearance then becomes one of the issues addressed in the vision account in 1 Kgs 19:11–13. Elijah is shown three apparitions, each of which might have been understood as a vision

---

11. Jon D. Levenson, *Sinai and Zion: An Entry into the Jewish Bible* (Minneapolis: Winston, 1985).

of YHWH, but each proves inadequate. The three visions include a great and mighty wind that splits mountains and shatters rocks, an earthquake, and a fire. Insofar as each of these visions has some degree of tangibility, none proves to be adequate to express fully the presence of YHWH as conceived in this narrative. Only when he hears the *qôl dĕmāmâ daqqâ* (often translated as "the still small voice," but better translated as "the sound of absolute silence") does Elijah recognizes the vision of YHWH, on account of its complete lack of tangibility.

At this point, we may recognize a priestly element in the portrayal of Elijah. The revelation of YHWH to Elijah is not the decisive factor; after all, revelation of YHWH is characteristic of prophets as well as priests. The manner of the revelation is what is decisive, insofar as the revelation is modeled on the encounter of the high priest with YHWH in the holy of holies of the Jerusalem temple. To be sure, such revelatory experience is not limited to the Jerusalem temple, but may be applied to other Israelite temples as well, such as Shiloh, where Samuel's vision of YHWH took place in the holy of holies, where the ark of the covenant resided in 1 Sam 3. Like Samuel, Elijah the prophet begins to look like Elijah the priest.

4. 2 Kings 1: Elijah and the King's Soldiers

The account in 2 Kgs 1 of Elijah's reception of the military units sent to fetch him at the time of the injury of King Ahaziah ben Ahab of Israel also comes into consideration.[12] The narrative begins with an account of Ahaziah's injury resulting from his fall through an upper story window of the royal palace in Samaria. In the aftermath of the king's injury, he sends messengers to inquire of Baal-Zebub, the god of Ekron, to determine whether or not he will heal. These messengers are confronted by Elijah, who condemns Ahaziah to death after demanding to know if there is no G-d in Israel, that the king sends to inquire of Baal-Zebub. When military units comprising fifty men are sent to summon Elijah, who is sitting atop a mountain, to appear before the king, fire from heaven kills the first two units. The third unit is spared when its captain appeals to Elijah for mercy, unlike his two predecessors who simply order the prophet to come down from the mountain and appear before the king. At the behest of the third captain, Elijah comes down from the mountain, appears before the

---

12. For discussion, see Sweeney, *I and II Kings*, 263–75.

king, and promptly condemns him to death for his apostasy in inquiring of Baal-Zebub instead of YHWH.

At first glance, this narrative simply takes up the power dynamics between Elijah the prophet and YHWH on the one hand and King Ahaziah and his soldiers on the other. But several factors signal that the power dynamics of the temple and priesthood also inform the roles of the primary characters, Elijah and the three military officers, as well as their interactions. The holiness of the temple and the need for a proper approach to the deity in the temple by human beings is a key factor here. Human beings do not approach the holy lightly in the Hebrew Bible. Boundaries are set at the foot of Mount Sinai in Exod 19 to prevent the people from approaching YHWH; any who might cross the boundary to touch the sacred precinct would be put to death. Uzzah dies as a result of touching the ark of the covenant as it is transported to Jerusalem in 2 Sam 6. When Solomon builds and dedicates the temple in 1 Kgs 6 and 8, only the priests and Levites are allowed to enter to bring in the ark of the covenant; the people of Israel remain in the courtyard before the temple throughout the entire dedication ceremony. As Lev 16, noted above, indicates, only the high priest would subsequently enter the holy of holies and then only on Yom Kippur, lest he die. And Lev 10 portrays the deaths of Aaron's sons, Nadab and Abihu, when they approach YHWH at an unauthorized time, compromising YHWH's holiness. A similar fate befalls Korah and his supporters in Num 15 when they offer strange incense before YHWH in an attempt to challenge Aaron's and Moses' authority to serve as priests before YHWH's holy presence.

The dynamics of temple holiness appear to inform the character of Elijah in this narrative. Throughout the narrative, Elijah is addressed by the military commanders as "man of G-d," a term that conveys Elijah's and Elisha's roles as representatives and even embodiments of divine power and presence. Elijah is situated atop a mountain when the commanders approach. Although the identity of the mountain is never given—it could be Mount Horeb again or it could be anywhere—the mountain setting evokes the settings of sanctuaries in ancient Israel which are typically conceived as atop mountains to represent the presumed residence of the Deity. The address of the first two captains to Elijah, "Man of G-d, thus says the king, come down (immediately)!" employs the cohortative imperative verb, *rēdāh*, "come down!" to convey the nature of the command presented to the prophet. There is no sense of honor or respect conveyed. Following the commands of the first two officers, fire comes down (*tēred*, corresponding to the officers' commands) from heaven in a manner reminiscent of the fire that ignited Elijah's altar at Mount Carmel. Only when the third officer approaches him, kneels before him in a manner befitting an approach to G-d, and begs him for mercy, does Elijah finally agree to come down from the mountain to appear before the king.

Here we see a somewhat different dynamic from our earlier narratives. Elijah does not appear to function as a priest per se. Instead, he appears to take on the role of G-d who is approached by the priests in the temple itself.

5. 2 Kings 2: Elijah's Ascent to Heaven

The narrative in 2 Kgs 2:1–18 concerning Elijah's transference of power to Elisha and his ascent to heaven in a fiery chariot again evokes images of priestly practice and temple imagery.[13] The narrative begins with the premise that G-d is about to take Elijah to heaven in a whirlwind. It builds on 1 Kgs 19, in which Elijah appointed Elisha as his successor, by portraying Elisha's refusal to abandon his master as he is about to meet his fate. While traveling on to the Jordan to meet his fate, Elijah parts the waters of the river by striking them with his rolled up mantle, and Elisha requests a double portion of Elijah's power when he will succeed his master. Shortly thereafter, a fiery chariot and horses appear to take Elijah to heaven. When Elisha picks up Elijah's fallen mantle, he finds he can part the waters of the Jordan much as Elijah had done, and his disciples recognize that the spirit of Elijah has now settled on Elisha. Throughout the subsequent narratives, Elisha functions as a man of G-d much like his master, but his powers appear to surpass those of Elijah.

Again, we may observe indications of priestly roles and imagery in the portrayal of Elijah and Elisha. The first pertains to the transference of power from Elijah to Elisha. As interpreters have long noted, there are tremendous parallels with the transference of power from Moses to Joshua ben Nun in Num 27:12–23 and Deut 31:16–21. Here, the priestly connotations remain ambiguous, due in large measure to the ambiguity of Moses' identity as a Levite in Exodus–Numbers and as a prophet in Deuteronomy. We may note that Moses employs his levitical rod to split the waters of the Red Sea, but Joshua does not bear a levitical rod and the waters of the

---

13. For discussion, see Sweeney, *I and II Kings*, 263–75.

Jordan split only when the priests bearing the ark of the covenant set foot in the waters. By contrast, Elijah employs his rolled up mantle to split the waters of the Jordan, and Elisha employs the mantle to perform the same act. Although Joshua is not formally designated as a priest, he does take on priestly roles, including his exhortations to the people to observe divine Torah as they take possession of the land of Israel in Josh 1 and again near the close of his life in Josh 23. Joshua also plays the key role in presiding over covenant ceremonies in Josh 8:30–33 and 24:1–28, although most interpreters see him fulfilling a royal function much like Josiah during Josiah's reforms. Although Elisha's succession of Elijah is suggestive of a potential priestly role, the evidence is not decisive.

But Elijah's ascent to heaven takes on a different character. Chariot motifs appear throughout the Elijah–Elisha narratives, sometimes in relation to the human combatants in the narratives and sometimes in relation to the heavenly army brought by YHWH to defeat the Arameans. We may also note that chariot imagery is a frequent means to portray YHWH's traversing of the heavens in hymnic literature such as Hab 3 or Ps 68 and 22 (= 2 Sam 22). But perhaps the most important aspect of this imagery for our purposes is the analogy it creates with the ʿôlâ or the "whole burnt offering," the standard form of sacrifice to YHWH in Israelite and Judean worship. To a certain extent, Elijah's ascent to heaven is portrayed in terms analogous to an ʿôlâ offering, in which he is conveyed to heaven as a presumably pleasing "presence" to YHWH. And of course Elijah's ascent to heaven without burial in a grave establishes another analogy with Moses, whose grave is likewise unknown to anyone but G-d.

6. 2 Kings 3: Elisha and Music

A little-noticed aspect of Elisha's role in 2 Kgs 3, which recounts the failed campaign against Moab carried out by King Jehoram ben Ahab of Israel and his allies, is his use of music to accompany his prophecy.[14] Elisha accompanies King Jehoram of Israel, King Jehoshaphat of Judah, and the unnamed king of Edom on a campaign to subdue King Mesha of Moab, who has refused to pay further tribute to Israel following the death of King Ahab ben Omri. When the allies find that they lack water for their animals while traveling around the southern end of the Dead Sea to attack

---

14. For discussion, see Sweeney, *I and II Kings*, 276–84.

Moab, King Jehoshaphat proposes that they consult Elisha ben Shaphat in an effort to determine the potential success or failure of their campaign. Despite obvious tension with the king of Israel, Elisha agrees to deliver an oracle, but demands a musician to accompany him as he speaks. Once the musician begins playing, Elisha delivers an oracle that promises abundant water and victory over Moab to the allies. Although Israel and its allies have a very clear advantage in the ensuing battle, they withdraw from action upon seeing Mesha sacrifice his own son on the walls of his city. Hence, the failure of the campaign is not due to any failing on the part of G-d or Elisha, but is due to the unwillingness of Israel to pursue the battle upon seeing such an objectionable act.

Two key features of this narrative address the concerns of this paper. The first is the depiction of Elisha's role as an oracular prophet who speaks as a result of an oracular inquiry. Although Elisha's action is clearly prophetic, readers must bear in mind the context in which oracular inquiry was made in the ancient world. It was fundamentally a ritual act in which the oracular figure would engage in a ritual of offering as a prelude to delivery of the oracle. An important example of such action is the portrayal of Balaam's oracles against Israel in Num 22–24. Balaam commissions seven incense altars and lights them in a ritual act of oracular inquiry. Such action illustrates the oracular delivery of the *baru* priests of ancient Mesopotamia and Aram, who engaged in such rituals to provide the basis on which an oracle might be discerned.[15] Such bases might include readings of smoke patterns from the incense altars, patterns of oil deposited into water, and other possibilities. That such oracular inquiry is a priestly function should come as no surprise. Even the Israelite high priests wear the Urim and Thumim as a breast piece, indicating that oracular inquiry is a recognized element of priestly identity. One sees such action also in the portrayal of Moses, who enters the tent of meeting to consult with YHWH. Aaron interprets for him when he emerges from his face-to-face conversation with G-d.

The second is the playing of music to accompany the oracular presentation. Musical accompaniment is not only a feature of oracular delivery; it is also a feature of temple worship. Indeed, the book of Chronicles portrays the levitical singers as prophetic figures who sing the temple liturgy.[16]

---

15. For discussion of *baru* priests in ancient Mesopotamia, see Cryer, *Divination*.
16. See David L. Petersen, *Late Israelite Prophecy: Studies in Deutero-Prophetic Literature and in Chronicles* (SBLMS 23; Missoula, Mont.: Scholars Press, 1977), 55–96.

Heman, the king's seer, is identified as the ancestor of a line of temple-based levitical singers who are identified as prophets in 1 Chr 25. Furthermore, there seems to be a development from the Deuteronomistic History to the Chronicler's History insofar as the Deuteronomistic History will refer to the priests and the prophets who were present at Josiah's reading of the Torah in 2 Kgs 23:2, whereas 2 Chr 34:30 identifies them as priests and Levites. Although we know little concerning the conduct of Judean liturgy, the portrayal of David's bringing the ark of the covenant into Jerusalem in 1 Chr 16 portrays the Levites singing psalms as the foundation of the liturgy to celebrate the occasion. We may also note that prophetic books frequently include liturgical psalms, such as Isa 12; Hab 3; and Joel 1–2. Jeremiah, identified as priest and prophet, composes lamentation psalms to express the difficulties in his relationship with YHWH and his fellow priests.[17]

Altogether, Elisha's actions are those of an oracular prophet—and indeed, the professional guild of the sons of the prophets that he leads appears to be devoted to oracular divination—such activity appears to have a setting in temple and levitical practice as well, particularly when we move to the later periods of Judean history.

7. The Well-Being of Creation

The final feature of the Elijah–Elisha narratives to consider is the focus on the well-being of creation, particularly in relation to the motif of drought that appears throughout the narratives, together with the well-being of individual human beings and the role of Elijah and Elisha in healing them and restoring them to life.[18]

The well-being of creation plays an important and pervasive role throughout the Elijah–Elisha narratives. We see the concern with creation at the outset of the Elijah narrative in 1 Kgs 17, when Elijah is commanded by YHWH to live in the Wadi Cherith, where he will be supported by the waters of the wadi and the food that the ravens bring him. That is to say, he will be supported by creation. We see it again in his encounter with the woman from Zarephath, a Canaanite/Phoenician city, who is starving to death because creation can no longer sustain her and her son. Scholars

---

17. On the relationship between Psalms and prophecy, see William H. Bellinger Jr., *Psalmody and Prophecy* (JSOTSup 27; Sheffield: JSOT Press, 1984).

18. For discussion of the texts taken up here, see Sweeney, *I and II Kings*, ad loc.

rightly see this as a jab against Baal, the Canaanite/Phoenician god of fertility whose role it is to sustain creation by bringing rain and fertility to the land. Obviously, as is portrayed throughout the narrative, Baal has failed in this essential task. The narrative claims this role for YHWH instead by portraying Elijah as YHWH's agent, who ensures that the woman and her son have enough to eat, and who brings the woman's son back to life after he nearly succumbs to starvation and illness. The motifs of the well-being of creation, drought, starvation, and recovery from near fatal illness appear repeatedly. We have seen the motif of drought in the Carmel episode, the motif of illness in the Ahaziah episode, and even power over creation in Elijah's splitting of the waters of the Jordan River. Other examples include the drought that permeates the Elisha narratives, the recovery of Naaman from leprosy, and the birth and recovery of the Shunammite woman's son, among others.

The importance of the motif of creation and the sustenance of life in the Elijah–Elisha narratives cannot be underestimated in relation to the question of the role that these narratives play in relation to the conceptualization of priesthood and temple. The Jerusalem temple—like temples throughout the ancient Near East at large—is conceived as the holy center of creation.[19] Insofar as the temple functions properly as a source for divine revelation and teaching in the world, so creation will function smoothly. If the temple is disrupted, then creation will be disrupted; and vice versa, if creation is disrupted, then something must be awry in the temple. This points to a basic motif of the Elijah–Elisha narratives: the introduction of Baal worship to the land of Israel.[20] Such apostasy on the part of Ahab and Jezebel constitutes a fundamental rejection of YHWH's role as creator and G-d of Israel. As such, it constitutes a fundamental rejection of the covenant with YHWH who grants the land of Canaan to Israel as the foundation of the covenant between G-d and people. As a result, creation suffers as drought emerges, starvation and illness ensue, enemies invade, and people die. Elijah and Elisha are engaged in a battle throughout the narratives on behalf of YHWH, which culminates in the overthrow of the house of Omri, the overthrow of Baal and his supporters, and the destruction of Baal's temple. When YHWH is acknowledged

---

19. Jon D. Levenson, "The Temple and the World," *JR* 64 (1984): 275–98.

20. For discussion of the pervasive role of Baal and Canaanite religion in the Elijah and Elisha narratives, see Leah L. Bronner, *The Stories of Elijah and Elisha as Polemics against Baal Worship* (POS 6; Leiden: Brill, 1968).

as the true G-d of creation and of Israel, creation returns to its normal state of equilibrium, in which the rains come, food grows, enemies are defeated, and people live.

Altogether, this concern for the proper acknowledgement of YHWH as G-d of creation and of Israel points to the fundamental concern of the Elijah–Elisha narratives. Restoration of the worship of YHWH entails the restoration of creation and the welfare of the people. Such restoration entails the restoration of YHWH's temple and priesthood as well.

8. Conclusion

Our discussion of priestly and temple motifs in the Elijah and Elisha narratives points to several important features. First, Elijah acts as a priest in preparing a Sukkot *ʿōlâ* offering for YHWH as part of his confrontation of the prophets of Baal on Mount Carmel. Second, Elijah's experience of YHWH's revelation on Mount Horeb is constructed as an analogy to the high priest's experience of YHWH in the holy of holies of the temple. Third, Elijah's encounter with the three military officers sent to fetch him portrays the prophet and the mountain on which he resides in terms analogous to a holy temple site. Fourth, Elijah's ascent to heaven employs the imagery of an *ʿōlâ* offering, and it presents a pattern of succession for Elijah and Elisha that is analogous to that of Moses and Joshua. Fifth, Elisha's use of music to accompany his oracular presentation employs a pattern known in the Jerusalem temple, where the levitical singers are also known as prophets. Sixth, the overriding concern with the proper worship of YHWH as G-d of creation and Israel signals the role played by the temple in insuring the integrity of creation and its ability to provide food for its inhabitants.

When taken together, these motifs signal significant priestly association for Elijah and Elisha as portrayed in the book of Kings. Nevertheless, neither is ever identified as a Levite or even as a first-born son. We cannot conclude with confidence that they are in fact bona fide priests. But their priestly associations point to the possibility that they may have functioned in some priestly capacity in northern Israel, much as an Ephraimite figure such as Samuel could be recognized as a priest in Shiloh, or as oracle diviners, such as the Mesopotamian *baru* priests functioned in a priestly capacity in their own cultures. Insofar as Israel and Judah were two autonomous kingdoms throughout their histories, we must reckon with the possibilities that they employed some very different conceptualizations of religious belief and practice, including constructions of their respective priesthoods that must be considered in any assessment of religion in northern Israel.

Court Prophets during the Monarchy and Literary Prophets in the So-Called Deuteronomistic History

Diana Edelman

Introduction

The kings of Judah had a range of cultic specialists at their disposal to use to determine the divine will; the ecstatic was only one alongside the interpreter of dreams, the omen priest, and practitioners of other forms of divination. The Deuteronomistic History has tended retrospectively to collapse many of these practitioners into a single category, the ecstatic, and to insist that kings were never without a person who could convey YHWH's will to the king directly. The implications of this literary construct will be explored.

In the Iron II period in the kingdom of Judah, a range of cultic personnel tended to the needs and will of the national gods and helped the king understand particularly what the head male deity, YHWH Sebaot, wanted him to do as his earthly vice-regent. The Bible mentions the כהן (kōhēn), the כמר (kōmēr), the נביא (nābî'), the ראה (rō'eh), the חזה (ḥōzeh), the בוקר (bôqēr), the חלם חלום (ḥōlēm ḥălôm), the מנחש (mĕnaḥēš), the צפה (ṣōpeh), the קסם (qōsēm), and the מעונן (mĕ'ônēn) in neutral terms at least once. In my recent study of these phenomena, I have concluded the term כהן (kōhēn) is a broad category that included a number of sub-specialties, including prophets, visionaries, oracle-givers, wielders of the 'ûrîm and tummîm, probably also omen-interpreters, dream interpreters, doctors/healers, and scribes who recorded tôrôt and other divine teaching and decisions forming a body of sacred knowledge restricted to use by trained כהנים (kōhănîm). The sacrifices they performed may well have been components of other rituals whose primary purpose was to ascertain the divine will and possibly influence it or change it. A more apt translation of כהן is probably "diviner" or "oracle-giver" than "priest."[1]

That was the reality, even if we lack sufficient detailed information to understand how each of these cultic specialists performed his task. It is also apparent that in the remembered past as construed in the books of the Hebrew Bible, these specializations have tended to be collapsed into two main "legitimate" categories: כהן and נביא, with a number being rejected as "illegitimate." In the remainder of my paper I will look at the roles in which the נביא is remembered or cast in the books of Deuteronomy, Joshua, Judges, Samuel, and Kings and the moves to combine this former specialization with other former specializations. Hereafter, I will use the standard "priest" as the translation of כהן and "prophet" as the translation of נביא.

The coherence of the scholarly construct dubbed the "Deuteronomistic History" is being challenged more and more, as indications that individual compositions have been joined together that create the sense of a larger periodization of the past are being enumerated.[2] This was not an

---

1. Diana Edelman, "From Prophets to Prophetic Books: The Fixing of the Divine Word," in *The Production of Prophecy: Construing Prophecy and Prophets in Yehud* (ed. Diana Edelman and Ehud Ben Zvi; Bible World; London: Equinox, 2009), 29–54.

2. For an excellent overview of the history of discussion for and against the concept of a Deuteronomistic History, see Thomas Römer and Albert de Pury, "Deuteronomistic Historiography (DH): History of Research and Debated Issues," in *Israel Constructs Its History: Deuteronomistic Historiography in Recent Research* (ed. Albert de Pury, Thomas Römer, and Jean-Daniel Macchi; translated from 1996 French original; JSOTSup 306; Sheffield: Sheffield Academic Press, 2000), 24–141. For those who have questioned the existence of the hypothetical Deuteronomistic History, see, for example, Claus Westermann, *Die Geschichtsbücher des Alten Testaments: Gab es ein deuteronomisches Geschichtswerk?* (TB 87; Gütersloh: Kaiser, 1994); Ernst Würthwein, "Erwägungen zum sog. Deuteronomistischen Geschichtswerk: Eine Skizze," in *Studien zum Deuteronomistischen Geschichtswerk* (ed. E. Würthwein; BZAW 227; Berlin: de Gruyter, 1994), 1–11; A. Graeme Auld, "The Deuteronomist and the Former Prophets, or 'What Makes the Former Prophets Deuteronomistic'?" in *Those Elusive Deuteronomists: The Phenomenon of Pan-Deuteronomism* (ed. Linda S. Schearing and Steven L. McKenzie; JSOTSup 268: Sheffield: Sheffield Academic Press, 1999), 116–26; Ernst Axel Knauf, "Does 'Deuteronomistic Historiography' (DtrH) Exist?" in *Israel Constructs Its History: Deuteronomistic Historiography in Recent Research* (ed. Albert de Pury, Thomas Römer, and Jean-Daniel Macchi; JSOTSup 306; Sheffield: Sheffield Academic Press, 2000), 388–98; relevant essays in Thomas B. Dozeman, Konrad Schmid, and Thomas Römer, eds., *Pentateuch, Hexateuch, or Enneateuch? Identifying*

epic written by a single author or even an extended project conceived by a single individual who decided to conceptualize his people's past as having five distinctive ages, who then set about collating sources and cutting and pasting to create what is before us, as Martin Noth had proposed.³ Thus, it might be profitable to examine the way in which "prophets of old" are conceived to have functioned within each book and then see similarities and differences within the larger collection of books and try to determine the significance readers of these books in the late Persian and early Hellenistic period would have associated with the נביא.

Prophets in Deuteronomy

In the book of Deuteronomy, a prophet is implicitly linked to a dreamer of dreams in 13:2–6, but it is unclear whether they are presented as two separate functionaries or a single one equated by an explicative *waw*. An explicit equation of the two is found in the Pentateuch, in Num 12:6, where YHWH announces he makes himself known to prophets in both dreams and visions.

In Deuteronomy the prophet never encounters YHWH "face to face" as Moses did (Deut 34:10), but the specific mechanisms for receiving YHWH's word are not given. Both he and the dreamer of dreams can "give" or announce a sign (אות; *'ôt*) or a portent (מופת; *môpēt*) as a means of confirming the veracity of their word and commands. As long as they name YHWH Elohim as the sole source of their inspiration, they are legit-

---

Literary Works in Genesis through Kings (SBLAIL 8; Atlanta: Society of Biblical Literature, 2011); and relevant essays in Konrad Schmid and Raymond F. Person Jr., eds., *Deuteronomy in the Pentateuch, Hexateuch, and the Deuteronomistic History* (FAT; Tübingen: Mohr Siebeck, 2012). The latter two publications are too new for me to access but are likely to contain articles challenging the concept of a Deuteronomistic History as conceived by Noth or others.

3. Martin Noth, *Überlieferungsgeschichtliche Studien: Die sammelnden und bearbeitenden Geschichtswerke im Alten Testament* (Halle: Niemeyer, 1943); the first part was translated and published as *The Deuteronomistic History* (JSOTSup 15; Sheffield: Sheffield Academic Press, 1994). The periodization he points out exists in the current sequence of these books, even if, as pointed out by Knauf, it never appears as a complete sequence in a "historical" summary in any narrative or psalm ("Does 'Deuteronomistic Historiography' (DtrH) Exist," 397). However, its existence need not be the result of the vision of a single author or editor working in the Neo-Babylonian period after the termination of the independent kingdom of Judah.

imate cultic personnel. As noted by Christophe Nihan, in this book prophecy is superior to all other political and religious institutions because it alone traces back to the revelation of torah and the covenant-making at Mount Horeb in Deut 5. The other offices and institutions are all linked to the people's establishment in the land (judge, levitical priest, and king). As a corollary, prophecy is also made subordinate to the initial set of revelations at Mount Horeb.[4]

In Deut 18:15-22, YHWH is to raise up a prophet like Moses, even though none will ever function in the same expanded capacity (cf. Deut 34:10-12), who is a native "member of the covenant people." He is to speak YHWH's words and commandments to the people, isolating them from direct contact with the divine as per their request at Horeb, when the direct encounter was overwhelming. Anyone who does not heed the prophet's words spoken in YHWH's name will be held accountable by God, and the proof of the legitimacy of any prophecy will be in its fulfilment.[5] Death is the punishment for a prophet who speaks in the name of any god other than YHWH, or speaks something not commanded by YHWH directly, claiming it has come from him.[6] The book is set on the plains of Moab. In

---

4. Christophe Nihan, "Deuteronomy 18 and the Emergence of the Pentateuch as Torah," *SEÅ* 75 (2010): 21-56, here 31-33. See also Thomas Römer, "Moses, Israel's First Prophet, and the Formation of the Deuteronomistic and Prophetic Libraries," in this volume. The latter point has been emphasized previously by Hans M. Barstad, "The Understanding of the Prophets in Deuteronomy," *SJOT* 8 (1994): 236-51, here 241.

5. Sven Tengström makes the important observation that the criterion in 18:20-22 for identifying a "true" prophet was never a functional rule since, logically, a true prophet would have needed to have been credentialed and recognized prior to his prophetic activity and its fulfilment. Instead, it is the basic principle of the deuteronomistic theology of history ("Moses and the Prophets in the Deuteronomistic History," *SJOT* 8 [1994]: 257-66, here 264). For the suggestion it might point redactionally to the rival viewpoints among prophets in the book of Jeremiah, see Romer, "Moses." For the suggestion that 18:21-22 is an addition dating to the fifth century, though belief in the literal fulfillment of the word of God is much older, see Alexander Rofé, "Classes in the Prophetical Stories: Didactic Legenda and Parable," in *Studies on Prophecy: A Collection of Twelve Papers* (ed. G. W. Anderson et al.; VTSup 26; Leiden: Brill, 1974), 143-64, here 156-57.

6. For a reconstruction of the growth of Deut 18:9-22, in which vv. 10-12a are considered the original core see, for example, Andrew David Hastings Mayes, *Deuteronomy* (NCBC; London: Marshall, Morgan, & Scott, 1981), 279-80. For the suggestion that vv. 15-22 are adapted from prescriptions copied from the *adê* loyalty oath

the story world, Moses is delivering YHWH's words and commands that were revealed to him at Sinai but that are only now being conveyed to the people because they apply to life within the promised land, Cisjordan.

Reflection over the information in Deut 18 indicates some uncertainty over the role conceived for the prophet. Following on from Moses, an apparent chain of successors is to mediate the words and commands of YHWH and any who do not heed these mediated words will be held accountable.[7] This definition of the role of prophet has two possible interpretations: it either makes him a conveyor of ongoing new revelation—which then accounts for the statement about distinguishing between a legitimate and illegitimate prophet by seeing whether his words will come true—or it makes him basically a teacher of revealed torah, not necessarily adding to it, but expounding it and warning of consequences for not following it. The need to distinguish between legitimate and illegitimate prophets is still there, because he can still misrepresent the divine teaching, in its spirit or in its words, or claim that it derives from a deity other than YHWH.[8] The latter position would already represent the distinction between the functioning ecstatic prophets in the Iron Age and the prophets as remembered in the past, from a present where their role had been modified significantly in light of the growing authority of torah.

It would seem initially that the former, newly revealed torah, is the more likely option here in light of the close association of levitical priests

---

of Esarhaddon (lines 108–123) and so is part of the original text of Deuteronomy, created in the reign of Josiah, see Römer, *So-Called Deuteronomistic History*, 75–78. He assigns the expanded law of the prophet in 18:9–22 to the exilic redactor (80, 131). For the view that it is secondary in its totality, see Tengström, "Moses and Prophets," 263–64.

7. The scholarly trend is to see Deut 18:15, 18 to have a distributive sense rather than an exclusive one, in which YHWH himself is instituting a chain of prophetic successors to Moses, in a creative redaction of the episode in Deut 5. See, conveniently, Nihan, "Deuteronomy 18," 27, 30. For a defense of the minority, exclusive, position, see Barstad, "Understanding of the Prophets," 247–49. For the subsequent undermining or "revision" of this scheme, making Abraham the first prophet, on the one hand, or making Elijah the new Moses and new patron of the prophets instead of Moses, see Römer, "Moses."

8. Nihan proposes a third, intermediary possibility: Mosaic torah or teaching becomes the model and norm for future prophecy, so that new revelation by subsequent prophets may not deviate from the revelation in the book of Deuteronomy ("Deuteronomy 18," 33). A similar view was expounded earlier by Barstad, though not in specific reference to Deut 18:9–22 ("Understanding of the Prophets," 241).

with the teaching, interpretation, and administration of torah elsewhere in the book. Torah is a key category in Deuteronomy; it describes the contents of some of the book or the book in its entirety (1:5; 4:8, 44; 17:11, 18–19; 27:3, 8, 26; 28:58, 61; 29:29; 30:10; 31:9, 11–12, 24, 26; 33:4, 10). It is levitical priests and the appointed judge "in the place YHWH will choose" who will adjudicate cases that are too difficult to resolve at the local level. They will interpret the torah and announce a ruling. A person must accept that decision or be killed (Deut 17:8–13). The priests, the sons of Levi, are also designated as those who are to read it out to all those assembled before YHWH in the place he will choose, so they may hear and learn to fear YHWH their God and observe diligently all the words of this law or teaching (31:11–12). In 33:10 it is Levi who is to teach Jacob YHWH's ordinances (*mišpāṭîm*) and Israel his law/teaching (*tôrâ*).

However, the second option of fixed torah needs to be reconsidered. Are prophets in Deut 13 and 18 being cast in a role similar to that of the priests, as purveyors of torah as well, but primarily as barometers of the morality of the nation at large and as broadcast systems for the calamitous consequences for falling away from the terms of the covenant in the forms of specific signs and portents? Are the passages about prophets part of the original composition or later scribal additions? Did this book originally only refer to a single category of cultic personnel, priests, which would have encompassed a range of subspecialities, so that those who taught and interpreted torah could well have been trained prophets?

Prophets in Joshua

There is no mention of a prophet in the book of Joshua. Joshua ben Nun is appointed as Moses' political successor, so to speak, not his spiritual successor. He is not "the" prophet like Moses, nor first in the chain of succession of prophets to be raised up by YHWH, as the need arises,[9] in spite of the emergence of this interpretation in the course of the history of the book's reception.[10] In the current sequence of books and ongoing story

---

9. Here I agree with Tengström ("Moses and Prophets," 261–62) and disagree with Barstad, who argues that Deut 18:15–19 has Joshua specifically in mind ("Understanding of the Prophets," 243–44, 246). He is followed by Knut Jeppesen ("Is Deuteronomy Hostile towards Prophets?" *SJOT* 8 [1994]: 252–56, here 255).

10. For Joshua as a prophet in the history of reception, see Eduard Noort, "Joshua: The History of Reception and Hermeneutics," in *Past, Present, Future: The Deuteron-*

world, Joshua is moving the people across the Jordan to occupy the land; it is only after this process that the divine commands and words contained in Deuteronomy are to come into force. So in the final sequence of books and editing, there was no need for a prophet.

Instead, priests feature in this book as the personnel needed to carry the ark of the covenant of YHWH, to bless the people, to blow the trumpets to capture Jericho, to divide up YHWH's נחלה (*naḥălâ* = "inherited property"), to distribute portions among the Israelites, to deal with the "illegitimate" altar built by the Transjordanian tribes, and to administer the cities of refuge (Josh 3:3, 6, 8, 14–15, 17; 4:3, 9–11, 16–18; 6:4, 6, 8, 9, 12, 13, 16; 8:33; 14:1; 17:4; 19:51; 20:6; 21:4, 13, 19; 22:13, 30, 31). Does this book use כהן (*kōhēn*) as an all-embracing term for cultic personnel, feeling no need to portray subspecialists at work?

Prophets in Judges

In the book of Judges,[11] after the people have settled in the land, surprisingly, only two incidents involving prophets are found (4:4; 6:8–10). Thus, while one might have expected, on the basis of Deut 18:15–22, that the narrative would contain an unbroken succession of prophets raised up by YHWH, now that the people are in the land this is not the case. As will be seen, priests are equally scarce in this book.

The first prophet encountered in Judges is Deborah, who is described in 4:4 as "a woman, a prophet," before being identified as the wife of Lappidoth.[12] Since her status as a female prophet precedes her identity as wife, emphasis is placed on her role as a prophet.[13] As the narrative unfolds, Israel is being oppressed at YHWH's instigation by Jabin, king of Canaan, and the people cry out to YHWH after twenty years for relief. Deborah's

---

omistic History and Prophets (ed. J. C. de Moor and H. F. van Rooy; OTS 44; Leiden: Brill, 2000), 199–215, here 207–15.

11. In the current macro storyline, the era of the Judges extends from Judg 2:11 to 1 Sam 12:25, so the prophet Samuel technically falls within this era.

12. Whether one chooses to translate Lappidot as a personal name or as "torches," if the ending is taken to convey a plural (*-ôt*), or as "flasher," if the ending is understood to signal an abstract noun (*-ût*), the fact that her status as a womanly prophet comes first highlights it over her status as wife or her characterization as "a woman of torches," usually taken to mean "a fiery woman."

13. This is noted also, e.g., by Tammi J. Schneider in *Judges* (Berit Olam; Collegeville, Minn.: Liturgical Press, 2000), 64–65.

status as (the) one judging Israel at that time (4:4), rendering the משפט (*mišpāṭ*), "justice," to all Israel (lit, "the children of Israel") under a particular palm tree in the central hill country of Mount Ephraim between Ramah and Bethel (4:5), becomes the basis of her ability to summon Barak from the Galilee to her so she can deliver the message of *yhwh 'ĕlōhê yiśrā'ēl* ("the Lord, God of Israel") to him. Barak is commanded to gather forces from Naphtali and Zebulon at Mount Tabor against Sisera, Jabin's commander (v. 2), who is to be joined in battle subsequently at the Wadi Kishon (4:6–7). Without explanation, Barak asks Deborah to accompany him into battle and says he will not go without her (4:8); she agrees to do so, and subsequently tells him when he is to initiate battle against Sisera at the Wadi Kishon (4:14). She also tells him when she agrees to accompany him that he will not gain glory on his chosen "path," because YHWH will sell Sisera into the hand of a woman (4:9).

The most emphasized "path" in the biblical texts is YHWH's, which involves living one's life according to the terms of his covenant. By choosing to involve YHWH's mouthpiece Deborah, Barak might be seen to take a pious stance in which he signals his intention to follow whatever YHWH tells him to do and to be his instrument to punish the foreign oppressor. However, YHWH's comment suggests Barak is thinking of Deborah as a "lucky charm," whose presence will guarantee his success, compelling divine support and victory, which in turn will earn him personal glory or fame for his prowess in war, so that he, not YHWH, receives credit for the deliverance. This same situation is highlighted twice in 1 Samuel. In the first instance, the people mistakenly think Jonathan has won a great victory against the Philistines at the Michmash Pass (14:45), even though Jonathan had correctly noted before the battle that it is YHWH who delivers by many or by few (14:6). In the second instance, Samuel learns that Saul has set up a victory stele on Mount Carmel after defeating the Amalekites, claiming the victory for himself rather than crediting YHWH (15:12) as he had correctly done when he had defeated Nahash the Ammonite (1 Sam 11:12–13). Indeed, YHWH is credited with the victory over Jabin in the end, not Deborah, Barak, or Yael (4:23).

It should be noted that the battle at the Wadi Kishon is to be fought by proxies on both sides: Sisera is the general of King Jabin, the actual oppressor, and Barak is commander of YHWH's human forces from Naphtali and Zebulon. Thus, on one level, neither general should expect to gain glory for himself; they are simply dutiful employees whose "bosses" win or lose.

However, as illustrated by Joab's fear that if David is not personally present at the capture of Rabbat-Ammon the victory will be credited to his name, not David's (2 Sam 11:1; 12:26–29), and also by the victory songs sung about David and Saul, which in their present narrative contexts have David as Saul's general but Saul inactive at or absent from the battlefront (1 Sam 18:5–9; 21:11), those who lead men into war and fight heroically are memorialized, whether they are kings or not. Thus, it is plausible for the character Barak to be able to think he might gain fame as a result of his unanticipated commission.

However one chooses to fill the gap concerning Barak's motivation for asking Deborah to accompany him to Mount Tabor,[14] it is important to bear in mind that he is not commissioned as a judge. This is a role already being played by Deborah.[15] As a woman, Deborah is able to fulfill the judicial aspect of the office of judge, but not the military aspect.[16] Thus, there

---

14. The LXX filled it by having Barak say, "For I do not know the day upon which the angel of YHWH will make me prosper." Although it is generally seen to be a later expansion, some have viewed it as the more original reading, with the MT version having been corrupted in transmission. See, for example, James S. Ackerman, "Prophecy and Warfare in Early Israel: A Study of the Deborah-Barak Story," *BASOR* 220 (1975): 5–13, here 8; and J. Alberto Soggin, *Judges: A Commentary* (trans. John Bowden; OTL; Philadelphia: Westminster, 1981), 65.

15. Yairah Amit correctly notes that there is no report of her being raised up (root קום = *qwm*) as a deliverer (root ישע = *yš'*) either. However, we meet her "judging" (root = שפט *špṭ*) all Israel. Since 2:11–19 tells us that one who judges also normally delivers (2:16), we assume she has been appointed judge at some point not narrated in the past, after Ehud's death (*The Book of Judges: The Art of Editing* [trans. J. Chipman; BibIntSer 38; Leiden, Brill, 1999], 202, 206). But perhaps we should, on reflection, understand this to be an indirect divine appointment; her establishment as a reliable prophet led to the people seeking her out for matters of "justice," or her abilities to dispense *mišpāṭ* seemed to indicate she had divine favor, and gained her a reputation that grew into a form of unconfirmed leadership in terms of observing *mišpāṭ*. The argument that Deborah is portrayed to fulfill the office of oracle-giver on the eve of battle and during it in the "source" material in Judg 4–5, with Barak the leader and protagonist, does not address how her portrayal as one judging and rendering "the justice" in the current form of the story affects such a hypothetical historical reconstruction (Ackerman, "Prophecy and Warfare," 6, 10; Barnabas Lindars, *Judges 1–5: A New Translation and Commentary* [Edinburgh: T&T Clark, 1995], 182–83). No example of a female serving this function for an army has been cited from ancient Near Eastern parallels, and it is likely that her portrayal in this capacity is itself an exception to the rule at whatever point it was framed.

16. Contrast the view of Robert G. Boling that Deborah was a "first-rate military

is a need for a temporary military leader. Working in tandem, the two can fulfill the normal roles expected of a judge—judicial and military—but working individually, they cannot.[17] For Susan Niditch, this explains why Barak asks Deborah to accompany him and will not command without her: she is the judge who, technically, is supposed to lead on and off the battlefield.[18]

It is ironic, then, that Sisera is ultimately dispatched by the hand of a woman but not by the hand of the judge Deborah. This might have endorsed the ability of a female to be a military leader. Instead, it is the hand of a non-Israelite, one whom Sisera mistakenly assumed would help him hide. In the culture of the time, this is quite an ignoble death. Women were not warriors; a solid insult to hurl at one's enemies was to wish that the hearts of their warriors would become like the heart of a woman in labor (Jer 48:41; 49:22), or more generally, that they themselves would become women, losing their strength (Jer 50:37; 51:30).[19]

Does this narrative imply that a prophet renders משפט, or is it a coincidence that this judge happens to be a prophet as well? It could do either. One thing is clear: Deborah commissions a military leader chosen by YHWH and then serves as his advisor in a way that foreshadows to some degree the roles of prophets in the monarchic eras. However, unlike

---

leader" and the ideal judge because she trusted God to decide the outcome of the battle, unlike male leaders (*Judges* [AB 6A; Garden City, N.Y.: Doubleday, 1975], 98).

17. Here I differ from Robert H. O'Connell, who says that Barak is the designated deliverer and, as such, should have served as the main character of the account (*The Rhetoric of the Book of Judges* [VTSup 63; Leiden: Brill, 1996], 107–8). He is only a military deliverer, serving only half of the office of judge. O'Connell does go on to note, however, that the failure to have YHWH "raise up" Barak is due to the unique situation in this narrative, in which no single character emerges as YHWH's sole deliverer (108).

18. Susan Niditch, *Judges: A Commentary* (OTL; London: Westminster John Knox, 2008), 65. The majority position assumes that Barak is insecure or afraid.

19. O'Connell sees Judg 4–5 as satirizing the half-heartedness of the men of Israel by contrasting it with the zealous attitude of the Israelite women (*Rhetoric*, 101). His observation fits nicely with the ancient worldview, in which women were ordinarily not warriors. He seems to build upon the view of Donald F. Murray that the story shows Barak and Sisera to share the tragic fate of "ignominious subjection to the effective power of a woman," which subsequently is characterized as "the ironic subjection of men of action to subservient women" ("Narrative Structure and Technique in the Deborah-Barak Story [Judges IV 4–22]," in *Studies in the Historical Books of the Old Testament* [ed. J. A. Emerton; VTSup 30; Leiden: Brill, 1979] 155–87, here 173, 183).

the subsequent prophets in the books of Samuel and Kings, she is not a prophet who warns the leader or the people to follow YHWH's revealed teaching, *tôrâ*, or else suffer disastrous consequences. Instead, her primary role as prophet is to proclaim YHWH's word to Barak.

But we may ask what we as readers are to envision is meant by her "judging" and her association with "the" *mišpāṭ*. As a singular noun, *mišpāṭ* can be understood as the abstract term "justice," a specific "ruling" or legal decision, a legal case or lawsuit, a legal claim, or preexisting rights, practices, or prototypes.[20] If it means she was making legal rulings (*mišpāṭîm*) as subsequent kings did (1 Kgs 20:39–40; 2 Kgs 6:26), the information would suggest her commitment to *mišpāṭ* as a central feature of Israelite identity and social fabric while reinforcing her depiction as the recognized leader. We can then ask whether there is an implied reference here to torah, which includes YHWH's *mišpāṭ*[21] and *mišpāṭîm*.[22]

However, another understanding is possible from the verbal forms and the syntax used in verses 4–5. Rather than construing Deborah as

---

20. The argument of Boling that it is an oracular response to a specific inquiry depends on the prior assumption that Deborah's location under the palm suggests she is performing a cultic function, which he then identifies as the giving of oracles (*Judges*, 95). This would require a special nuance to the normal legal overtones of *mišpāṭ*, though some biblical texts portray the casting of lots or use of Urim and Thummim as rendering decisions of a quasilegal nature, which he might argue could extend to oracular decisions as well. His reconstruction of Deborah's status as an oracle-giver is possible; the location of Deborah's seat at a palm tree in Mount Ephraim—not a natural environment for a palm—might hint that, in earlier tradition, Deborah was renowned as a cultic functionary at a shrine or "high place" (*bāmâ*) dedicated to a female goddess, since sacred trees are often, though not exclusively, symbols of female deities. For a discussion of the range of meanings associated with palms and tree imagery see, conveniently, Diana Edelman, "The Iconography of Wisdom," in *Essays on Ancient Israel in Its Near Eastern Context: A Tribute to Nadav Na'aman* (ed. Y. Amit et al.; Winona Lake, Ind.: Eisenbrauns, 2006), 149–52. However, Boling seems to be confusing "history" with "literature." He seems to think Deborah played this role historically, and so is playing it in the current story as well. That is a dangerous leap to make when she appears in a collection of stories that focus on an office called "judge" (*šōpēṭ*).

21. Looking at Exodus and Deuteronomy as the core texts that deliver YHWH's torah in covenantal contexts, *mišpāṭ* occurs in Exod 21:9, 31; 23:6; Deut 1:17; 10:18; 16:18–19; 17:8–9, 11; 18:3; 19:6; 21:17, 22; 24:17; 25:1; 27:19; 32:4, 41. It is also used frequently in Leviticus and Numbers.

22. Again limiting the search to Exodus and Deuteronomy, the plural form *mišpāṭîm* occurs in Exod 21:1; 24:3; Deut 4:1, 5, 8, 14, 45; 5:1, 31; 6:1, 20; 7:11, 12; 8:11; 11:1, 32; 21:1; 26:12, 17; 30:16; 33:10, 21, but also regularly in Leviticus and Numbers.

rendering binding legal decisions for individuals who would seek her out when they had specific issues needing resolution, it would be possible to understand instead that she presided over regularly recurring public assemblies in which YHWH's earthly representative made a appeal for help, entering into judgment with the people before YHWH, as Samuel does in 1 Sam 7:6 during a ritual assembly at Mizpah, and again in 12:7 during an assembly at Gilgal. It is unclear whether, during his annual circuit to Bethel, Gilgal, and Mizpah, he heard individual cases and rendered legal decisions, or whether he presided over the celebration of a public ritual, during which he served as the mediator between the people and YHWH in what resembled a lawsuit. If this option is followed, "the" *mišpāṭ* in verse 4 could refer to a ritual structured in large part as a lawsuit. Whichever understanding is favored, it is still uncertain whether Deborah's role as one judging and establishing individual or corporate "justice" is an integral part of her role as prophet, or whether it is associated with her authority as a recognized leader.

Samuel is another example of a prophet (1 Sam 3:1, 19–21; 19:20, 24) who is also a judge (1 Sam 3:20; 7:6, 15; 12:7)—as well as a priest (1 Sam 7:9–10, 17; 9:12, 23–24; 10:8; 13:8–13). But since he appears in a different book, we should not automatically assume consistency in function between the two overlapping offices. While both Deborah and Samuel are depicted as conveying the word of YHWH to a third party, both are also associated with the administration of justice in their functions as judges. However, Samuel's "judging" of the people in 1 Sam 7:6, 15–17, and 12:7 is never directly connected with the rendering of a ruling (*mišpāṭ*) in a legal debate, even if it might imply or allow for such a situation.[23] At YHWH's insistence, he explained to them the *mišpāṭ* of the king, which in the context refers to the customary rights and privileges claimed by the king (1 Sam 8:9, 11; 10:25). Instead, Samuel's judging follows the more standard form of warning the people about their failure to adhere to the covenant (1 Sam 7:3–4, 6) and, after rehearsing the deeds done by YHWH for his people, warning them of the possibility that, due to this failure, YHWH will sweep away both the people and king (12:6–25). Prayer on behalf of the people, while not an explicit element of Deborah's dispensing

---

23. It could be argued that 1 Sam 12:3–5 depicts Samuel as rendering a legal decision in which he is both defendant and judge. On the other hand, this might be a necessary part of a larger procedure in which he is confirmed as worthy to serve as the mediator in a ritualized lawsuit between YHWH and his people.

of *mišpāṭ*, is an integral part of Samuel's role (7:5; 12:19). Thus, while it is possible that readers are meant to assume the dispensing of justice as an integral part of the prophetic role in Deborah's story world, this remains a possibility only,[24] and it is unclear whether Deborah came to be remembered as resembling Samuel in her performance of office, or as contrasting with him.

The second appearance of a prophet is in Judg 6:8–10. There, an anonymous prophet introduces YHWH's response to the people's cries for deliverance from Midianite raids that served as divine punishment for doing what was evil in YHWH's opinion (6:1). Various scholars have noted that a link is drawn between this prophet and Deborah by their being introduced at the same point in their respective narrative units, and by use of the parallel, unique phrase, "a woman, a prophet" (4:4) and "a man, a prophet" (6:8) to describe each of them.[25] In this way, the two prophetic figures in the book become closely linked. Lilian R. Klein argues that the linkage establishes a contrast; Deborah was effective, successfully implementing YHWH's will, while the unnamed male prophet is unsuccessful at changing the attitudes or behavior of the people who rebelled against YHWH.[26] Amit, in contrast, notes that the prophetic rebuke plays two roles narratologically in the Gideon story proper. Elaborating the "crying out" stage of the larger cyclical framework, it convinces Gideon that God's acts of deliverance are distant memories and cannot be expected in the present, explaining why he and the people doubt YHWH's current interest in their welfare, and accounting for his harsh words and insistence on reassuring signs. At the same time, it emphasizes the justice of God's path and his attempt to convey providential ways to his people, who tend not to listen.[27]

This anonymous prophet is specifically sent by YHWH, and the word he delivers from YHWH summarizes God's deliverance from the house of slavery in Egypt and from all oppressors, whom YHWH drives out, giving their land to Israel (v. 9). Thus, it presumes events narrated in Deuteronomy, possibly Exodus, and Joshua. After that, YHWH reminds them that

---

24. See above, n. 20.
25. So, for example, Barry G. Webb, *The Book of Judges: An Integrated Reading* (JSOTSup 46; Sheffield: JSOT, 1987), 145; Lilian R. Klein, *The Triumph of Irony in the Book of Judges* (JSOTSup 68; BLS14; Sheffield: Sheffield Academic Press, 1988) 50; Schneider, *Judges*, 102.
26. Klein, *Triumph of Irony*, 50.
27. Amit, *Book of Judges*, 250–51.

he is their divinity (*'ĕlōhîm*), and that they were commanded not to honor the gods of the Amorites in whose land they now live, before accusing them of not having listened to his voice (v. 10). John E. Harvey has linked the reference to the deliverance from Egypt in the prophetic summary to a wider rhetorical strategy in the Gideon story to establish parallels between Moses and Gideon by referring back to events directly associated with the activities of Moses.[28]

These three verses illustrate the statements in Deut 18:15, 19 that Israel is to heed any prophet YHWH will raise up, and will hold accountable anyone who does not. This prophet functions to warn Israel that they have been disobedient. While Deuteronomy does not specify that the people are not to worship the Amorite gods in Canaan, these fall under the prohibition of worshiping other gods. Thus, it is unclear here whether the prophet is conveying a newly received word of God or is explaining how the people have disobeyed a word that was already revealed. In either case, the prophet indicates that their disobedience is the reason for the Midianite raids and implies that they need to return to YHWH. Since they are crying out to YHWH already, there may be no need to state this explicitly, though the need to draw the chain of cause and effect suggests they have not fully understood this on their own and that their crying to YHWH for help is not the same as turning to him in repentance. Most scholars consider these three verses to be a late scribal addition to the book.[29]

It may not be coincidental that this anonymous prophet appears in the narrative where the people ask Gideon and his son and grandson to rule over them, effectively initiating kingship. It thereby draws on the close association of prophets as royal advisors to kings in Samuel and Kings, but inverts it, so that the prophet warns the people rather than the king.

---

28. John E. Harvey, *Retelling the Torah: The Deuteronomistic Historian's Use of Tetrateuchal Narratives* (JSOTSup 403; London: T&T Clark, 2004), 72. He also notes this is one of almost seventy references to the exodus found in the so-called Deuteronomistic History (11), making it a key story in Deuteronom(ist)ic thought.

29. See, e.g., Wolfgang Richter, *Die Bearbeitungen des "Retterbuches" in der deuteronomischen Epoche* (BBB 21; Bonn: Peter Hanstein, 1964). Soggin has argued, however, that the prophetic episode is incomplete, lacking a logical conclusion. He concludes that it might have been included in an older version of the story, though in a different context and in a much less "mutilated" form than the present on, having been moved to its current location to give the Deuteronomistic writer's interpretation greater authority (*Judges*, 112–13).

After chapter 6, there is no further prophetic activity,[30] even though the people cyclically fall afoul of the same commandment as soon as the divinely raised up judge dies, leaving them without an earthly leader.[31] In this book, the judge substitutes in some measure for the prophet; (s)he is raised up by YHWH,[32] in most instances receives divine spirit that prompts him/her to military victory over the punishing oppressors, and then settles into holding the people to the observance of YHWH's commandments. If they do this job adequately, there is no need to send a prophet as an early warning system. The book can be said, then, to illustrate that life can be lived without prophets if people adhere to the divine commandments. Priests only appear in the book of Judges in the story in chapters 17–18, in which the tribe of Dan takes the idol of Micah and its priest, Jonathan son of Gershom son of Moses, to minister before the idol until the land goes into captivity.[33] These are often understood to be later scribal additions to

---

30. It may be argued that Samuel's status as a judge belongs to the era of judgeship, which only ends in 1 Sam 12:25. My comment refers to the current boundaries of the book of Judges.

31. Robert Polzin has argued that, in Judg 4:1, Ehud's death is placed after the report of the Israelites' "continuing" to do evil in YHWH's eyes in order to demonstrate that the eighty years of peace did not result from Israel's repentance, but was simply the length of Ehud's life (*Moses and the Deuteronomist: Deuteronomy, Joshua, Judges* [Part 1 of *A Literary Study of the Deuteronomic History*; New York: Seabury, 1980], 161). Its absence in the LXX might mean it is a later addition but, assuming that it is to be understood as an integral form of the MT, this is not the most obvious interpretation of the verse. First, the idiom *yāsap* + infinitive, meaning "to do more of something," often translates into the sense of "continuing" an action, but there is no necessary implication of an unbroken chain of activity. Secondly, the concluding phrase ואהוד מת (*wĕ'ēhûd mēt*) is a parenthetical aside that both explains what precedes and prepares for the information introduced in v. 2 about YHWH having sold Israel into the power of King Jabin. The verb can be construed either as a *qal* participle or as a 3ms *qal* perfect, representing the pluperfect here. In the first instance, the people's new falling away takes place as Ehud is dying; in the second, it takes place after he dies. Polzin's chronological interpretation would likely have been conveyed by using the normal *waw* consecutive + 3ms *qal* imperfect, followed by Ehud's name, as in normal syntax (וי[ו]מת אהוד) (*wayyāmot* [or *wayyûmat*] *ēhûd*). Thus, I would not see 4:1 as contradicting the cycle outlined in 2:16–23, where v. 19 clarifies that v. 17 also refers to the situation once a judge is gone.

32. This verbal connection between prophet and judge has been noted by Mayes (*Deuteronomy*, 280).

33. The story contains an implicit condemnation of a Mosaic or Mushite priestly line. This raises an interesting question about underlying motivation. Does it perhaps

the core book of saviors.³⁴ Thus, neither priest nor prophet plays a vital role in Judges.

Prophets in Samuel

Moving to the books of Samuel, we begin to find prophetic activity regularly in connection with kingship.³⁵ Prophets are kingmakers who anoint the king-elect (1 Sam 10:1; 16:1–13)³⁶ and then serve as advisors and mediators between YHWH and his chosen earthly vice-regents (Samuel:

---

undercut Moses' historical role as founder of a line of priestly specialists, in order to allow his later role as prophet and mediator of torah to be foregrounded? Gale A. Yee suggests it arises from priestly rivalry between Mushite and Zadokite families in which the former are condemned in favor of the latter, who are to control the centralized cult in Jerusalem under Josiah ("Ideological Criticism: Judges 17–21 and the Dismembered Body," in *Judges and Method: New Approaches in Biblical Studies* [ed. Gale A. Yee; 2nd ed.; Minneapolis: Fortress, 2007], 138–60, here 151). For the possible function of Moses in tradition before he became the supreme law mediator, see Diana Edelman, "Taking the Torah out of Moses: Moses' Claim to Fame before He Became the Quintessential Law-Giver," in *La construction de la figure de Moïse/The Construction of the Figure of Moses* (ed. Thomas Römer; Transeuphratène Supplément 13; Paris: Gabalda, 2007), 13–42.

34. So, e.g., Noth, *Deuteronomistic History*, 49; Richter, *Bearbeitungen*; Van Seters, *In Search of History*, 345; Uwe Becker, *Richterzeit und Königtum: Redaktionsgeschichtliche Studien zum Richterbuch* (BZAW 192; Berlin: de Gruyter, 1990), 296–99; Niditch, *Judges*, 11–13. However, for the view, based on syntax throughout the book, that it is original, see John Lübbe, "The Danite Invasion of Laish and the Purpose of the Book of Judges," *OTE* 23 (2010): 681–92. For its status as part of an original narrative of seven cycles dating to the end of the eighth century B.C.E., see Amit, *Book of Judges*, 310, 316, 336, 375. For an argument that Judg 17–18 is part of the original, Josianic-era work (seventh century B.C.E.) created by the Deuteronomist, see Yee, "Ideological Criticism," 144.

35. These books contain the end of the era of the judges (1 Sam 1–12) and most of the account of the era of the united monarchy, which could also be characterized as the reigns of Saul, David and Solomon over all Israel (1 Sam 13:1–1 Kgs 2:11). Mark A. O'Brien prefers to combine the more traditional subdivision between the united monarchy and divided monarchies into the final of three periodizations he thinks punctuate the Deuteronomistic History. Each period has a different form of leadership: the period under Moses and Joshua; the period of Israel from the judges to the monarchy, and the period of Israel under the prophets and kings (*The Deuteronomistic History Hypothesis: A Reassessment* [OBO 92; Freiburg: Universitätsverlag, 1989], 288).

36. An anonymous prophet anoints Jehu to be king of Israel in place of Joram (2 Kgs 9:1–10), recalling the role of Samuel and Nathan in anointing Saul and David in Samuel.

1 Sam 12–15; Gad: 1 Sam 22:5; Nathan: 2 Sam 7:2; 12:1–15; 12:25). They also appear in ecstatic groups (1 Sam 10; 19) and are equated with other cultic personnel.

In chapter 3, Samuel is commissioned by YHWH as a prophet in a time when the word of YHWH had become rare and visions were not widespread (3:1). In this incident, Samuel does not seem to fit into the line of prophetic spokesmen that YHWH would raise up, as announced in Deut 18:15–22. He is not warning the people more generally, but is pronouncing divine judgment against the house of the priest-*šōpēṭ* leader Eli specifically, for his failure to restrain his sons from blaspheming once he learned about their misdeeds (3:11–14). However, he passes the test of a legitimate prophet, since YHWH does not let any of his words fall to the ground, and all Israel from Dan to Beersheba knows he is a trustworthy prophet of YHWH (vv. 19–20). He seems to fulfil the role envisioned in Deut 18, however, in 1 Sam 12, in his speech to the people after Saul's coronation.

A move can be seen in Samuel to collapse what almost certainly would have been former specializations among cultic personnel in the Iron II period into the solitary category of נביא.[37] In 3:1, the rare דבר יהוה (*dĕbar yhwh* = "word of YHWH") seems implicitly to be equated with the lack of a vision (חזון = *ḥazôn*), and Gad is described as both נביא (1 Sam 22:5) and חזה, "seer" (1 Sam 22:5; 2 Sam 24:11; 1 Chr 21:9). Outside of Samuel, reference is made to records of Gad the חזה alongside records of Samuel the ראה and Nathan the נביא in 1 Chr 29:29. In 1 Sam 9:9, the ראה is identified with the נביא just before the story of the encounter between Samuel and Saul, implying that Samuel was traditionally remembered as a ראה as well as an איש אלוהים (*'îš 'ĕlōhîm*, 9:6). This resonates with the claim in Num 12:6 that "when there are prophets among you, I, YHWH, make myself known to them by means of the vision (במראה) and I speak to them by means of the dream (בחלום)." Yet, interestingly, the "dreamer of dreams" has not yet been fully integrated with the ecstatic in 1 Sam 28:15, where Saul tells the ghost of Samuel that he has tried to contact Elohim through the two legitimate means of prophets and dreams with no success, before turning in desperation to illegitimate necromancy. As noted earlier,

---

37. This has been emphasized already by A. Graeme Auld ("Prophets through the Looking Glass: Between Writing and Moses," *JSOT* 2 [1983]: 3–23); Bruce Vawter, "Were the Prophets Nabî'?s?" *Bib* 66 (1985): 206–20. The same move has been observed within the minor prophets by Edgar W. Conrad, "The End of Prophecy and the Appearance of Angels/Messengers in the Book of the Twelve," *JSOT* 73 (1997): 65–79.

it is unclear whether the נביא is being equated with the dreamer of dreams (חלום חלם) in Deut 13:1 via an explicative *waw* or whether these are two independent categories of legitimate religious specialists.

The use of signs to confirm the words pronounced by Samuel as he anoints Saul king-elect of Israel in 1 Sam 10, and by Nathan in 2 Sam 12:11–14, is consistent with the use of the sign (האות; *hā'ôt*) and the portent (המופת; *hammôpēt*) by the prophet or dreamer of dreams in Deut 13:2. In Samuel, an individual who bears the title נביא can also act on his own initiative as a flawed human being who is using his own judgment to act (Samuel in 1 Sam 8).

Prophets in Kings

The book of Kings[38] contains anonymous groups of prophets and anonymous individual prophets, as well as named individual prophets. Ehud Ben Zvi has undertaken a study of the anonymous "prophets of old" in the books of Kings in order to identify the ways in which they are evoked and remembered for a postmonarchic readership and audience. He identifies five functions associated with them. Prophets are (1) a faithful minority of servants of YHWH who are likely to be persecuted if the ruling leader is sinful; (2) a group aware of Israel's history of misconduct that justified the extreme divine punishment against monarchic Israel; (3) a group that unsuccessfully tried to bring Israel to YHWH; (4) a group that embodies a reminder of Israel's history of rejecting YHWH and disregarding the advice of YHWH's servants; and (5) a group that stands first in the chain of transmission of YHWH's essential teachings that leads directly to the readers and rereaders of the book of Kings.[39] To this can be added a view that prophets who disobey YHWH are killed by him directly, with lions the favorite means of demise (1 Kgs 13; 20:35–36).

We can see from this list that the third and fourth points above cohere closely with the prophetic role as articulated in Deut 13 and 18: the prophets try to help an errant Israel return to YHWH and his covenant stipula-

---

38. The final era in the books of Deuteromy–2 Kings, the period of the divided monarchy or the period of the kingdoms of Israel and Judah, is narrated in 1 Kgs 2:12–25:30.

39. Ehud Ben Zvi, "'The Prophets'—Generic Prophets and Their Role in the Construction of the Image of the 'Prophets of Old' within the Postmonarchic Readership/s of the Book of Kings," *ZAW* 116 (2004): 555–67.

tions, and come to embody the history of the failure of those attempts when Israel does not listen to their warnings and divine proclamations. The latter point is an elaboration of the first that encompasses the disobedience of the people during the conquest, the time of the Judges (2 Kgs 17:8), and the reigns of Saul, David, and Solomon (1 Kgs 11:31–39). Yet in its development in various passages in Kings, it refers to events outside the Deuteronomistic History and thus already embraces a more developed Mosaic age, as may be reflected in Exodus (2 Kgs 17:7) as well as the patriarchal era (1 Kgs 18:31, 36).

In addition, the second point resonates strongly with Deuteronomy, which warns that those who fail to heed prophetic messages will be held accountable. Kings uses this as the basis of meaning for the terminations in 721 B.C.E. and 586 B.C.E. of Israel and Judah as independent kingdoms. The first point about prophets as a persecuted minority is a new emphasis found only in this book within the larger span of Deuteronomy–2 Kings. The fifth point about the prophets in a chain of transmission of YHWH's teachings down to those who read and reread Kings may need more emphasis on what is being transmitted: torah specifically, which embodies YHWH's revealed commands. In this way, the prophets are YHWH's "torah police," who warn people to heed it and warn of consequences they can expect when they do not, though this specific connection is only found in 2 Kgs 17. There, prophets and seers are remembered as having been sent by YHWH to warn Israel and Judah to keep the commandments and statutes in accordance with all the laws he commanded their ancestors and sent to them by his servants the prophets (2 Kgs 17:13). At the end of the same scene, this torah, which must be observed, is said to have been written by YHWH (17:37). Mosaic mediation of the law is specifically being denied here. And, unlike Samuel, Kings distinguishes between prophets and seers as cultic personnel.

Priests are not remembered to have administered torah in Kings. Instead, the book associates torah-keeping and administration specifically with kings: David admonishes Solomon to walk in the written torah of Moses (1 Kgs 2:3); Jehu was not careful to follow the torah of YHWH the God of Israel (2 Kg 10:31); Joash followed the commandment written in the book of the law of Moses and did not put to death the children of convicted murderers (2 Kgs 14:6). Manasseh had a chance to observe what YHWH had commanded directly, as well as what Moses had mediated, but he chose instead to disobey (2 Kgs 21:8). The master copy of the book of torah is "rediscovered" during temple repairs in the reign of

Josiah (2 Kgs 22:8, 11), and after hearing its contents, the king sets about to establish the words of the law of Moses written in the book (2 Kgs 23:24–25). In this respect, Kings builds on the idea expressed in Deut 17:18–20 that the king should have a copy of "this torah" written for him in the presence of the levitical priests and should read it all the days of his life to learn to fear YHWH and diligently observe all the words of this torah and these statutes, so he and his descendants may reign long over his kingdom in Israel. It was the failure of kings to do this regularly, then, that contributed to the demise of both kingdoms for readers of the larger sequence of books.[40]

If we turn to the individually named prophets in Kings, we can see an attempt to establish a chain of prophets raised up by YHWH after Moses in the monarchic era, prophets who warned kings and people about their repeated disobedience to torah, announcing signs and consequences.[41] This seems to resonate with the announcement made by YHWH about raising up a prophet like Moses as circumstances dictated in Deut 18:15–20. In Kings itself, this is not yet an unbroken chain,[42] but as Ernst Knauf

---

40. My comments agree in some points with observations made in Rudolph Smend in proposing a redactional layer that focused on obedience to torah, which he designated DtrN ("Das Gesetz und die Völker: Ein Beitrag zur Deuteronomistischen Redaktionsgeschichte," in *Probleme Biblischer Theologie* [ed. H. W. Wolff; Munich: Chr. Kaiser, 1971], 494–509; *Die Entstehung des Alten Testaments* [Stuttgart: Kohlhammer, 1981], 110–25). However, I would date these additions in the Persian or even early Hellenistic period, and think the verses in Deuteronomy are secondary, not original.

41. My observations overlap to some degree with those made by Walter Dietrich, which led him to posit a redactional layer within the "Deuteronomistic History" focused on prophecy and its fulfillment, which he associated with a DtrP redactor: the prophetic Deuteronomist (*Prophetie und Geschichte* [FRLANT 108; Göttingen: Vandenhoeck & Ruprecht, 1972). For the addition of references to Moses, though not to Moses the prophet explicitly, in the MT texts of Isa 63:11–12, Jer 3:1, Mic 6:4, and Mal 3:22, see Nihan, "Deuteronomy 18," 22–23. While Nihan thinks that they serve to align prophetic traditions about the exodus and wilderness with the Pentateuch, they could be seen as another indirect strategy for strengthening this desired chain of "prophets like Moses" by recalling the founder of the chain.

42. The growth of this chain over time has been postulated by various scholars; the anecdotal stories associated with Elijah and Elisha (except perhaps 1 Kgs 21) and the man of God proclaiming the destruction of Bethel in 1 Kgs 12:33–13:33 are argued to be Persian additions by, e.g., Rofé ("Classes in the Prophetical Stories," 143–64); McKenzie (*Trouble with Kings*, 81–100); Susanne Otto ("The Composition of the Elijah-Elisha Stories and the Deuteronomistic History," *JSOT* 27 [2003]: 487–508). For

has noted, if Kings is combined with the date superscriptions in the latter prophets, an unbroken chain is produced.[43] He concludes from this that Kings came to serve as the introduction to the prophetic corpus, rather than as the end of the so-called Deuteronomistic History. It can be added that the books of Samuel extend this trend backward to the foundations of monarchy with Saul. Knauf emphasizes that the themes of Jerusalem and torah are central in Kings, suggesting that these were primary concerns in the time of the book's readers.

Conclusion

The books that Noth argued formed a coherent composition that he dubbed the "Deuteronomistic History" only came to have a semblance of intentional coherence over time, through expansions designed to draw them more closely together. The passages about prophets in Deut 13 and 18[44] are likely to be secondary additions made when the prophetic corpus began to

---

a claim that stories about the prophet Isaiah in 2 Kgs 18:13–20:19 are postexilic additions, see Römer, *So-Called Deuteronomistic History,* 154–55. See also his comments in his contribution in this volume, "Moses."

43. Ernst A. Knauf, "Kings among the Prophets," in *The Production of Prophecy: Constructing Prophecy and Prophets in Yehud* (ed. Diana Edelman and Ehud Ben Zvi; Bible World; London: Equinox, 2009), 133. For attempts to explain why Hosea, Amos, and Micah, associated with prophetic books, are not mentioned in the books of Kings, see for example, Klaus Koch, "Das Prophetenschweigen des deuteronomistischen Geschichtswerks," in *Die Botschaft und die Boten* (ed. J. Jeremias and L. Perlitt; Neukirchen-Vluyn: Neukirchener, 1981), 115–28; Christopher Begg, "The Non-Mention of Amos, Hosea, and Micah in the Deuteronomistic History," *BN* 32 (1986): 41–53. For attempts to explain the absence of Jeremiah in the 2 Kings, see for example, Norbert Lohfink, "Gab es eine deuteronomistischen Bewegung?" in *Jeremiah und die "deuteronomistische Bewegung"* (ed. W. Gross; BBB 98; Weinheim: Beltz Athenäum, 1995), 313–82 [358–67]; Marius D. Terblanche, "No Need for a Prophet Like Jeremiah: The Absence of the Prophet Jeremiah in Kings," in *Past, Present, Future: The Deuteronomistic History and Prophets* (ed. J. C. de Moor and H. F. van Rooy; OTS 44; Leiden: Brill, 2000), 306–14.

44. Deut 18:9–22 is deemed secondary by Reinhard G. Kratz because it does not contain information found in the Book of the Covenant, does not relate to cult centralization, and has second person plurals. He thinks the earliest form of Deuteronomy had second person singulars only (*The Composition of the Narrative Books of the Old Testament* [trans. J. Bowden; London: T&T Clark, 2005], 119–20, 133). He notes that 17:4–20, 18:1–8, and 18:9–22 interrupt the ordering of the law in 16:18–20 + 17:8–13 and 19:1–3, making a comprehensive law about offices out of the additions (120).

gain importance and needed better integration into the expanding collection of authoritative books being read and reread in Jewish scribal circles, with Kings edited as well to serve as its introduction. This allowed a chain of prophetic successors to Moses to be built artificially, making room for entire collections of prophetic warnings and explications of torah to be created or incorporated, read, and contemplated.

The reference to the king and to his need to read a copy of the book of the law all his life in Deut 17:14–20 is also likely a secondary expansion,[45] made with the same purpose in mind. Both strategies convert ecstatic prophecy, omen interpretation, and oracle-giving that were practices undertaken in the monarchic past into a written collection of expanded, fixed torah that now needs to be taught to emerging Jewish communities and interpreted by cultic personnel, כהנים,[46] so that all understand the way of YHWH Elohim, what he requires of his people, and what sort of consequences they could expect for failure to comply.[47]

---

45. It is deemed to belong to the "original Josianic edition" by, e.g., Gary N. Knoppers ("The Deuteronomist and the Deuteronomic Law of the King: A Reexamination of a Relationship," *ZAW* 108 [1996]: 329–46); Bernard M. Levinson ("The Reconceptualization of Kingship in Deuteronomy and the Deuteronomistic History's Transformation of the Torah," *VT* 51 [2001]: 511–34); Patricia Dutcher-Walls ("The Circumscription of the King: Deuteronomy 17:16–17 in its Ancient Social Context," *JBL* 121 [2002]: 601–16). Verses 14–20 are considered to be part of an exilic redaction by, e.g., Kratz (*Composition of Narrative Books*, 119, 133); Römer (*So-Called Deuteronomistic History*, 80, 131). Römer points out that it serves as "a table of contents" for the accounts of monarchy in Judges, Samuel, and Kings (139), with v. 14 foreshadowing the installation of kingship where the king will judge, recalling Judges. This is a more viable observation than the argument made by Kratz that everything in Deuteronomy that is not associated directly with cultic centralization or taken from the Book of the Covenant is secondary.

46. I agree with Römer that the king is portrayed as the addressee of torah rather than its mediator, as would have been the case in reality, and that he is made dependent on the transmitters of the law, beginning with Moses. But I want to qualify his point that Moses' successors are considered the Deuteronomistic scribes, the descendants of the Jerusalemite scribes and court officials. In the texts, they are the prophets who will be raised up by YHWH as he feels is necessary (Deut 18:5–20) (*So-Called Deuteronomistic History*, 140). In reality, they are likely to be the so, but they do not play this role in the story world.

47. My work would suggest the need to collapse the DtrN and the DtrP redactions into a single one, since the two are closely related and are part of the same larger thought complex in my understanding. The prophet advisor reminds the king of YHWH's commands, implicitly written in the copy of the book he should be reading

The decision to make the נביא the chosen legitimate means of conveying the divine will in the past must have had something to do with the role of the נביא as the mouthpiece for spontaneous divinely initiated communication to humans. The decision might have been motivated by a desire to emphasize that YHWH, the sole god, could not be consulted, manipulated, or held to a revealed course of action.

---

daily, and warns about consequences for failing to obey. Kratz has noted "DtrP is not far removed from DtrN and sometimes identical with it; it was inserted and revised either before or after the law or between one stratum of the law and the next" (*Composition of Narrative Books*, 170). However, I am not yet convinced that we can assume systematic redactions; the growth of these books, both individually and as a set, was probably a more complicated process, with individual scribes adding smaller illustrations that built on earlier trends, making explicit what was implicit in some cases and solidifying the explicit in others, both within and between books. Kratz has argued this in connection with DtrP; it is not a unitary redaction but rather sporadic yet deliberate insertions of blocks of material (*Composition of the Narrative Books*, 170). Here I have an understanding somewhat similar to that of Raymond F. Person Jr., that we should not think of individual redactors making extensive, systematic revisions of the entire collection of scrolls but of individual scribes making changes in single scrolls over a long period of time (*Deuteronomic School*, 8–9, 16).

Prophetic Memories in the Deuteronomistic Historical and the Prophetic Collections of Books

Ehud Ben Zvi

Introductory Issues

This essay is not about what monarchic or, for that matter, premonarchic prophets might have been or what they did or did not do. It is about how they were imagined by Persian period Jerusalem-centered literati whose memories of prophets of old were based on their readings of the Deuteronomistic historical and the prophetic collections of books. This essay is about why these prophets of old were imagined and remembered in certain ways and about the basic, general conceptual prototypes of prophecy and prophets that these literati shared among themselves, and about their social mindscape, which was underlying, generating, and reflecting itself in these memories

This type of exploration is consonant with the actual historical roles of Deuteronomistic and prophetic collections of books in Persian Yehud. They served above all as tools for didactic instruction and socialization among the literati who produced, read, and reread them, and likely—through the intermediation of these literati—for other groups in Yehud as well. These collections could serve such a role because reading these collections brought to the present of their rereading communities memories of the past and of the characters that populated it. These remembered and thus constantly construed characters became sites of memory within the community. The collection of fifteen prophetic books (hereafter PBC) and the Deuteronomistic historical collection (hereafter DHC) served to a large extent as platforms for a crucial social activity: evoking, exploring, and instilling a shared social memory. Through the process, readers construed and remembered characters. Connective features shared by characters in some group (e.g., prophets, priests, etc.) created a web of attributes that reflected the implied understanding of the basic nature of the group, or one may say of a conceptual prototype of a "generic" (nonindividualized) member of the group was (e.g., a prophet). Conversely, this prototype contributed to the shaping of social memories of members of the group (e.g., prophets).

It is worth stressing that for the most part the main sites of memory were not the very books in either the DHC or the PBC that evoked these central figures of old (e.g., the book of Judges, or the book of Isaiah), but the places, events and, above all, prophetic characters whose memory the books were seen to encode, and which the literati decoded as they imagined and vicariously experienced the past in their present. Thus, it is not by chance that, for instance, although all (or almost all) the information the literati in the Persian and later periods could gather about their main prophets of old was based on the prophetic books in their repertoire, they constantly referred to prophets and to their words, *not* to the prophetic books associated with them (see, for instance, Jer 26:18; Zech 1:4; 7:7; 2 Chr 24:19).[1] This is not to say that the prophetic books were not important as such, but that the "person" of the particular prophet that the readers shaped in their minds through shared readings and social interaction symbolized—and embodied, as it were—the contents and messages of the

---

1. The case of the or ספר התורה or משה/ספר תורת יהוה (e.g., Josh 1:8; 2 Kgs 14:6; 22:10–11; cf. 2 Chr 17:9; 34:14) is different. This "book" served both as a core site of memory by itself—unlike books of, e.g., Isaiah, Ezekiel or Judges—and as a book whose reading brought to the present of the remembering community central figures, events, and texts from the past. To the extent that this book was imagined only as Deuteronomy, in itself a problematic assumption in some cases (e.g., 2 Kgs 22:10–11; see Ehud Ben Zvi, "Imagining Josiah's Book and the Implications of Imagining It in Early Persian Yehud," in *Berührungspunkte: Studien zur Sozial- und Religionsgeschichte Israels und seiner Umwelt* (ed. R. Schmitt, I. Kottsieper, and J. Wöhrle; AOAT 250; Münster: Ugarit, 2008), 193–212, here 201–8), this characterization would have been a unique case of a prophetic book calling much mindshare to itself (see below), and as such it would have accentuated existing patterns of similarities and dissimilarities between Moses and the other prophets. See Ehud Ben Zvi, "Exploring the Memory of Moses the Prophet in Late Persian/Early Hellenistic Period Yehud/Judah," in *Remembering Biblical Figures in the Late Persian and Early Hellenistic Periods: Social Memory and Imagination* (ed. Diana V. Edelman and Ehud Ben Zvi; Oxford: Oxford University Press, 2013), 335–64.

book. The book was the means to recreate and encounter the "person." Reading the book made such a "person" of old present in the remembering community.²

This holds true, of course, for the DHC as well. The collection did not call attention to itself directly, but to what happened to Israel, the main protagonist of the history, through time. Through reading and rereading the DHC, the literati in Yehud imagined and vicariously experienced main events of Israel's past, and encountered time and again the multiple characters that populated the past as remembered and construed. All of these characters evoked memories of particular places, events, concepts, and even texts. Remembered characters became signs embodying and secreting meanings. Of course, much social mindshare was devoted to those that evoked and embodied concepts and events that were at the core of the collective social memory of the literati and that played important roles for identity formation. Thus, for instance, Abraham, Jacob, Moses, Joshua, David, and the like were sites that commanded much memory mindshare, while others, for instance, עדיה, Adaiah, (the father of ידידה, Jedidah, the mother of Josiah; see 2 Kgs 22:1) had very little. To be sure, a positive feedback loop was at work as well: the more important the character, the larger the mindshare that was associated with him or her, and conversely, the larger the mindshare he or she commanded, the more likely that some core concepts and images would end up being embodied in the character. Of course, these characters, or sites of memory, were imagined and (virtually) encountered within particular contexts associated with particular periods of the agreed-upon, shared, and remembered past. Thus they drew meaning, at least in part, within the context of the remembered circumstances of their relevant period. This memory-anchoring principle plays a central role in the shaping of both characterizations of core personages in "historical" (i.e., social memory) narratives about the past that existed in ancient Yehud (see below) and of crucial periods as remembered by the community. As it did both, it contributed much to the construction of their discursive significance.³

---

2. This process may have facilitated redactional activities in the books. After all, the books were meant to provide the messages of the prophets of old. An exploration of this point is, however, beyond the scope of this essay.

3. To be sure, (human) personages who were anchored to particular periods that existed in the memory of the community did not constitute all the (main) sites of memory that shaped the mentioned memoryscape. Particular (construed and remem-

Prophetic characters were as a group among the most salient sites of memory in the memoryscape of the Yehudite literati, and they appear in dramatically different periods within the basic narrative of Israel about itself. It is impossible to engage thoroughly with memory of each of monarchic or premonarchic prophetic figures in Yehud, even if one restricted the scope of the analysis only to those who were strongly evoked by the reading and rereading of the DHC, the PBC, or both in a way that informed each other in Yehud.[4] It is feasible, within the boundaries of a chapter, to explore *some* of the ways in which prophets and prophetic figures were remembered, the basic narratives that shaped their characterizations, and some aspects of the system of preferences that shaped the representation of prophets and prophecy in the DHB and the PBC.

Of course, this line of research will not tell us much about any "historical" Elijah or Zephaniah. But it will help us understand why prophets were remembered the way they were, and why they tended to be associated with certain periods and not others. Above all, it will shed some light on what it does to the literati to continuously remember a past in which monarchic or premonarchic prophets were imagined and vicariously encountered the way they were.[5] The point is to go beyond the obviously correct, and widely acknowledged understandings such as (1) that the shared social activity of creating a *present* past contributed much to identity formation and social

---

bered) spaces (e.g., Jerusalem, temple, "the land"), and transtemporal or perhaps panchronic characters such as YHWH and Israel were also among the main sites of memory. Yet *particular* periods, as socially construed and remembered by the community, became reenacted, as it were, as the literati who read, for instance, the prophetic books actually had to speak the voices of the prophets of old and YHWH's words to them. To do so implied vicariously experiencing the context in which the words were set (within the remembered past agreed upon by the literati). Even when the process of speaking voices of the past was not at work (e.g., in third person narratives), the readers still imagined a past and closely identified with many of the main characters, their experiences, and the spaces they walked through within the mentioned circumstances (e.g., the monarchic temple they construed as they read many texts set in that place).

4. That is, even if one leaves aside prophetic characters that are evoked primarily in Genesis–Numbers, Chronicles, or Ezra–Nehemiah. Even if one restricts the endeavor to those in the PBC alone, the matter would be well beyond the scope of even a lengthy monograph.

5. Or, in other words, what kind of impact such continuous remembering had upon literati engaged time and again in this process of remembering the past and, to a large extent, of mentally reenacting it within a socially shared imagination.

cohesion among the literati; (2) that it influenced nonliterati members of the community whose discourse was influenced by the former, and (3) that it set some boundaries between in-groups and out-groups. After all, like other communities, this one was one comprised of shared memory and imagination. Instead, I plan to begin to explore, for instance, some aspects of the grammar implied in the structure of the social memory that was shared and reenacted through shared readings and rereadings of these collections and its generative powers.

The emphasis above on remembering and shaping so-called "historical"—but actually social memory—*narratives* is not accidental. As is well known, social memories take the form of narratives or interrelated sets of narratives informing and balancing each other.[6] Readers assign significance to the characters populating a narrative as they internalize the basic plot and the communicative messages they find in it. Social memory among the literati in Yehud was construed as an interrelated set of narratives structured and, above all, remembered in terms of many individuals, heroes and villains, each of whom became a site of memory in a large, socially shared memoryscape of the literati (although from a later period, cf. Sir 44–49). In this context, prophetic memories in Yehud should be explored for the present purposes.

To explore the matters mentioned above, I will refer to prophetic memories, basic narratives, connective features, and underlying system of preferences shaping the representations of prophets and prophecy in the DHC, and will look into the social mindscape about prophecy that they suggest. I will focus mainly on (1) a few highly salient personages, because the more centrally they figured as sites of memory for the community, the more they attracted to themselves and thus embodied and communicated what was crucial for the community and because, conversely, the more they embodied and communicated these crucial concepts, the more central they became; and (2) "generic" prophetic characters or groups that reflect more clearly central conceptual images of what a prophet of old should be—that is, more than highly individualized portrayals of a certain individual or group.[7] Then I will continue with a

---

6. On the cross-cultural construction of social memories as narratives see, for instance, Eviatar Zerubavel, *Social Mindscapes: An Invitation to Cognitive Sociology* (Cambridge: Harvard University Press, 1997); idem, *Time Maps: Collective Memory and the Social Shape of the Past* (Chicago: University of Chicago Press, 2003).

7. For a fuller explanation of this approach, which is particularly relevant to the

similar study of the PBC. I will conclude with some observations about the interplay between the discussed features, since both PBC and DHC were read as part of one ideological discourse, namely that of the (at least ideologically) Jerusalem-centered literati of Yehud, and since the memories evoked by each of these collections informed each other and together shaped the comprehensive memory of the very same remembering community of literati.[8] Needless to say, this exploration will have to focus on paradigmatic (or at least potentially paradigmatic) cases, and to refrain from any attempt at comprehensiveness.

Two related caveats must be addressed before embarking on this exploration. First, the reconstructed "remembering community" of literati stands for an "ideal" community that conflates a number of historical communities of literati in Yehud that existed for a few generations. The crucial features that characterized these related communities are (1) a shared intellectual discourse; (2) a repertoire of central or authoritative books that included the DHC and the PBC or something very close to them; and (3) social memories about prophets that were shaped mainly by the two collections mentioned above, but not Chronicles.

These considerations lead to the second caveat: The "ideal" community discussed here must be a pre-Chronicles community. The comprehensive social memory of the pre-Chronicles period cannot be equated with that of the Chronicles and of post-Chronicles Yehud, because the composition and, above all, the reading and rereading of Chronicles by itself shaped and drew attention to complementary sets of memories of prophets that balanced, informed, and were in turn also balanced and informed

---

case of Kings, see Ehud Ben Zvi, "The Prophets," republished with minor changes under the same title in *The Books of Kings: Sources, Composition, Historiography, and Reception* (ed. Baruch Levine and André Lemaire; VTSup 129; Leiden: Brill, 2010), 387–99.

8. Whatever the origin of the sources or literary forerunners of each of books in their respective collections might be, the PBC and the DHC were read by the same literati and *together* shaped the comprehensive social memory of the late Persian, Jerusalem-centered, Yehudite literati.

It is worth stressing that the approach proposed here is a "bird's-eye view" approach. A colleague—who is both an historian and a field archaeologist—compared it to focusing on patterns that emerge when an helicopter overviews a site and its region, in contradistinction to advancing a detailed (ground-perspective) study of each building or room in a particular site. Of course, both approaches are necessary to advance knowledge on the site or issue, because they raise different questions.

by, the memories evoked by the two others collections. As a result, a new system of social memory interactions emerged. Texts construed as encoding memory are decoded within their *Sitz im Diskurs*. Or from a slightly different perspective, sites of memory become meaningful to the community not as standalone sites, but as part of a large memoryscape populated by other sites of memory. As the memoryscape shifts, by the reading and rereading of Chronicles, to some extent so does the meaning of each site of memory. This said, a significant result of the present study is that Chronicles follows, in a number of substantial cases, (ideological) generative grammars, and responds explicitly to implied questions and issues that existed within the pre-Chronicles communities and, conversely, that many features associated with prophecy and prophetic characters in the DHC particularly—but also in the PBC—come strongly and explicitly to the forefront in Chronicles. To put it in other words, Chronicles did not represent a radical departure from the pre-Chronicles discourse in Yehud, but quite the opposite: it shows significant continuity, at least in terms of prophecy and prophetic and prophetic characters.⁹

THE DHC, MEMORIES OF PROPHETIC CHARACTERS, AND THEIR IMPLICATIONS

The DHC communicated and shaped social memory in the form of a narrative. As is well known, the starting point of a "national" narrative is often particularly meaningful. To illustrate with a present day example, whether the historical narrative of "modern Germany" begins with Bismarck or with a plethora of great philosophers, writers, and musicians is clearly not a minor issue devoid of any discursive importance. The DHC begins with Moses the prophet. Significantly, he is *also* a prophet. Moreover, the opening of Deuteronomy (1:1) is reminiscent of those of prophetic books. Deuteronomy is *also* a prophetic book. These basic observations already sug-

---

9. See Ehud Ben Zvi, "Observations on Lines of Thought Concerning the Concepts of Prophecy and Prophets in Yehud, with an Emphasis on Deuteronomy–2 Kings and Chronicles," in *Words, Ideas, Worlds: Biblical Essays in Honour of Yairah Amit* (ed. Athalya Brenner and Frank H. Polak; Sheffield: Sheffield Phoenix, 2012), 1–19; idem, "Are There Any Bridges Out There? How Wide Was the Conceptual Gap between the Deuteronomistic History and Chronicles?" in *Community Identity in Judean Historiography: Biblical and Comparative Perspectives* (ed. Gary N. Knoppers and Kenneth A. Ristau; Winona Lake, Ind.: Eisenbrauns, 2009), 59–86.

gest blurred or fuzzy boundaries. Moses is a prophet *and* a lawgiver, *and* a few other things (e.g., a [super]kingly and priestly figure);[10] Deuteronomy is a prophetic book *and* a historical book *and* a pentateuchal book and so on. In addition, memories of Moses the prophet were encoded not only in Deuteronomy, but also in other pre-Chronicles texts (Exodus–Numbers). Obviously, this essay is not the appropriate place for any kind of significant study of the memories of Moses.[11] For present purposes, a few observations suffice. First, Moses was a central site of memory that came to embody in one person virtually every feature associated with prophecy. He was, among other things, a foreteller, a wonder maker, a historian, a teacher, a writer, a singer, an intercessor; a person who prayed for people, who admonished them, who suffered rejection, a conveyor of divine messages for the people, a doom announcer, and a hope maker.[12]

In other words, Moses was construed as the prophetic exemplar; he embodied all possible attributes assigned to prophets. Thus, it comes as no surprise that neither the DHC nor any other book available within the community evokes the image of another prophet to whom the full range of attributes is attached. In fact, only a few of them fulfilled even a significant number of them, and some features (e.g., singer) were not embodied in entire books (e.g., "singer" in Kings).

To remember Moses, presented at the beginning of historical narrative as extremely worthy of being remembered, was to remember and to internalize a particular organization of the past. There was (1) a pre-Mosaic and thus primarily nonprophetic period; (2) the time of Moses the paradigmatic prophet period; and (3) the post-Moses period or, better, the period of the Mosaic prophets (Deut 18:15, 18).[13] Prophets are intermediaries, and since the main divine communication that Moses transmitted to the people was "the torah," this structural periodization of the memory of the past was tantamount to the following: (1) the (mainly) pre-torah era (2) the period of Moses' prophetic communication, or torah, and (3) a torahic

---

10. See, for instance, John Lierman, *The New Testament Moses: Christian Perceptions of Moses and Israel in the Setting of the Jewish Religion* (Tübingen: Mohr Siebeck, 2004), which discusses perceptions of Moses in Yehud as well.

11. For my own contribution to the topic, see Ben Zvi, "Exploring the Memory of Moses."

12. See note above.

13. For the point that these prophets can only be Mosaic, not equal to Moses, see Deut 34:10.

period (cf. 2 Kgs 17:13). The overlap of these structures was consistent with the way in which Israel figured as a "torah-centered community" within the social mindscape of the literati. It created a clear overlap between the torahic period and the period of the Mosaic prophets.

This being said, it is particularly worth noting that, on the *surface*, the historiographical narratives addressing the beginning of the torahic period of Mosaic prophets in the DHC did not draw the attention of its primary readers and rereaders toward memories of prophets. To illustrate, Joshua is never called a prophet or even "man of god,"[14] and the term נביא does not appear in the book at all. The crossing of the Jordan, although clearly reminiscent of the crossing of the Sea of Reeds,[15] was shaped in social memory far more as a liturgical enterprise than as "divine miracle" associated with a prophetic intermediary.

Yet Joshua was remembered as a leader who followed Moses as the main divine intermediary (see Josh 1:1–2). Moreover, the memory of Joshua is that of a person who consistently referred to Moses and to the contents of the divine message that he communicated, namely "torah." He was imagined as learning "torah," reminding people of "torah," encouraging them to follow it, admonishing them about the consequences of abandoning it, writing its words, and so on (e.g., Josh 1:8; 8:31–32; 22:5; 23:6). Thus, Joshua becomes an exemplar of a Mosaic prophet as construed by texts such as 2 Kgs 17:13, which reads:

שבו מדרכיכם הרעים ושמרו מצותי חקותי ככל התורה אשר צויתי את
אבתיכם ואשר שלחתי אליכם ביד עבדי הנביאים

This text communicates YHWH's memory of "the prophets" as a chain of transmission for the Mosaic torah. The community of readers was supposed to orient their memory to YHWH's and to make YHWH's their own collective memory (cf. Zech 1:6).

---

14. The only one referred to as a "man of God" in Joshua is Moses (see Josh 14:6; cf. Deut 33:1).

15. On these matters, see, among others, Jan Wagenaar, "Crossing the Sea of Reeds (Exod 13–14) and the Jordan (Josh 3–4): A Priestly Framework for the Wilderness Wandering Studies in the Book of Exodus," in *Studies in the Book of Exodus: Redaction, Reception, Interpretation* (ed. M. Vervenne; BETL 126; Leuven: Peeters, 1996), 461–70 and bibliography.

The texts of 2 Kgs 17:13 and Zech 1:6, along with others, reflected and shaped a sense of *partial* conceptual blending between prophetic characters and YHWH's servants within the discourse of the community.¹⁶ One may note the use of the *exact epithet* עבד יהוה in the book of Joshua. It was associated time and again with Moses.¹⁷ But significantly, it was also used for Joshua. This choice, especially given the context in which the exact epithet was used (see Josh 24:29–30; see also Judg 2:8–9), served pragmatically to underline the role of Joshua as the successor of Moses, as YHWH's intermediary—similar to Moses, but not his equal (compare and contrast with Deut 34:5–10).¹⁸ The expression evoked also a sense of participation

---

16. Other texts include 1 Kgs 14:18; 15:29; 2 Kgs 9:7, 36; 10:10; 14:25; 17:13, 23; 21:10; 24:2; Isa 20:3; Jer 7:25; 25:4; 26:5; 29:19; 35:15; 44:4; Ezek 38:17; Amos 3:7. I emphasize "partial" because the realm of YHWH's servants included nonprophetic characters (see, for instance, Isa 41:8–9; 56:6; Jer 27:6; 30:10; Job 1:8). A partial blending of concepts of YHWH's servants and prophets is well attested in later literature as well. See for instance Ezra 9:11; Dan 9:6, 10.

17. See, e.g., Jos 1:1, 13, 15; 8:31, 33; 11:12; 12:6; 13:8; 14:7; 18:7; 22:2, 4, 5.

18. For the use of עבד יהוה as an epithet of Moses, see also 2 Kgs 18:12; 2 Chr 1:3; 24:6 (cf. 1 Chr 6:34; and see also Neh 10:30; Dan 9:11). Among the intended primary readers of the DHC (and Chronicles), the epithet brought up associations with the figure of Moses. In Psalms, the epithet עבד יהוה evoked the image of David; see Ps 18:1; 36:1 (cf. 1 Kgs 8:66; Isa 37:35; Ezek 34:23; Ps 132:10; 2 Chr 6:15–17; 6:42). In the PBC, there is, of course, Isa 42:19 (cf. Isa 42:1; 52:13; 53:11). The question of whether, within the discourse of Persian-period Yehud, readers of Isaiah would have read some play, at least at some level, between the image of servant Israel and their own image of Moses, the servant of YHWH (inasmuch as in Greek literature Achilles was "the swift of foot") is beyond the scope of this essay. But it relates directly to the investigation of the concept "Israel" in the shared social mindscape of the literati, which involved both transtemporal Israel and the literati themselves, as they identified with it. The matter should be addressed in a separate essay.

Many other personages populating the past were characterized as YHWH's servants (e.g., Abraham, Caleb, Ahijah, Elijah, Isaiah, Nebuchadnezzar and Zerubbabel), but the epithet עבד יהוה was not associated with them. There are additional texts that underline the role of Joshua as the successor of Moses, though clearly not his equal. One may note, for instance, the command to Joshua in Josh 5:15 to remove his sandals, which evokes the memory of Moses' removal of his sandals (Exod 3:5). One may note, however, that, among other differences, it was YHWH who gave the command to Moses, but an angelic figure, namely, שר צבא יהוה to Joshua. For another example, compare and contrast Deut 34:7 with Josh 24:29.

in a long chain of prophets who were remembered as YHWH's עבדים, even if the exact epithet was not used in relation to them.[19]

Joshua was remembered as one who was contacted directly by the deity, not through an intermediary, just as Moses was (cf. Deut 31:23; Josh 1:6 with Deut 31:7).[20] Moreover, the literati imagined that YHWH explicitly chose to inform Moses, in Joshua's presence, of the future exile and the promise of restoration afterwards (see Deut 31:14–21 and cf. Amos 3:7; and note the obligation to teach this prophecy in Deut 31).[21] One may note also the choice of the plural verbal form כתבו in reference to this prophecy in verse 19. This choice explicitly asks the readers to imagine Joshua as included, despite the expected use of singular form in verse 22 that signals the centrality and incomparability of Moses.

The memory of Joshua is evoked and clearly "prophetized" in 1 Kgs 16:34. One may note that the clause X כדבר יהוה אשר דבר ביד is used elsewhere, with prophets standing for X (see 1 Kgs 14:18; 15:29; 17:16; 2 Kgs 24:2).

Moreover, Persian-period readers of Joshua likely understood Josh 24:19–20 as prophetic, in the sense of foreseeing the future. Within the discourse of the period, Joshua's construction of the present of his time in terms of the fulfillment of all YHWH's good promises (Josh 21:45; 23:14) was pregnant with significance, since from their perspective, all the "bad" promises were fulfilled as well.

In fact, the literati were supposed to construe Joshua's great present in a way reminiscent of that of Solomon, and *vice versa* (cf. Josh 21:45; 23:14 with 1 Kgs 8:56). The purposeful use of the same language drew attention to some narrative/mnemonic similarities. In both cases, once the remembered narrative reaches its highest point, memories of the following periods had

---

19. See, for instance, 2 Kgs 9:7; 17:13; 21:10; Jer 7:25; 26:5; 35:15; 44:4; Ezek 38:17; Zech 1:6; see also 1 Kgs 14:18; 15:29; 2 Kgs 10:10; 14:25; Isa 20:3. As mentioned above, not only prophets were characterized as "servants of YHWH," but, leaving aside patriarchal figures that belong to an earlier period in Israel's mnemonic map and David, the vast majority of *persons* who were remembered as YHWH's servants and who populated the period from Moses to the catastrophe were prophets.

20. One may still note a difference in the choice of verbal forms, namely, ויאמר versus ויצו. The first tends to be used in this literary unit for YHWH's talk with Moses; the second for YHWH's talk with Joshua, and for Moses' talk with the people (see Deut 31:10, 14, 16, 23, 25), but see Josh 1:1.

21. Note the motif of the prophet as teacher. This motif is clearly assumed and considered central in 2 Kgs 17:13, and later on in Chronicles.

to be structured in terms of a general decline plot. In the case of 1 Kgs 8, the underlying concept of (future) exile, bubbles quite saliently to the surface of the "highest point" narrative (see 1 Kgs 8:46–53 [cf. 2 Chr 6:36–39]; cf. 1 Chr 16:35). Likewise, the dramatic future downturn is implied and clearly evoked in Persian-period readings of Josh 21:45; 23:14. Moreover, both speakers (Joshua and Solomon) were construed as sharing an understanding of history (future and past) as a sequence of fulfillments of YHWH's promises. This message was clearly "prophetic."[22] In addition, both Joshua and Moses were characterized as prophetic because they foresaw the future,[23] and because they explained to the people the causality governing history (namely, YHWH's will and responses).

Joshua was also imagined as a memory maker or "national" historian, a person telling the people of his generation their (hi)story, and indirectly the Persian-period literati who overhear him—as they virtually "experience" the event through their readings, so they may learn from it (see Josh 23:3–4; 24:2–13). Although "summaries of history" may appear in different contexts,[24] within the DHC, they tend to be associated with prophetic voices (see 1 Sam 12:8–15; Judg 6:8–10; see also Judg 10:11–14, in which a prophetic personage is implied).[25] Along with the construction of prophets as those who admonished Israel by recalling their past (e.g., Jer 16:10–13; Ezekiel 20), this tendency contributed to the prophetization of the memory of Joshua.

---

22. See Deut 18:14–22; 1 Kgs 12:15; 14:18; 15:29; 16:12; 17:16; 2 Kgs 9:36; 10:10; 14:25; 17:23; 24:2; cf. 1 Kgs 11:31–35 with 1 Kgs 12:15; 1 Kgs 14:7–11 with 1 Kgs 15:29; 2 Kgs 15:12 with 2 Kgs 10:30. These texts carry a potentially "misleading" interpretation that had no place in the discourse of the community (e.g., things simply happened because prophets prophesied them). As one would expect, this potential generated the development of notes and comments meant to counter such potential "misinterpretation." For a discussion of these and other aspects see Ehud Ben Zvi, "Prophets and Prophecy in the Compositional and Redactional Notes in I–II Kings," *ZAW* 105 (1993): 331–51.

23. On 1 Chr 16:35 and David's knowledge of the future see Ehud Ben Zvi, "Who Knew What? The Construction of the Monarchic Past in Chronicles and Implications for the Intellectual Setting of Chronicles," in *Judah and the Judeans in the Fourth Century B.C.E.* (ed. Oded Lipschits, Gary N. Knoppers, and Rainer Albertz; Winona Lake, Ind.: Eisenbrauns, 2007), 349–60.

24. See, for instance, Jer 16:10–13; Ezekiel 20; Psalms 78, 105, 106, 107, 136; Neh 9:6–37; Jdt 5:3–23; 1 Macc 2:50–68.

25. The alternative, that is, to imagine a kind of direct divine revelation to the entire people as in Sinai, seems very unlikely.

Like Moses, Joshua is not remembered only as a prophet, but *also* as a prophet. It is worth noting that in this case the prophetization of Joshua does not lead to memories of a miracle-worker, healer, or king-maker prophet (though he is a covenant-maker),[26] but implies some of the characteristic features of prophecy that are similar to those that emerge as dominant in Chronicles.[27] Significantly, Chronicles depicts characters who fulfill clear prophetic roles, and thus are imagined as "prophetic," but who are not explicitly designated as "prophets," and who fulfill other roles as well.[28]

---

26. Joshua, like Moses, is a covenant maker. He also writes a covenantal text (Josh 24:25–26). Memories of Samuel evoked by 1 Sam 12 were clearly reminiscent of those of Moses and to a minor extent those of Joshua. (See also Jer 11.) The question of whether prophetic roles and covenant making were closely associated within the mindscape of the literati cannot be discussed here. To be sure, the usual presence of historical reviews in the introduction to covenants, of statements exhorting the subordinate to fulfill its obligations, and common warnings about the punishments that would fall on those who break it, created a certain amount of overlap between prophetic roles and figures and covenant making. However, it is unclear whether connections between the two went beyond these shared generic roles within the Persian-period literati's mindscape.

27. I have dealt elsewhere with prophets in Chronicles. See Ehud Ben Zvi, "Chronicles and Its Reshaping of Memories of Monarchic Period Prophets: Some Observations," in *Prophets and Prophecy in Ancient Israelite Historiography* (ed. Mark Boda and Lissa M. Beale; Winona Lake, Ind.: Eisenbrauns, 2013), 167–88.

28. Yairah Amit, among others, maintains that in Chronicles, "a king, a Levite or any other person, functions as prophet when he utters prophetic statements in the Chronistic sermonizing style," Yairah Amit, "The Role of Prophecy and Prophets in the Chronicler's World," in *Prophets, Prophecy, and Prophetic Texts in Second Temple Judaism* (ed. Michael H. Floyd and Robert D. Haak; LHBOTS 427; London: T&T Clark, 2006), 80–101, here 89. The "Chronistic sermonizing style" to which she refers is the style of the "Levitical sermon" as discussed in Gerhard von Rad, "The Levitical Sermon in I and II Chronicles," in *The Problem of the Hexateuch and Other Essays* (Edinburgh: Oliver & Boyd, 1966), 267–80. Contrast Amit's position with Schniedewind's, for whom prophets are *only* those that Chronicles explicitly designate as such (e.g., William M. Schniedewind, "Prophets and Prophecy in the Books of Chronicles," in *The Chronicler as Historian* [ed. M. Patrick Graham, Kenneth G. Hoglund, and Steven L. McKenzie; JSOTSup 238; Sheffield: Sheffield Academic Press, 1997], 204–24, here 214). Suffice it to say that Chronicles reflects and shapes a conceptual field populated by both "prophets" and prophetic characters who deliver prophecies, even if they are not *explicitly* called prophets. This shared conceptual field strongly associates one image with the other. On these matters, see Ben Zvi, "Chronicles and Its Reshaping of Memories."

The fact that there are no explicit references to "prophets" in Joshua is significant,[29] but so is the fact that Joshua was imagined as a prophetic character, that is, as one who embodies and fulfills attributes associated with prophecy. It is also significant that several of the prophetic attributes associated with Joshua point at a trend that emerges saliently and explicitly in Chronicles.

The situation is not essentially different in Judges.[30] To be sure, Deborah is designated אשה נביאה in Judg 4:4. Significantly, she is *also* a prophet (like others, she "judges" Israel; see Judg 4:4–5) and her most memorable prophetic contribution is singing a song that construes memory (cf. Deut 31:22, 30; 32; and Exod 15:20; note the characterization of singers as prophets in 1 Chr 25:1).[31] Moreover, it is worth noting that in Judg 5:1 the song is associated with both Deborah (the main character and the "prophet") and Barak the military leader, who partakes in a prophetic role (cf. Chronicles' characterization of some kings and military leaders as people who uttered prophetic speeches).[32]

The only other explicit reference to a נביא is in Judg 6:8–10, in which, significantly a "summary of history" along with the its lessons is communicated (and see Chronicles and see above).[33]

---

29. See my previous "Prophets and Prophecy in the Compositional and Redactional Notes."

30. On prophecy in Judges, see Christoph Levin, "Prophecy in the Book of Judges," paper presented at the 2002 Annual Meeting of the Society of Biblical Literature, November 23–26, 2002.

31. The memory "category" of singing prophetess includes Miriam and Deborah. But due to Hannah's song (1 Sam 2:1–10), her memory was at least partially "prophetized." Clearly within the book of Samuel, her song was presented as proleptic, and thus likely read as "prophetic" from the perspective of a remembering community in late Persian Yehud and early Hellenistic Judah (see, e.g., v. 10).

At a later time Targum Jonathan made the implicit association of Hannah and her song with prophecy explicit. See *Tg.* 1 Sam 2:1: צליאת חנה ברוח נבואה ("And Hannah prayed in a prophetic spirit"; Eveline Van Staalduine-Sulman, *The Targum of Samuel* [Leiden: Brill, 2002], 204–5). On evidence for a characterization of Hannah as a prophetess in Septuagint traditions (e.g., L), see Stanley D. Walters, "Hannah and Anna: The Greek and Hebrew Texts of 1 Samuel 1," *JBL* 107 (1988): 400 n. 24. On Hannah's partially prophetic characterization in 1 Sam 2, see James W. Watts, *Psalm and Story: Inset Hymns in Hebrew Narrative* (JSOTSup 139; Sheffield: JSOT, 1992), 30–32.

32. See Amit, "Role of Prophecy," and Ben Zvi, "Chronicles and its Reshaping of Memories."

33. The text of Judges preserved in 4QJudg[a] demonstrates the existence of a text

It may be noted also that in Judg 6:8–10 the role of the prophet is reminiscent of that of the מלאך יהוה of Judg 2:1–3, and reflects a social mindscape in which these two conceptual realms already partially overlap and partially "blend" with one another (see Isa 44:26; Hag 1:13; Mal 1:1; 2 Chr 36:15–16).

In addition, within the discourse of the Persian period, people upon whom רוח יהוה descended included not only judges but prophets (see Isa 61:1). The community was asked to remember Gideon as one who consulted the deity through a kind of trial to ascertain whether to wage war or not, an activity usually associated with prophecy (see 1 Kgs 22; cf. 2 Chr 18).

More importantly, the community was supposed to remember that, in the period of Judges of their shared memory, Jotham played a crucial role as speaker who made sense of the events described in the historical narrative (cf. 1 Sam 12; prophetic speeches in Chronicles). In addition, within the context of a Persian-period remembering community, the core of Jotham's speech, namely the parable in Judg 9:8–15 was most likely construed as significant not only to its immediate context in the world portrayed in Judg 9, but also as a prophetic comment about future kings. This speech, oriented to the longterm future, is clearly at work in the prophetic characters in the PBC, and in Moses and Joshua. This case also attests to a tendency to construe a multi-temporality of prophetic words: Jotham clearly refers to Abimelech, but his words could apply to numerous other events.[34]

The most memorable prophet in the book of Samuel is Samuel himself, even though he is preceded by the איש אלהים of 1 Sam 2:27–36. A substantial study of the memory of Samuel in Yehud demands a separate research venue. A few observations about memories of him, however, suf-

---

of Judges in which Judg 6:11–13 immediately followed 6:2–6. It is possible that the note mentioned above was a late addition to the text. If this is the case, it would only demonstrate the discursive generative power of the considerations advanced in this essay. Certain approaches to memories of prophets existed that would tend to create explicit, particular memories like those expressed in these verses. On the possible text-critical issues, see Julio C. Trebolle Barrera, "Textual Variants in 4QJudg[a] and the Textual and Editorial History of the Book of Judges," *RevQ* 14 (1990): 229–45; and Richard S. Hess, "The Dead Sea Scrolls and Higher Criticism of the Hebrew Bible: The Case of 4QJudg[a]," in *The Scrolls and the Scriptures: Qumran Fifty Years After* (ed. Stanley E. Porter and Craig A. Evans; Sheffield: Sheffield Academic Press, 1997), 122–28.

34. The concept of multitemporality of prophetic words is clearly at work in Chronicles. See Ben Zvi, "Who Knew What?"

fice for the present purpose. He was among the individual prophets in Samuel–Kings with largest narrative space, and one with highest evaluation and mindshare (see not only the narratives about him in 1 Samuel, but also Jer 15:1; Ps 99:6). The tendency to remember such a great prophet of the past in ways reminiscent of Moses is at work here too, just like the tendency to shape him as a great figure, though still of less stature than Moses (cf. the case of Elijah, another individual prophet with much mindshare; see below).

Given the focus in this essay on general systemic trends and tendencies rather than on particular individual traits, it is worth stressing that Samuel is reminiscent of Moses—as is usually noticed[35]—but that, unlike Moses, he begins a long line of named individual prophets associated with the establishment of kings and royal dynasties.[36] This chain of prophets plays an important role for the Saul-David-Solomon transition, and for the basic narrative about the northern kingdom reflected in and remembered in Yehud on the basis of the book of Kings.[37] Conversely, a systemic preference for emphasizing this aspect within memories about monarchic prophets developed.[38] Given that the book of Kings and the memories it evoked were structured around kings, it is only to

---

35. See, for instance, Andries Breytenbach, "Who Is Behind the Samuel Narrative?" in *Past, Present, Future: The Deuteronomistic History and the Prophets* (ed. J. C. de Moor and H. F. van Rooy; OTS 44; Leiden, Brill, 2000), 50–61.

36. Moses does not appoint kings, but he is a kingly figure himself, far more than Samuel. In fact, in the Hebrew Bible Moses is also characterized as a royal figure, one far more powerful than the deuteronomic king envisaged in Deut 17:14-20, as I discussed in "Exploring the Memory of Moses." On the royal image of Moses in the Hebrew Bible see Lierman, *New Testament Moses*, 79–89. Moses is clearly a royal figure in some later Second Temple texts, e.g., Philo, *De vita Mosis* 1:334 (see Wayne A. Meeks, *The Prophet-King: Moses Traditions and the Johannine Christology* [NovTSup 14; Leiden: Brill, 1967], 107–16), and later on in some rabbinic texts (see Exod. Rab. 40:2; 48:4; Num. Rab. 15:13; Midr. Tehillim Ps 1; b. Zebah. 102a).

37. The chain of violent replacements of leaders begins actually with the איש אלהים of 1 Sam 2:27-36. Yet this prophet, whose role was narratively and mnemonically necessary to allow for the rise of Samuel, did not depose a reigning king. This said that the presence of the crucial temporal term עַד־עוֹלָם in both 1 Sam 2:30 and 2 Sam 7:16 suggests that at some level 1 Sam 2:30 served as an interpretive note looking forward to the rest of the DHC and balancing other positions there. The issue is, regrettably, beyond the scope of this essay.

38. Note, for instance, how the image of Elijah suddenly departs from its comparative Mosaic framework in 1 Kgs 19:15b-16. On Moses and Elijah see below.

be expected that this chain of prophets should be given salience, and that eventually the rereading community should develop a mindshare commensurate with the narrative space given to the relevant prophetic characters in Samuel–Kings. It is also to be expected that it would cause a substantial decrease in the number of individualized prophets associated with Judah after Nathan, and certainly after Rehoboam, for neither the agreed-upon collective and comprehensive memory of the period nor its basic ideological discourse could have allowed for a story about a prophet of YHWH anointing a new dynasty in Judah instead of the Davidic/Solomonic one. This lack of individualized prophetic memories for monarchic Judah, with the salient exception of Isaiah,[39] characterizes the book of Kings. Of course, it was balanced by the PBC for the crucial late monarchic period (see below), and later in a less memorable, but from a temporal perspective far more comprehensive way by Chronicles.

Nathan, the most salient prophet in the second part of the book of Samuel and 1 Kgs 1, is, of course, a central member of the mentioned chain of prophets. But the Nathan of memory, like all larger characters, fulfills more than one memory role. To remember Nathan was to remember the temple and David. Yet it is also to remember the role of the prophet in leading David to recognize his past sin and in announcing his punishment. This is particularly relevant within the context of a Persian-period community. The latter likely saw a reflection of themselves in the suffering, weakened בן מות David, fully aware of having grievously sinned[40] and thoroughly humiliated, as he is characterized in the latter part of Samuel. This David stood typologically for "their" Israel. Nathan as a site of memory embodied and reminded the community of the suffering, humiliated David of the present, and of the great temple of the future, and of the late monarchic period prophets of the PBC.

Since I have written elsewhere about prophets and prophecy in the book of Kings,[41] only a few observations are in order for present purposes.

---

39. Significantly, even Jeremiah is not mentioned in Kings.

40. For a reading of the David of Samuel that develops, among others, a portrayal in which David's "consciousness of having sinned" plays an important role, see Frank H. Polak, "David's Kingship—A Precarious Equilibrium," in *Politics and Theopolitics in the Bible and Postbiblical Literature* (ed. H. G. Reventlow, Y. Hoffman and B. Uffenheimer; JSOTSup 171; Sheffield: Sheffield Academic Press, 1994), 119–47.

41. See Ben Zvi, "Generic Prophets"; idem, "Prophets and Prophecy in the Compositional and Redactional Notes."

The first is that Kings reflects and contributes to the shaping of a general concept of the prophets of old as a group—to be distinguished from particular highly individual prophets—who are: (1) a faithful minority of servants of YHWH who were likely to become an object of persecution if the ruling leader was sinful; (2) a group that was aware of Israel's history of misconduct that justified the extreme divine punishment against monarchic Israel, and that unsuccessfully tried to bring Israel to YHWH; (3) a group that embodied a reminder of Israel's history of rejecting YHWH and of disregarding the advise of YHWH's servants; and (4) a group associated with transmission of YHWH's teachings, standing at the earliest spot in the chain of transmission of these teachings and leading directly to the remembering community (see, explicitly, 2 Kgs 17:13).[42] In other words, these "generic" prophets were clearly and explicitly Mosaic prophets.[43]

As for the strongly individualized prophets, the two most memorable prophets that populated the book were Elijah and Isaiah.[44] Not surprisingly, both characters, or sites of memory, were encoded in other books in addition to Kings (see the book of Isaiah; Mal 3:23 [most ET. 4:5]; 2 Chr 21:12–15). Many stories contribute to the construction of Elijah and Elisha, but it is particularly noteworthy that Elijah's narrative, and thus his memory, was shaped so as to be reminiscent in many ways of that of Moses the prophet, while at the same time making sure that Elijah remains secondary to him.[45] The focus on remembering Isaiah and on his worthiness to be remembered, so strongly encoded in Kings, directly relates to the fact that he (along with Hezekiah) embodied the memory of the glorious deliverance of Jerusalem in 701 B.C.E. that stood as a direct counterpoint to the catastrophe of 586 B.C.E. This issue, as will be noted below, is central to the way in which the PBC organizes knowledge about the past and its prophetic voices.

---

42. See Ben Zvi, "Generic Prophets."

43. See ibid.

44. As important as Elisha is, he remains the person who "poured water on the hands of Elihu" (2 Kgs 3:11) and secondary to his master. Note Mal 3:23 [most ET 4:5], which mentions Elijah not Elisha, and 2 Chr 21:12–15 of which, "theoretically," the sender should have been Elisha, but which was attributed to Elijah, most likely because he was more saliently in the mindshare of the community.

45. For some comparisons between memories associated with Elijah and Moses see, for instance, Jerome T. Walsh, *1 Kings* (Berit Olam; Collegeville, Minn.: Liturgical Press, 1996), 284–89. The presence of a significant number of "parallels" has been widely acknowledged.

But before turning to the PBC, another important aspect of the ways in which the DHC contributed to the shaping of social memory about prophets and prophecy demands attention. The memory world of the community could not have started with the catastrophe of 586 B.C.E., but had to go back to the remembered establishment of a torah-centered community in the days of Moses, the prophet who mirrored their ideological image of themselves as a torah-centered community. It could not have concluded with the events of 586 or those narrated in 2 Kgs 25:27–30. To be sure, there were genre and discursive reasons to conclude the collection with the fall of the polity and its aftermath,[46] but the collection served as a tool to organize knowledge and shape a general social mindscape, including those involving prophecy and prophets. Although the DHC, like any historiographical collection, evoked memories of past prophets, it also generated tendencies towards the shaping of memories about prophetic characters in the pre-utopian future.[47] Reading the DHC suggested to the remembering community that these future personages, unlike many of the former prophets, would most likely not be involved in deposing and anointing Israelite kings, but would be Mosaic and absolutely necessary in the future as well. This is so because they are required to warn Israel and urge it to keep YHWH's commandments and statutes, in accordance with all the torah that YHWH commanded Israel and that was sent to Israel by the prophets, to paraphrase 2 Kgs 17:13. Within the underlying ideological discourse of the community, the prophets were associated with the divine teaching, and they were and necessary for its transmission.

The PBC, Memories of Prophets, and Their Implications

Even if there is little explicit narrative in the prophetic books, the PBC contributed much to the creation of social memories, which were organized and remembered in narrative form.[48]

---

46. E.g., Kings being a book about, and structured around (Israelite) kings; the centrality of the catastrophe of 586 B.C.E. within the discourse of the community, and its construction as a watershed, etc.

47. Like most historiographical narratives, the DHC does not address the real utopian future. These matters are addressed by the PBC, and it is the latter that evokes many memories of utopian futures.

48. As memories usually are. See above, n. 5.

Narratively shaped social memories behave as all narratives do. They have beginnings and endings, and their plots are rarely uniform in terms of temporal density. They emphasize certain periods and deemphasize others. Since each prophetic book within the collection was meant to bring to the present a particular prophetic character of the past, it could not but structure time in terms of prophetic figures. Although this is an obvious genre requirement, it does something to the community to remember a past that is structured around prophetic characters, and it does tell something about the mindscape of the community that it developed a strong social preference for books about prophets of old rather than about other possible characters (e.g., priests, sages, or the like).

Unlike the DHC, the main narrative implied and communicated by the PBC, as a whole, begins with the crisis in the Assyrian period, mainly in terms of both a prefiguration of and a counterpoint to the catastrophe of 586 B.C.E. (e.g., Micah, Hosea, Isaiah). The second period it draws attention to is set around that catastrophe, preceding and directly leading to it, and including its immediate aftermath (e.g., Zephaniah, Jeremiah, Ezekiel). The third main period with which prophetic characters were associated was that of the early restoration.

To be sure this does not mean that readers of these books had to imagine that there were no prophets before Amos or Hosea—in fact, they could not have done so—but it means that these books focused the readers' and rereaders' mindshare mainly on prophetic characters associated with these three periods. As such, they reflect a mnemonic narrative shaped around the catastrophe, explaining time and again its causes and the didactic lessons to be learned from it, and providing hope for the future.

The PBC shaped a social mnemonic narrative about the late monarchic past characterized by a guiding concept of decline and constant slide toward the catastrophe from the period of Hezekiah on. Significantly, there was no room in that narrative for Josiah as a salient, positive site of memory. In fact, it is particularly worth noting that the second main period did not begin with the time of Manasseh (which is fully ignored) but with that Josiah.[49] Even the glorious period of Isaiah and Hezekiah was seen as inexorably leading toward the destruction (Isa 39:1–8; this section directly leads the reader to Isaiah 40). Within this implied narra-

---

49. See Ehud Ben Zvi, "Josiah and the Prophetic Books: Some Observations," in *Good Kings and Bad Kings* (ed. Lester L. Grabbe; LHBOTS 393; EABS 5; London: T&T Clark, 2005).

tive about the past, the late monarchic prophets had to be imagined as: (a) aware of the incoming and justified catastrophe—after all, YHWH had informed the prophets of the deity's plans for Israel (cf. Amos 3:7); (b) warning voices (both of this attribute and the previous one are consistent with a mindscape in which YHWH is construed as a deity who warns before punishment); (c) on the whole unsuccessful in terms of their generation, since the catastrophe did happen; and (d) successful in the sense that their words as encoded in the relevant books, and they themselves, became important sites of social memory for the later community, which stood in both continuity and discontinuity with late monarchic Israel/Judah.

The latter point is worth elaborating. Of course, within this scheme late monarchic Israel/Judah had to be imagined as on the whole rejecting their prophets, so as to fulfill their role as sinners meriting the catastrophe that came to them (cf. Jer 35:15; Zech 1:4–6; cf. 7:12–14). This explicitly reflects and communicates a central feature of the collective memory of monarchic-period prophets: they voiced unsuccessful warnings to their own time and society (cf. also Jer 7:25; 25:4; 26:9; 35:15; 44:4).[50] Yet, because they were unsuccessful, they and their contemporaries became successful sites of memory for the remembering community in Yehud. In fact, memories of both the prophets of old and of those who rejected them were structured and didactically used to communicate what, within the story, the late monarchic prophets could not accomplish in their own generation. Thus matters of continuity and discontinuity between the literati in Yehud and monarchic Israel/Judah were negotiated.

This narrative clearly reflected and reinforced the crucial role of the memory of the catastrophe and the related concept of exile and overcoming exile had in the discourse of Yehud. This is not surprising, given the general ideological discourse of the period and the numerous material reminders of the catastrophe that confronted Yehudites and especially Jerusalemites at the time, since the ruins of monarchic Judah that were all around them. It is also fully consistent with the very basic metanarrative directly evoked by the collection, namely, that late monarchic Israel sinned, was severely punished. But, loved by YHWH, they will be led to an utopian future. In the meantime there exists a measure of partial relief to Israel in the form of a Jerusalemite temple and community in Yehud.

---

50. See also, for later periods, Neh 9:30.

Yet it is worth stressing that the implied narrative and the underlying systemic preferences that led to the above-mentioned temporal mindshare within the collection of prophetic books, and the organization of memories of the past in terms of individual prophetic characters, as powerful and significant as they were to the community, had to be, and were, placed in proportion within the PBC itself because of other features within their *Sitz im Diskurs*. In other words, demands that were implied in the discursive logic of the community and the "rules" of social memory called for and required that the above-mentioned features be balanced.

As central as a catastrophe may have been in the collective memory of a particular group, Israelite memory could not have its starting point in the catastrophe itself or in its surrounding era, just as Armenian and Jewish arrays of social memories cannot begin with their respective catastrophes in the last century, but must include a very substantial and substantive precatastrophe period. Similarly, remembering and explaining Israel's catastrophe in 586 B.C.E. required a story about Israel that well preceded the events of 586 B.C.E., and those directly related to them in terms of the social memory of the period (e.g., Sennacherib's invasion and the nondestruction of Jerusalem in 701, and the rebuilding of the temple in the Persian period). Not only did the PBC require other memory-evoking texts within the community to balance itself, but even within the PBC there are crucial references to sites of memory situated well before the late monarchic period (e.g., Isa 63:11–12; Hos 2:15; 9:9–10; 10:9; 12:14; Mic 6:4; Mal 3:22 [most ET 4:4]).

In addition, and most importantly, the community was to remember the figure of Moses, the prophetic exemplar par excellence within its ideological discourse and social memory. The prophetic book of Moses (i.e., Deuteronomy) already called into question any implicit claims that the prophets worthy of being remembered are only those in the PBC. In fact, it called into question the temporal boundaries of the PBC, since Deuteronomy was to some extent *also* a prophetic book.

Moreover, the figure of Moses clearly influenced the ways in which the prophetic characters in the PBC were construed and vice versa, creating a sense of connection among all these prophetic figures. This is true not only in more or less obvious cases such as Jeremiah and Ezekiel,[51] but also at a

---

51. See Henry McKeating, "Ezekiel the 'Prophet Like Moses'?" *JSOT* 101 (1994): 97–109; Christopher R. Seitz, "The Prophet Moses and the Canonical Shape of Jeremiah," *ZAW* 101 (1989): 3–27. For a brief survey of research (with bibliography) on

more basic level, given that within the social memory of the community, all worthy prophets, explicitly or implicitly, called Israel to follow YHWH's Mosaic teachings, and they therefore had to be construed as Mosaic as well.[52] Within the discourse of the community, reading prophetic books was remembering to follow these teachings, as is stated explicitly in Mal 3:22 [most ET. 4:4] and implicitly elsewhere. This interrelation within the collective memory of the community between Moses, the prophetic exemplar, and the later Mosaic prophets is explicitly reflected and encoded in Deuteronomy, which was presented to the community as *also* the prophetic book of Moses, and thus as expanding and breaking the temporal constraints of the PBC.[53]

The discursive necessity both to keep a relatively narrow temporal focus in the PBC while at the same time expanding the temporal focus toward the past probably generated a tendency toward potential time fuzziness, in which sites of memory embody at least potential temporal slippage. For instance, the book of Obadiah might have evoked a reading of the book in which the prophetic character was imagined in a way informed by 1 Kgs 18.[54] The book of Jonah almost certainly asked its primary and intended readerships to imagine the prophetic character in a way informed by 2 Kgs 14:25–27, but not always or necessarily so,[55] and thus contributed to the development of multiple images of the prophet informing each other and a general sense of fuzziness that was, not incidentally, consistent with one of the basic communicative messages of the book, namely that there are serious and systemic limits to the literati's ability to construe "secure" knowledge from authoritative texts, even though

---

the potential link between the figures of Jeremiah and Moses, see Mark Roncace, *Jeremiah, Zedekiah, and the Fall of Jerusalem: A Study of Prophetic Narrative* (LHBOTS 423; London: T&T Clark, 2005), 20.

52. See Ben Zvi, "Exploring The Memory of Moses."

53. It goes without saying that temporal relations shaped in a memoryscape belong to this memoryscape. To illustrate, whereas a particular representation/social memory of President Lincoln may be historically later than one of President Obama, from the perspective of the remembering community, their remembered President Lincoln always precedes their remembered President Obama.

54. See Ehud Ben Zvi, *A Historical-Critical Study of The Book of Obadiah* (BZAW 242; Berlin: de Gruyter, 1996).

55. See Ehud Ben Zvi, *Signs of Jonah: Reading and Rereading in Ancient Yehud* (JSOTSup 367; Sheffield: Sheffield Academic Press, 2003), 40–64.

this is their role in society. A book like Joel may be read against multiple temporal backgrounds.

But even more important than balancing the message of the collection by selecting memories of the past was the balancing of the past with images of the future. Remembering a past in which YHWH announced Israel's future utopias in the midst of, and against the background of, a particularly sinful Israel was especially significant because it shaped the fundamental relationship between YHWH and Israel as unconditional, and thus provided unconditional hope. Therefore, to remember such a terrible past was also to remember the future, that is the utopian future. The PBC is at the very same time focused on a relatively narrow past and exuberantly, far more than any other ancient Israelite collection, enmeshed in the future.[56]

Most significantly for the present purposes of understanding the conceptualization of prophets and prophecy, whereas the prophets evoked by the PBC served as central sites of memory in the pastscape of the remembering community, the very same books asked them to imagine and remember a future devoid such characters. Memories of prophets structured and organized the past, but memories of future prophets played no role in utopia.

This was not a minor matter. It went well beyond matters of balancing continuity and discontinuity between past and future Israel. It directly relates to core features of the community's conceptualization of prophets and prophecy, as temporary features, historically contingent institutions necessary at particular times, but not others.

Some of the reasons for the absence of prophets in utopia are obvious, such as the following: (1) voices warning Israel were not imagined as part of utopia; (2) since the prophecies of the monarchic prophets about an utopian future were imagined as fulfilled, then there would be no need for new prophecies; moreover, (3) prophecies about utopia were remembered as closely associated with periods constructed as sinful.

But there is more. Other factors have more to do with the generative logic of utopian future. For instance, prophets were intermediaries, but when utopia was imagined and remembered in terms of a successful marriage between YHWH and Israel (e.g., Hos 2), there was no possible role

---

56. It is precisely this close association of memories of the tragic past and the utopian future that provided significance to both from the perspective of the remembering community.

for intermediaries between husband and wife. In these instances, the intellectual discourse of the community required that divine gifts be endowed to Israel so as to allow her to become a faithful wife. These gifts would perform the job that the prophets of old could not. They would turn Israel into a necessarily faithful wife (Hos 2:21–22). A similar generative logic, though without the marital imagery, was at work when Israel was imagined as being divinely endowed with a new heart, unable to sin (e.g., Jer 31:31–34; 32:38–41; Ezek 11:19–20; 36:25–28), or living in a radically reshaped, idyllic world (e.g., Isa 11; 65:17). In none of these cases could there be any significant role for prophets like those populating the PBC. The authorities that commanded the mindshare of the future remembering community were king YHWH (e.g., Isaiah 40–66;[57] Jer 50:4–5, 19–20; Hos 2:18–22; 14:6–9;[58] Obadiah; Zeph 3), at times a highly elevated Davidic king, who did not look like any previous king in either the PBC or the DHC[59] and, very rarely, judge figures (see Obad 19–21; cf. Neh 9:27).[60] Prophets were conspicuous for their absence.

What about the prophetic books? Were they also imagined as temporary, or as historically contingent institutions or sites of memory meant to play no significant role in the future? Certainly a utopian future without conspicuous prophets was one in which new prophetic books would not

---

57. See H. G. M. Williamson, "The Messianic Texts in Isa 1–39," in *King and Messiah in Israel and the Ancient Near East: Proceedings of the Oxford Old Testament Seminar* (ed. J. Day; JSOTSup 270; Sheffield: Sheffield Academic Press, 1998), 238–70, here 239.

58. See Ehud Ben Zvi, *Hosea* (FOTL 21a.1; Grand Rapids: Eerdmans, 2005), 307–8; and note that the Targum felt the necessity to add an explicit note about a messianic king in v. 8 ("they shall dwell in the shade of the Anointed One").

59. For memories of a future David see, e.g., Isa 9:5–6; 11:1–9; Jer 23:5–6; 30:8–11; 33:14–26; Ezek 34:23–30; 37:1–28; Hos 3:5; Amos 9:11–15; Mic 5:1; cf. Zech 9:9–10). Very often the future David and the circumstances of his reign are portrayed as highly elevated (e.g., Isa 9:5–7; 11:1–9; Hos 3:5). Most significantly, the memories of this future are far different from the memories of the reign of David (or Solomon) reflected in the books of Samuel, Kings, or even Chronicles, which in its own way lionizes the past David (and Solomon).

60. See Ben Zvi, *Obadiah*, 197–229 (228). See also Paul R. Raabe, *Obadiah* (AB 24D; New York: Doubleday, 1996) 255–73, here 269; cf. Johan Renkema, *Obadiah* (HCOT; Leuven: Peeters, 2003) 215–19; and John Barton, *Joel and Obadiah: A Commentary* (OTL; Louisville: Westminster John Knox, 2001), 157. It is worth noting that even in a text such as Isa 19:20, in which the portrayed world clearly evokes images of the exodus, the prophetic Moses is replaced by a מושיע.

be written. But what about those that were so central to the present community? Texts such as Jer 31:31–34 may suggest that there might be no need for them.

Yet even the very activity of remembering and imaginatively experiencing these periods was grounded upon reading prophetic books. Prophetic books were implicitly present in the preutopian, worldly future that looked not much different from the present of the remembering community, and in which, certainly, prophetic memories played a major role. Significantly, even within the PBC, these memories might refer to characters whose memories were encoded primarily outside the PBC (e.g., Moses and Elijah, as in Mal 3:22 [most ET 4:4]). A process of setting memories of past and future, multiple collections, and roles of prophecy is at work here as well.[61]

A Few Final Considerations

Explorations may raise significant issues and point at lines for future research. The present study is just an exploration, as befits the scope of a chapter in a collected essays volume, but it brings up substantial issues. For instance, it not only indicates that the DHC and the PBC shaped prophetic memories in Yehud, but also points at the multiple, closely intertwined ways in which their roles as prophetic memories and memory shapers were fulfilled. The PBC shaped prophetic memories, but it could not have done so or emerged in the present form within a community in which the DHC, or some similar large historiographical, memory-evoking narrative, were absent. This is true not only at the basic level of shaping an image of a monarchic past to provide a mnemonic background for the prophetic characters and statements set in the books included in the PBC—which is obvious—but also at a deeper discursive level, because the balancing role of the historical narrative allowed for the development of a more temporally concentrated corpus of prophetic books. A community without the DHC or any similar narrative would have been a community in which the PBC would have never emerged.

---

61. Much more can be written about "memories of prophets" in the PBC. After all, the entire collection is about creating such memories. This said, the selected observations advanced here suffice for the argument advanced in this particular essay. See below.

Yet both collections balanced and informed each other. The PBC provided the most memorable examples of the late monarchic warning: unheeded prophets that the DHC called for. Both collections shared basic ideological tenets and central memory structures and sites of memory. Among these, one may mention the importance of the catastrophe, the hope for a new beginning after the catastrophe, a similar sense of causality in history, similar constructions of the character of YHWH, the centrality of torah and Moses, the necessity (in the preutopian period) of Mosaic, or torahic, prophets, the potential multitemporality of prophetic utterances (i.e., their words' relation to the circumstances in which they were reportedly uttered, but also potentially to other circumstances in both the future and the past, fulfilled multiple times), and a certain preference for fuzziness about boundaries concerning collections, prophecy, prophetic characters, and even between torah and דבר יהוה(cf. Isa 2:3; Mic 4:2; and note the multiple roles of Deuteronomy as a book of legislation, a prophetic book, and a historiographical book as well). Coming from differing perspectives and literary genres, these two collections mutually reinforced their central messages and shaped a memory of prophetic figures and prophecies that was supportive of them. Moreover, it shaped together a conceptual realm for prophetic figures and prophecies within the shared social mindscape of the remembering community.

At the same time, each collection made some particular contributions to the shaping of the comprehensive memory of the remembering community concerning the prophets of old, going beyond patterns of temporal density or tendencies emerging from the highly individualized characters of the various prophets appearing in these collections. In fact, some of these particular contributions touched on central aspects of what was evoked by terms and concepts such as prophetic character or prophecy.

To illustrate, it is easier to notice in the DHC trends toward prophetizing characters and toward providing prophetic figures with many of the attributes that become explicitly and saliently associated with prophetic characters in Chronicles (see above). But one is to take into account that both the DHC and Chronicles are historical narratives, unlike the PBC.

More importantly, although the prophets of the prophetic books may address worldly matters directly relevant to the people populating the world in which the books and the prophetic characters were set, much of their message was focused in the far future and the hope that remembering this future provided to the present community. To be sure, these features set the prophets who were remembered through the reading of the prophetic books, and the latter to some extent, in contradistinction with many of the memories evoked by the DHC concerning monarchic period prophets and their messages. Of course, it does not follow from this observation that there did not exist a socially shared mindscape within the Persian period community in which both collections were read and reread. First, the DHC is a historiographical work, and as such has clear genre constraints in terms of its ability to ask its readers to experience and remember a future. Moreover, the main prophetic character in the DHC, Moses, was remembered as actually foreseeing and teaching (along with Joshua) a far future, well beyond the horizon of his time. The entire DHC may in fact be seen as a detailed elaboration of the fulfillment of Deut 30:1 and 31:26–29. This would suggest that, from the perspective of the readers of Joshua–Kings, the subsequent chapter in their history is pregnant with the fulfillment of Deut 30:2–10.

One may mention also that, unlike the PBC, the DHC does not bring up memories of a future without prophets and without need for them. As such, it does not raise a concept of prophetic characters and books as temporary, contingent features that while absolutely necessary in the preutopian period have no role in the utopian. Yet historiographical narratives, unlike prophetic books, were not supposed to focus on the far future. Neither, for the most part, could their prophets do so. From the perspective of the remembering community, each collection made its contribution to the shaping of social memory. Each contribution was understood simultaneously in terms of the literary genre in which it was written and in terms of the larger *Sitz im Diskurs* in which it was read. An awareness of both interpretive lenses contributed to the significance given to the memories of the prophetic figures and books that the collections evoked among the Persian period literati, and allowed for the construction of a basic, shared conceptual range for what was prophetic within their intellectual discourse.

Prophets and Prophecy in Joshua–Kings: A Near Eastern Perspective

Martti Nissinen

Prophecy is one of the major literary ingredients of the multilayered narrative in the so-called Deuteronomistic History. Whether the result of a specific redaction (DtrP)[1] or continuing textual growth, stories of prophets span over large textual entities and play a crucial ideological role in the overall design of the work. The significant role given to prophets in the historical narrative raises the question of the relation of the narrative to the historical phenomenon of prophecy and the familiarity of its writers[2] with it. Fictitious as the stories on prophets probably are for the most part, they nevertheless represent the storytellers' imaginative understanding of prophets and prophecy. These imaginative portrayals are likely to be based on the storytellers' knowledge, experience, and appreciation of prophetic activities in their own socioreligious environment.

It is neither my aim to test the historical veracity or accuracy of the image of prophecy in Joshua–Kings, nor to develop a theory of interdependencies between the texts and their editorial history. The purpose of this essay is rather to view the portrayal of prophets and prophecy in Joshua–Kings against the background of the Near Eastern prophetic phenomenon as represented by the available sources, paying attention to commonalities as well as discrepancies between the constructs of prophecy in these different source materials. I will conclude that the biblical narrators,

---

1. Thus the classic work of Walter Dietrich, *Prophetie und Geschichte* (FRLANT 108; Göttingen: Vandenhoeck & Ruprecht, 1972).
2. The complex literary history of Joshua–Kings, or the Deuteronomistic History, has been amply demonstrated; however, it is not my purpose in this essay to adhere to any specific theory concerning its emergence; hence, I am consistently referring to its "writers" assuming that they are many.

to all appearances, were familiar with the prophetic phenomenon as an ancient tradition not essentially different from that reflected by Near Eastern prophetic sources. However, constructs of prophecy in Joshua–Kings, postdating the destruction of Jerusalem, belong to a very different textual and ideological context. This necessarily causes the biblical portrayal of prophets to diverge from Near Eastern constructs as well.

Prophecy and Divination

In the ancient Near East, prophecy was one of several methods of acquiring divine knowledge and becoming conversant with the will of the gods. Prophecy was probably never the foremost method of divination, but certainly one that at times enjoyed high appreciation by Near Eastern kings. Zimri-Lim of Mari maintained a regular correspondence with diviners, including receiving reports on prophecies addressed to him in different cities,[3] and the same is true for Kings Esarhaddon and Assurbanipal of Assyria,[4] who in their inscriptions juxtapose prophetic oracles (*šipir mahhê*) with other kinds of omens.[5]

In the ancient Near Eastern sources, prophecy is much less represented than, say, extispicy or astrology, but in Joshua–Kings, the significance of prophecy clearly exceeds that of other divinatory techniques. This may be explained by the compliance of the writers to the general ban of divination as expressed in Deut 18:9–14, where anyone "who practises divination, or is a soothsayer, or an augur, or a sorcerer, or one who casts spells, or who consults ghosts or spirits, or who seeks oracles from the dead"[6] is declared as abhorrent to YHWH, God of Israel, and the only diviner to be listened

---

3. Jean-Marie Durand, *Archives épistolaires de Mari I/1* (ARM 26/1; Paris: Éditions Recherche sur les Civilisations, 1988); Dominique Charpin, Francis Joannès, Sylvie Lackenbacher, and Bertrand Lafont, eds., *Archives épistolaires de Mari I/2* (ARM 26/2; Paris: Éditions Recherche sur les Civilisations, 1988).

4. Hermann Hunger, *Astrological Reports to Assyrian Kings* (SAA 8; Helsinki: Helsinki University Press, 1992); Simo Parpola, *Assyrian Prophecies* (SAA 9; Helsinki: Helsinki University Press, 1997); idem, *Letters from Assyrian and Babylonian Scholars* (SAA 10; Helsinki: Helsinki University Press, 1993).

5. Esarhaddon Nin. A ii 3–11; Ass. A ii 12–26; Assurbanipal Prism T ii 7–24; see Nissinen, *Prophets and Prophecy in the Ancient Near East*, nos. 97, 98, and 99. This work is henceforth referred to as SBLWAW 12 in this essay.

6. No translation will do justice to the Hebrew terminology, and the exact point of reference of each diviner listed here is conjectural.

to is a prophet like Moses. King Manasseh of Judah is condemned because of allowing such divinatory practices (2 Kgs 21:6), perhaps referring to Mesopotamian kind of methods of divination employed in Jerusalem.

In spite of such a categorical prohibition, however, divination is not absent from Joshua–Kings—on the contrary, it is reported many times without the slightest hesitation, and asking (*drš*) direction from YHWH— in other words, divination—is something the people are expected to do.[7] Joshua, for example, uses lot-casting, not only to find out who had confiscated the *ḥerem* and caused the defeat at the city of Ai (Josh 7:14–18), but even to divide the promised land to the Israelite tribes and to allot towns to the Levites (Josh 13–21). Gideon ventures to attack the Midianites on the basis of dream interpretation (Judg 7:13–15), and Saul, the first king of the Israelites, is recognized by Samuel by means of lot-casting (1 Sam 10:20–21). The oracle device called ephod appears in somewhat suspicious light when mentioned together with idols of cast metal and the teraphim in Micah's sanctuary (Judg 17:5; 18:11–20), but David's use of it is reported with approval:[8]

> When David learned that Saul was plotting evil against him, he said to the priest Abiathar, "Bring the ephod here." David said, "O LORD, the God of Israel, your servant has heard that Saul seeks to come to Keilah, to destroy the city on my account. And now, will Saul come down as your servant has heard? O LORD, the God of Israel, I beseech you, tell your servant." The LORD said, "He will come down." Then David said, "Will the men of Keilah surrender me and my men into the hand of Saul?" The LORD said, "They will surrender you." (1 Sam 23:9–12; cf. 30:7–8)[9]

Likewise, urim and thummin appear as a legitimate means to find out why YHWH does not answer his inquiry concerning his attempted attack against the Philistines (1 Sam 14:41–42).

---

7. See Thelle, *Ask God*.

8. See Timo Veijola, "David in Keïla: Tradition und Interpretation in 1Sam 23, 1–13," *RB* 91 (1984): 51–87 = idem, *David: Gesammelte Studien zur Davidüberlieferungen des Alten Testaments* (Schriften der Finnischen Exegetischen Gesellschaft 52; Helsinki: Finnische Exegetische Gesellschaft, 1990). Veijola finds David's oracle consultation possibly "einen der wenigen Züge, die uns von der Religion des historischen David erhalten sind."

9. Henceforth, all biblical quotations in English are according to the NRSV.

Technical methods of divination, such as the ephod or the urim and thummin, are used to answer a binary question that can only be replied "yes" or "no" and, obviously, always require an act of solicitation. Even prophecy is often actively sought for in Samuel–Kings by Judahite and Israelite kings (and even by Ben-Hadad of Damascus, 2 Kgs 8:7–15). Saul, facing the Philistine troops in Gilboa, resorts to the necromancer in En-Dor, but only after having failed to receive an answer from YHWH by means of dreams, urim, and prophets (1 Sam 28:6). Prophecy, hence, is unmistakably understood as another technique of consulting God.[10] There are also cases where an unprovoked divine revelation is confirmed by another divinatory act, using a different method, such as the election of Saul that is first revealed to Samuel by the direct word of God (1 Sam 9:15–17) and subsequently confirmed by lot-casting (1 Sam 10:20–24).[11] The practice of mantic confirmation is well-known from Near Eastern sources[12] and is also used in order to verify prophetic oracles, especially at Mari, where the prophet's "hair and hem" (*šārtum u sissiktum*) were often taken to cross-check the prophecy through another method of divination, probably extispicy.[13]

Sometimes the consultation of God is based on questions and answers, which resemble technical inquiries, but the answer is not necessarily of the binary type:

> After this David inquired of the LORD, "Shall I go up into any of the cities of Judah?" The LORD said to him, "Go up." David said, "To which shall I go up?" He said, "To Hebron." (2 Sam 2:1)

> David inquired of the LORD, "Shall I go up against the Philistines? Will you give them into my hand?" The LORD said to David, "Go up; for I will

---

10. See Esther J. Hamori, "The Prophet and the Necromancer: Women's Divination for Kings," *JBL*, forthcoming.

11. See Jeffrey L. Cooley, "The Story of Saul's Election (1 Samuel 9–10) in the Light of Mantic Practice in Ancient Iraq," *JBL* 130 (2011): 247–61. Cooley does not deny that the acts of election in 1 Sam 9–10 may derive from different traditions, but takes it for granted that "an editor chose to weave these traditions together to make what he believed to be a single logical narrative" (249).

12. Ibid., 250–56.

13. See, e.g., Jean-Marie Durand, "Mari," in *Mythologie et religion des sémites occidentaux* (ed. Gregorio del Olmo Lete; 2 vols.; OLA 162; Leuven: Peeters, 2008), 1:163–631, esp. 514–518; Esther J. Hamori, "Gender and the Verification of Prophecy at Mari," *WO* 42 (2012): 1–22.

certainly give the Philistines into your hand." ... When David inquired of the Lord, he said, "You shall not go up; go around to their rear, and come upon them opposite the balsam trees. When you hear the sound of marching in the tops of the balsam trees, then be on the alert; for then the Lord has gone out before you to strike down the army of the Philistines." (2 Sam 5:19, 23)

In both cases the first question allows an answer of the binary type ("Shall I go up?"—"Go up!"/"Do not go up!"), but the second one cannot be answered with a simple "yes" or "no." The method of the inquiry is not revealed to the reader and seems to be indifferent from the point of view of the writer, who either did not care or did not know how technical divination works. The quasi-realistic question-answer pattern is turned into a literary conversation between King Ahab and the anonymous prophet with a special foresight in 1 Kgs 20:13–14:

> Then a certain prophet [*nābî' 'eḥad*] came up to King Ahab of Israel and said, "Thus says the Lord, Have you seen all this great multitude? Look, I will give it into your hand today; and you shall know that I am the Lord." Ahab said, "By whom?" He said, "Thus says the Lord, By the young men who serve the district governors." Then he said, "Who shall begin the battle?" He answered, "You."

In the case of the joint attempt of Jehoshaphat of Judah and Ahab of Israel, the question to the four hundred prophets whom the kings are consulting (*drš*), and eventually to Micaiah ben Imlah, is formulated exactly the same way as inquiries addressed to a technical oracle, for instance: "Shall I go to battle against Ramoth-gilead, or shall I refrain?" resulting in the yes-answer: "Go up; for YHWH will give it into the hand of the king" (1 Kgs 22:6, 15). This could suggest that the *nĕbî'îm* consulted by Jehoshaphat and Ahab are, in fact, to be seen as technical diviners, but this is difficult to reconcile with the prophets "prophesying" (*mitnabbě'îm*) by symbolic gestures and shouting, which points toward ecstatic behavior (1 Kgs 22:10–12). The result, hence, is an interesting mixture of features of technical and nontechnical divination difficult to find in Near Eastern sources of prophecy,[14] but more common in Greek sources. For instance the Delphic Pythia, known for her hexametric oracles, is also associated

---

14. The activity of the group of *nabûs* of the Haneans in ARM 26 216 (SBLWAW 12 26) may actually refer to technical divination; this is suggested by the form of

with lot-casting[15] and the inquiries addressed to the women prophets of Dodona are formulated in a strictly binary manner.[16] Indeed, Micaiah's assertion, "whatever the LORD says to me, that I will speak" (1 Kgs 22:14), is almost verbatim the same as that of the Pythia in Aeschylus' *Eumenides*: "For as the god doth lead, so do I prophesy."[17]

The fluidity of the boundary between prophecy and technical divination in the narrative world of Joshua–Kings may indicate that even in the writers' real world, the socioreligious boundary of technical/nontechnical divination was somewhat less strict than it was at Mari or in Assyria. What may have mattered more was the distinction of accepted and prohibited kinds of divination; lot-casting is practised by the narrative characters without hesitation, but astrology and extispicy are never employed in Joshua–Kings and necromancy (1 Sam 28) appears in a dubious light— even though it eventually works!

The writers of Joshua–Kings appear perfectly on a par with their Near Eastern colleagues in understanding the role of prophecy, as divination in general, as a normal way of acquiring the *Herrschaftswissen* necessary for the kings (or their predecessors) to have their (quasi-)royal functions fulfilled.[18] Prophecy is used as another method of divination, and it is

---

the question posed to them: "Will my lord, when performing [his] ablution rite and [st]aying seven days ou[tside the city walls], [return] safe[ly] to the ci]ty [...]?"

15. E.g., Plutarch, *Moralia* 492b; see Sarah Iles Johnston, *Ancient Greek Divination* (Blackwell Ancient Religions; Chichester: Wiley-Blackwell, 2008), 52–55.

16. For the Dodona oracle, see Esther Eidinow, *Oracles, Curses, and Risk among the Ancient Greeks* (Oxford: Oxford University Press, 2007). According to Kallisthenes, an oracle was given to the ambassadors of the Spartans by collecting lots in a pot and letting the prophetess make the choice (*FGrH* 124 F 222a and b; the story of Kallisthenes is quoted by Cicero, *De Divinatione* 1.34.76 and 2.32.69).

17. Aeschylus, *Eum.* 29–33. The prophecy of Micaiah has also been compared with the oracle of the Pythia to Croesus, king of Lydia (Herodotos 1.46–49) by Wolfgang Oswald ("Ahab als Krösus: Anmerkungen zu 1Kön 22," *ZTK* 105 [2008]: 1–14). Oswald concluded, "Beide, Ahab und Krösus, erhalten je ein zweideutiges Orakel, das sie jeweils in ihrem Sinne interpretieren, dessen tatsächlicher Sinn aber eine Unheilsankündigung ist. In beiden Fällen ist es im Übrigen so, dass die Interpretation der Könige ohne Zweifel die nächstliegende ist. Krösus' Annahme, das Orakel müsse das Reich des Kyros meinen, ist ebenso verständlich wie die des Ahab, dass Jhwh ihm Ramot-Gilead in die Hand geben werde" (8–9).

18. See Beate Pongratz-Leisten, *Herrschaftswissen in Mesopotamien: Formen der Kommunikation zwischen Gott und König im 2. und 1. Jahrtausend v.Chr.* (SAAS 10; Helsinki: The Neo-Assyrian Text Corpus Project, 1999).

practised especially in connection with kings. However, unlike the Near Eastern sources, the prophets in Joshua–Kings occupy more prominent seats than other diviners.

It is noteworthy that, apart from Deborah in Judg 4:4 and the anonymous prophet in Judg 6:8–10,[19] prophets do not feature at all in the premonarchical settings of Joshua–Judges. Joshua receives divine words akin to prophecies addressed to kings, but this always happens without the mediation of prophets: "Be strong and courageous; do not be frightened or dismayed, for the LORD your God is with you wherever you go" (Josh 1:9, cf. 10:8). Prophets become significant actors only when monarchy is introduced: Samuel, the first king-maker, is not only the last judge but also marks the rise of prophecy as the preferred method of divination in Samuel–Kings. The first kings still keep utilizing divinatory methods, Saul turning to a necromancer (1 Sam 28) and David using the ephod (1 Sam 23:9–12; 30:7–8; cf. 2 Sam 2:1; 5:19,23), but after them, explicit references to diviners other than prophets become rare. Ahaziah's turning to Baal-zebub, the god of Ekron, sounds like a technical inquiry, but it is condemned by the prophecy of Elijah and eventually becomes the reason of Ahaziah's death—not because of the divinatory method, however, but because of turning to a wrong god, "as if there was no God in Israel" (2 Kgs 1).

PROPHETS AND KINGS

Prophecy appears in Joshua–Kings predominantly in a royal setting. The divine word is almost without exception addressed to men who already are kings or to whom kingship is promised. The only prophets in Joshua–Kings who do *not* communicate with kings belong to premonarchical contexts: Deborah in Judg 4:4, the anonymous prophet speaking to the Israelites in Judg 6:7–10, and the man of God addressing Eli in 1 Sam 2:27–36—even the old prophet from Bethel in 1 Kgs 13:11–32 is indirectly connected with Jeroboam through the man of God's prediction of the destruction of the altar in Bethel. The royal association of prophecy in the narrative world of Joshua–Kings, and probably also in the mental map of the writers of the texts, is reinforced by the absence of prophets in the book of Joshua and their rarity in Judges.

The royal focus of prophecy in Joshua–Kings is perfectly in line with other ancient Near Eastern documents, whether from Mari or from

---

19. Cf. Judg 13:6, where the "man of God" is actually an angel.

Assyria, in which prophecy mostly fulfills the function of *Herrschaftswissen* and the divine messages transmitted by prophets are almost always addressed to kings or members of the royal family. Unlike Greek texts, in which oracle sites are visited by kings and private individuals alike,[20] the Near Eastern documents are virtually silent about nonroyal individuals being addressed by prophets.[21] One might wonder to what extent this corresponds with historical reality; even sparse hints are enough to suggest that prophecy, among other divinatory means, was perceived of as available even to nonroyal persons, as implied by 1 Sam 9:9: "Formerly in Israel, anyone who went to inquire of God would say, 'Come, let us go to the seer.'" In the textual world of the preserved documents from the ancient Near East, however, prophecy is inextricably linked with kingship and royal ideology—and the same holds true for Joshua–Kings, even though the connection between prophecy and ideology is rather more intricate in the Hebrew Bible, thanks to its complicated literary history.

It is most intriguing to find some basic features of ancient Near Eastern royal ideology expressed by David in his "last words" in 2 Sam 23:1–7. The late origin of this text reveals itself in the very fact that the words are designated as an oracle (*nĕ'um*) of David who himself is presented as a prophet through whom the spirit of God speaks (v. 2); this marks the beginning of the prophetic career of David to be continued in later texts, such as the Dead Sea Scrolls,[22] the New Testament (Acts 2:30), and even in the Qur'an.[23] Otherwise, the image emerging from the poem of the king "who rules over people justly, ruling in the fear of God" (v. 3), with whom God has made "an everlasting covenant, ordered in all things and secure" (v. 5), and whose godless adversaries "are all like thorns that are thrown away" (v. 6), matches exactly with the image of the ideal Near Eastern king who rules justly, has an exclusive relationship with the divine world, and tramples his enemies underfoot.

---

20. See Michael Attyah Flower, *The Seer in Ancient Greece* (Berkeley: University of California Press, 2008).

21. The few exceptions include the scholar Urad-Gula (SAA 10 284 = SBLWAW 12 108) and the recipient of the Lachish Ostracon 3, possibly the official Tobiah (Lak[6]:1.3 = SBLWAW 12 139).

22. See Peter W. Flint, "The Prophet David at Qumran," in *Biblical Interpretation at Qumran* (ed. Matthias Henze; SDSRL; Grand Rapids: Eerdmans, 2005), 158–67.

23. See Peter Matthews Wright, "The Qur'anic David," in *Constructs of Prophecy in the Former and Latter Prophets and Other Texts* (ed. Lester L. Grabbe and Martti Nissinen; ANEM 4; Atlanta: Society of Biblical Literature, 2011), 197–206.

Ancient Near Eastern royal prophecies typically consist of divine expressions of support, instruction, warning, and indictment/judgment, but the distribution of these aspects varies according to source materials. It is easy to observe that in the extant prophetic oracles from Assyria, the divine support for the king is the actual *cantus firmus*, while the prophecies quoted in the letters form Mari give more expression to warning,[24] instruction,[25] and indictment/judgment.[26] This does not warrant the conclusion that the other aspects were absent from Assyrian prophecy, since there are traces of them even in the Assyrian sources;[27] it is rather the accident of discovery and preservation that causes the differences between the source materials in this respect.

Prophetic support, instruction, warning, and indictment/judgment can be found in Joshua–Kings as well, again in different proportions. A couple of times the judgment relates to an individual king whose recovery from accident or illness is denied: Ahaziah is condemned to death because he had inquired a wrong god (2 Kgs 1) and Elisha's prophecy concerning the death of Ben-Hadad, the sick king of Damascus, comes true by the hand of his follower, Hazael (2 Kgs 8:7–15).

It has often been noted that the most significant dissimilarity between biblical and Near Eastern prophecy is the categorical judgment of the prophets of their own king or people in the Hebrew Bible, a feature that may be due to historical circumstances but also to literary developments.

---

24. E.g., ARM 26 195 (= SBLWAW 12 5); ARM 26 197 (= SBLWAW 12 7); ARM 26 199 (= SBLWAW 12 9); ARM 26 202 (= SBLWAW 12 12); ARM 26 213 (= SBLWAW 12 23); ARM 26 216 (= SBLWAW 12 26); ARM 26 238 (= SBLWAW 12 43).

25. E.g., FM 7 39 (= SBLWAW 12 1); FM 7 38 (= SBLWAW 12 2); ARM 26 194 (= SBLWAW 12 4); ARM 26 199 (= SBLWAW 12 9); ARM 26 204 (= SBLWAW 12 14); ARM 26 205 (= SBLWAW 12 15); ARM 26 195 (= SBLWAW 12 5); ARM 26 206 (= SBLWAW 12 16); ARM 26 215 (= SBLWAW 12 25); ARM 26 217 (= SBLWAW 12 27); ARM 26 220 (= SBLWAW 12 30); ARM 26 221 (= SBLWAW 12 31); ARM 26 221bis (= SBLWAW 12 32); ARM 26 234 (= SBLWAW 12 39).

26. E.g., FM 7 39 (= SBLWAW 12 1); ARM 26 198 (= SBLWAW 12 8); ARM 26 206 (= SBLWAW 12 16); ARM 26 215 (= SBLWAW 12 25); ARM 26 217 (= SBLWAW 12 27); ARM 26 219 (= SBLWAW 12 29); ARM 26 221bis (= SBLWAW 12 32); ARM 26 233 (= SBLWAW 12 38). See the table in John H. Walton, *Ancient Near Eastern Thought and the Old Testament: Introducing the Conceptual World of the Hebrew Bible* (Grand Rapids: Baker Academic, 2006), 245–47.

27. See Martti Nissinen, "Das kritische Potential in der altorientalischen Prophetie," in *Prophetie in Mari, Assyrien und Israel* (ed. Matthias Köckert and Martti Nissinen; FRLANT 201; Göttingen: Vandenhoeck & Ruprecht, 2003), 1–32, esp. 10–14.

This holds true even for Joshua–Kings, where the divine judgment more often than not concerns the offspring of the king. In the extant Near Eastern documents, a divine word predicting the end of the royal dynasty is extremely rare but not totally unheard of. For example, as reported to Esarhaddon concerning a prophecy in Harran, the god Nusku proclaimed that the name and seed of Sennacherib will be destroyed (SAA 16 59).[28] In the Hebrew Bible, the *locus classicus* of such a reversal of a dynastic promise is the prediction of the annihilation of the eradication of the progeny of Jerobeam I by the prophet Ahijah the Shilonite (1 Kgs 14:10–11, 14):

> I will bring evil upon the house of Jeroboam. I will cut off from Jeroboam every male, both bond and free, in Israel and will consume the house of Jeroboam, just as one burns up dung until it is all gone. Anyone belonging to Jeroboam who dies in the city, the dogs shall eat; and anyone who dies in the open country, the birds of the air shall eat; for the Lord has spoken. … Moreover, the Lord will raise up for himself a king over Israel, who shall cut off the house of Jeroboam today, even now!

This prophecy reverses diametrically the dynastic promise pronounced by the prophet Ahijah to Jeroboam, according to which God would build him an enduring house, as he did for David (1 Kgs 11:37–39). The prophecy eventually comes true when Baasha kills Jeroboam's son Nadab and becomes king of Israel; according to 2 Kgs 15:29, Baasha "left to the house of Jeroboam not one that breathed, until he had destroyed it, according to the word of the Lord that he spoke by his servant Ahijah the Shilonite— because of the sins of Jeroboam that he committed and that he caused Israel to commit, and because of the anger to which he provoked the Lord, the God of Israel." The principal sin of Jeroboam, of course, was the worship of the golden calves at Bethel and Dan, and since Baasha himself continued this practice, the same judgment is pronounced over him by Jehu, son of Hanani (1 Kgs 16:1–3). The third king to receive the very same judgment, this time by Elijah, is Ahab together with his queen Jeze-

---

28. For this text, see Martti Nissinen, *References to Prophecy in Neo-Assyrian Sources* (SAAS 7; Helsinki: The Neo-Assyrian Text Corpus Project, 1998), 108–52, and cf. the discussion on the historical background of the letter in S. W. Holloway, *Aššur is King! Aššur is King! Religion in the Exercise of Power in the Neo-Assyrian Empire* (CHANE 10; Leiden: Brill, 2002), 410–12; and Matthijs de Jong, *Isaiah among the Ancient Near Eastern Prophets: A Comparative Study of the Earliest Stages of the Isaiah Tradition and the Neo-Assyrian Prophecies* (VTSup 117; Leiden: Brill, 2007), 271–74.

bel, with an explicit reference to the fate of Jeroboam and Baasha (1 Kgs 21:20-24; 2 Kgs 9:9-10). Even this prophecy comes true as predicted (1 Kgs 22:37-38; 2 Kgs 9:30-37).

The prophetic judgment in these interconnected texts is the key element of the narrative of the northern kingdom from the beginning (cf. 1 Kgs 12:15) to the end (cf. 2 Kgs 17:21-23). It does not represent any kind of royal ideology of the kingdoms of Israel and Judah, but the ideologies and narrative strategies of the writers of Joshua-Kings, for whom the destruction of the kingdom of Israel was an essential constitutent of their collective memory.

While prophetic judgment plays a crucial role in the narrative of Kings concerning the northern kingdom, it is not such an overwhelming feature of prophecy in Joshua-Kings as it is in the prophetic books of the Hebrew Bible; even other aspects of royal prophecy are well represented in Joshua-Kings. Quite the same way as Zimri-Lim of Mari is warned by prophets,[29] David receives a word of warning from the prophet Gad to leave his stronghold (1 Sam 22:5), and Rehoboam is warned by the man of God called Shemaiah not to wage war against the people of Israel who had made Jeroboam their king (1 Kgs 12:22-24). These prophetic warnings are not condemnatory as such, but they do function within the narrative plots of David's rise to power and the division of Solomon's kingdom.

The divine word pronounced to kings and other leaders of people in Joshua-Kings is, in fact, quite as often supportive as it is condemnatory. The divine promise to deliver enemies into the king's hands is one of the most typical features in ancient Near Eastern prophecy.[30] A similar promise is given directly by God to Joshua (Josh 6:2; 8:1, 18; 10:8), by the prophetess Deborah to Barak (Judg 4:6-7), by the mouth of an angel

---

29. ARM 26 197 (= SBLWAW 12 7): 21-24: "Now protect yourself! Without consulting an oracle do not enter the city!"; ARM 26 213 (= SBLWAW 12 23): 7-19: "Thus says Annunitum: Zimri-Lim, you will be tested in a revolt! Protect yourself! Let your most favored servants whom you love surround you, and make them stay there to protect you! Do not go around on your own!"

30. E.g., Mari: ARM 26 194 (= SBLWAW 12 4); ARM 26 195 (= SBLWAW 12 5); ARM 26 197 (= SBLWAW 12 7); ARM 26 211 (= SBLWAW 12 21); ARM 26 214 (= SBLWAW 12 24); ARM 26 217 (= SBLWAW 12 27); ARM 26 233 (= SBLWAW 12 38); Assyria: SAA 9 1.1 (= SBLWAW 12 68); SAA 9 1.2 (= SBLWAW 12 69); SAA 9 1.6 (= SBLWAW 12 73); SAA 9 1.7 (= SBLWAW 12 74); SAA 9 2.3 (= SBLWAW 12 80); SAA 9 2.5 (= SBLWAW 12 82); SAA 9 3.2 (= SBLWAW 12 86); SAA 9 3.5 (= SBLWAW 12 88); SAA 9 4 (= SBLWAW 12 89); SAA 9 7 (SBLWAW 12 92); SAA 9 8 (SBLWAW 12 93).

to Gideon (Judg 6:16; 7:9); and later by an anonymous prophet to Ahab (1 Kgs 20:13), by Elisha to Jehoram and Jehoshaphath (2 Kgs 3:18), and by Isaiah to Hezekiah (2 Kgs 19:6–7); moreover, Jeroboam II is said to have restored the previous borders of the northern kingdom according to the word of God pronounced by the prophet Jonah, son of Amittai (2 Kgs 14:25), which also implies a divine promise of military conquest. Personal divine promises concerning the fate of an individual king are given by Isaiah to Hezekiah concerning his recovery form the illness (2 Kgs 20:5–6), as well as by Huldah to Josiah who is said to die in peace—a prediction that, eventually, does not come true (2 Kgs 22:20, cf. 23:29).

Considering the strong link between prophecy and kingship, it is not surprising to find prophecy accompanying ancient Near Eastern kings' way to the throne. Prophets appear to have played a role in the investiture and enthronement of the Assyrian crown princes Esarhaddon and Assurbanipal.[31] The royal succession appears as an emphatically prophetic concern and Esarhaddon received oracles from the mouth of the prophet Ladagil-ili that sound like a dynastic promise: "Your son and grandson will exercise kingship in the lap of Ninurta."[32] In the Old Babylonian sources of prophecy preserved to us, prophets do not appear as actual king-makers. However, some prophecies from that period are best understood as coronation oracles, such as the oracle from Eshnunna to Ibalpiel II[33] and the prophecy of Adad reported to Zimri-Lim of Mari by Nur-Sin, his representative in Aleppo.[34]

The letter of Nur-Sin is probably the oldest reference to anointing kings in the Near East, but it says nothing about prophetic involvement in the

---

[31]. See Parpola, *Assyrian Prophecies*, xxxvi–xliv; Nissinen, *References to Prophecy*, 14–34; de Jong, *Isaiah among Ancient Near Eastern Prophets*, 251–59; Kateřina Šašková, "Esarhaddon's Accession to the Assyrian Throne," in *Shepherds of the Black-Headed People: The Royal Office vis-à-vis Godhead in Ancient Mesopotamia* (ed. Kateřina Šašková, Lucáš Pecha, and Petr Charvát; Plzeň: Západočeská univerzita, 2010), 147–79.

[32]. SAA 9 1.10 (= SBLWAW 12 77) vi 27–29; SAA 9 2.3 (= SBLWAW 12 80) ii 13–14.

[33]. FLP 1674 (= SBLWAW 12 66); see Maria de Jong Ellis, "The Goddess Kititum Speaks to King Ibalpiel: Oracle Texts from Ishchali," *MARI* 5 (1987): 235–66.

[34]. FM 7 38 (= SBLWAW 12 2); see Jean-Georges Heintz, "Des textes sémitiques anciens à la Bible hébraïque: Un comparatisme légitime?" in *Le comparatisme en histoire des religions: Pour un état de la question* (ed. F. Bœspflug and F. Dunand; Paris: Boccard, 1997), 127–56, esp. 146–50.

act of anointing. In Samuel-Kings, a king is anointed four times. Samuel anoints Saul the first king of the Israelites, thus fulfilling their request to have a king (1 Sam 10:1); however, as the first king turns out to be a failure, Samuel repeats the act with David (1 Sam 16:13). In both cases, the spirit of God is bestowed upon the anointed king. David receives the spirit immediately as if belonging to the very act of anointing, and Saul the very same day as he encounters the band of prophets at Gebah (1 Sam 10:10). In the case of Solomon, the act of anointing is technically performed by the priest Zadok, but this is done in the presence of the prophet Nathan who is likewise presented as protagonist of the anointing ritual (1 Kgs 1:32-53, esp. v. 34, 39, 45). The fourth case is Jehu to whom Elisha sent one of his "sons" to anoint him king of Israel and to perform the eradication of the progeny of Ahab (2 Kgs 9:6-10). All four biblical cases of anointing a king thus involve a prophet.

The anointing of Solomon and the role of the prophet Nathan therein is part and parcel of the narrative of David's succession which also includes the dynastic promise pronounced to David by Nathan (2 Sam 7:12-16), according to which God will establish the kingdom of David's offspring: "I will be a father to him, and he shall be a son to me. ... Your house and your kingdom shall be made sure forever before me; your throne shall be established forever." Nathan's oracle has plausibly been interpreted as reflecting a common Near Eastern royal ideology.[35] Indeed, the biblical prophet Nathan is quite as actively involved in king-making as his Assyrian colleagues seem to have been, even though Nathan's relationship to David seems rather more intimate than what is known of the Assyrian prophets' connection to their kings.

The function of prophecy in the Succession Narrative is too manifold and multilayered to match anything we know from the ancient Near East; one common feature is interesting, however: the role of the queen mother. We know how crucial the role played by Naqia, Esarhaddon's mother, was in the succession of her husband Sennacherib,[36] and a similarly important

---

35. E.g., Michael Avioz, *Nathan's Oracle (2 Samuel 7) and Its Interpreters* (Bible in History; Bern: Lang, 2005). Avioz interprets 2 Sam 7 as reflecting the vassal treaty ideology.

36. See Sarah C. Melville, *The Role of Naqia/Zakutu in Sargonid Politics* (SAAS 9; Helsinki: The Neo-Assyrian Text Corpus Project, 1999); Saana Svärd, *Women's Roles in the Neo-Assyrian Era: Female Agency in the Empire* (Saarbrücken: VDM Verlag, 2008), 31-33; Šašková, "Esarhaddon's Accession to the Assyrian Throne," 153-54, 170-71.

role is ascribed to Bathsheba, the mother of Solomon, in the Succession Narrative. Even prophecy is part of the picture in both cases: Naqia demonstrably turned to prophets on behalf of her son[37] and Solomon's kingship is presented as a joint project of Bathsheba and the prophet Nathan in 1 Kgs 1.

Prophets and Cult Places

Prophets and temples coincide in the ancient Near Eastern and Greek sources often enough to warrant the assumption that prophecy was at home in temples and cult places all over the Eastern Mediterranean. This is neither to say that prophecy was exclusively confined to temples, nor that a specific class of "cultic prophets," as distinct from "court prophets" or "free prophets," should or could be postulated. Anyhow, there is plenty of evidence of temples as venues of prophetic performances. At Mari, prophets are reported to have "arisen" (*tebû*) or "gone into trance" (*mahû*) in a temple to deliver an oracle:

> Another matter: a prophetess arose in the temple of Annunitum and spoke: "Zimri-Lim, do not go on campaign! Stay in Mari, and I shall continue to answer."[38]

> In the temple of Annunitum in the city, Ahatum, a servant girl of Dagan-Malik, went into trance and spoke: "Zimri-Lim (...)"[39]

Prophetic messages may be transmitted by priests like Ahum, the priest of the temple of Annunitum,[40] or the Assyrian priests Adad-ahu-iddina, Aššur-hamatu'a, and Nabû-reši-išši,[41] who report what had happened in their temples, including prophetic performances.

In spite of the recurrent appearances of prophets in temples, the affiliation of the prophets with temples at Mari is somewhat unclear.[42] It is not

---

37. SAA 9 1.8 (= SBLWAW 12 75); cf. SAA 9 5 (= SBLWAW 12 90).
38. ARM 26 237 (SBLWAW 12 42): 21–26; cf. ARM 26 219 (SBLWAW 12 29): 4–5; ARM 26 195 (SBLWAW 12 5): 5–6.
39. ARM 26 214 (SBLWAW 12 42): 5–8; cf. ARM 26 213 (SBLWAW 12 23): 5–7.
40. ARM 26 200 (SBLWAW 12 10) and ARM 26 201 (SBLWAW 12 11).
41. SAA 13 37 (SBLWAW 12 111); SAA 13 139 (SBLWAW 12 112); SAA 13 144 (SBLWAW 12 113).
42. See Daniel E. Fleming, "Prophets and Temple Personnel in the Mari Archives," in *The Priests in the Prophets: The Portrayal of Priests, Prophets and Other Religious*

impossible to find prophets participating in cultic practices,[43] but this is not very common either. The Assyrian sources, on the other hand, explicitly mention prophets as belonging to the temple personnel. A Middle-Assyrian provisions list from Kar-Tukulti-Ninurta (ca. eleventh century B.C.E.) lists prophets and prophetesses (*mahhû/mahhūtu*) together with the *assinnu*s of the Ištar temple as recipients of a ration of barley,[44] and a decree of expenditures for ceremonies in the temple of Ešarra in Assur from 809 B.C.E. mentions prophetesses (*mahhūtu*) as recipients of barley as a part of the expenditure for the divine council.[45] One of the preserved Assyrian prophecies from the seventh century B.C.E. is spoken by Issar-beli-da"ini, the votaress (*šēlūtu*) of the king, that is, a person who had been donated by the king to the temple.[46] A poorly preserved fragment of a text sent by another votaress to the king may also be a remnant of a prophetic oracle.[47] In fact, the domicile of several prophets in Arbela implies an affiliation with the prominent temple of Ištar in the same city.[48]

Specialists in the Latter Prophets (ed. Lester L. Grabbe and Alice Ogden Bellis; JSOT-Sup 408; London: T & T Clark 2004), 44–64.

43. FM 3 3 (= SBLWAW 12 52); see Jean-Marie Durand and Michaël Guichard, "Les rituels de Mari," in *Florilegium Marianum 3: Recueil d'études à la mémoire d'André Parrot* (ed. Dominique Charpin and Jean-Marie Durand; Mémoires de NABU 7; Paris: SEPOA, 1997), 19–78, esp. 59–63; Martti Nissinen, "Prophetic Madness: Prophecy and Ecstasy in the Ancient Near East and in Greece," in *Raising Up a Faithful Exegete: Essays in Honor of Richard D. Nelson* (ed. K. L. Noll and Brooks Schramm; Winona Lake: Eisenbrauns, 2010), 1–30, esp. 9–11.

44. VS 19 1 (= SBLWAW 12 123) i 37–39; see Brigitte Lion, "Les mentions de 'prophètes' dans la seconde moitié du IIe millénaire av. J.-C.," *RA* 94 (2000): 21–32.

45. SAA 12 69 (= SBLWAW 12 110): 27–31; see Martti Nissinen, "Prophets and the Divine Council," in *Kein Land für sich allein: Studien zum Kulturkontakt in Kanaan, Israel/Palästina und Ebirnâri für Manfred Weippert zum 65. Geburtstag* (ed. Ernst-Axel Knauf and Ulrich Hübner; OBO 186; Fribourg: Universitätsverlag; Göttingen: Vandenhoeck & Ruprecht, 2002), 4–19, esp. 16–17.

46. SAA 9 1.7 (= SBLWAW 12 74); see Svärd, *Women's Roles in the Neo-Assyrian Era*, 79–80.

47. SAA 13 148 (= SBLWAW 12 114).

48. See Parpola, *Assyrian Prophecies*, xlvii–lii; de Jong, *Isaiah among Ancient Near Eastern Prophets*, 294–98, Martti Nissinen, "City Lofty as Heaven: Arbela and Other Cities in Neo-Assyrian Prophecy," in *"Every City Shall Be Forsaken": Urbanism and Prophecy in Ancient Israel and the Near East* (ed. Lester L. Grabbe and Robert D. Haak; JSOTSup 330; Sheffield: Sheffield Academic Press, 2001), 172–209, esp. 176–83.

Whatever functions the prophets may have fulfilled in relation to the temples at Mari, they repeatedly appear as advocates of worship, reproaching the king for neglecting his ritual duties[49] and giving orders to him concerning ritual performances such as *pagrā'um* and *kispum* offerings[50] or sacrifices to a commemorative monument (*humūsum*).[51] Similar prophetic orders can also be found on the recently published tenth–ninth century B.C.E. Luwian stele of Hamiyata, king of Mazuwari (Til Barsip), who mentions a prophet ordering the establishment of the statue of the storm-god Tarhunza.[52] In Neo-Assyrian texts, prophets are usually not found expressing ritual demands, except for one case, where Ištar requires offerings from the newly enthroned Esarhaddon.[53] However, even in Assyrian sources, the welfare of the temples appears as a prophetic concern. Two letters of the Assyrian temple officials report prophecies concerning temple property[54] and Assurbanipal in his inscription mentions dreams and prophetic oracles as the source of divine orders to renovate the temple of the Lady of Kidmuri, that is, Ištar of Calah.[55]

While not yielding an accurate picture of the function of prophets in the worship of gods, the ancient Near Eastern sources confirm the close connection between temples and prophets. Prophetic messages, for sure, could be uttered in different environments, but the temples provided a sacred space where divine-human encounters, even prophetic ones, were

---

49. ARM 26 219 (SBLWAW 12 29): 4–9.

50. ARM 26 220 (SBLWAW 12 30): 20–23; ARM 26 221 (SBLWAW 12 31): 7–17. For these offerings, associated with the cult of the dead, see Durand and Guichard, "Les rituels de Mari," 19–78; Jean-Marie Durand, "Le *kispum* dans les traditions amorrites," in *Les vivants et leurs morts: Actes du colloque organisé par le Collège de France, Paris, les 14–15 avril 2010* (ed. Jean-Marie Durand, Thomas Römer, and Jürg Hutzli; OBO 257; Fribourg: Academic Press; Göttingen: Vandenhoeck & Ruprecht, 2012), 33–52.

51. ARM 26 218 (SBLWAW 12 28: 5–13; for *humūsum*, see Durand and Guichard, "Les rituels de Mari," 33.

52. Tell Ahmar 6 §§ 21–23 (cf. 5 §§ 12–15): "I destroyed for myself the enemies, and the god-inspired (one) said to me: 'Establish Tarhunza of the Army!'" Editio princeps: J. David Hawkins, "Inscription," in *A New Luwian Stele and the Cult of the Storm-God at Til Barsib–Masuwari* (ed. Guy Bunnens; Tell Ahmar 2; Leuven: Peeters, 2006), 11–31, esp. p. 15, 27–28. For the historical context of this text, see Bunnens, *New Luwian Stele*, 85–102.

53. SAA 9 3.5 (SBLWAW 12 88).

54. Adad-ahu-iddina: SAA 13 37 (SBLWAW 12 111); Nabû-reši-išši: SAA 13 114 (SBLWAW 12 113].

55. Prism T ii (SBLWAW 12 99): 16–17.

believed to take place; therefore, temples were an ideal venue for communication with the divine by means of prophecy.[56] The constructs of prophecy in texts from Mari and Assyria present the prophets as sharing the symbolic worlds of both the temple communities and the (implied) authors of the texts and, for their part, contributing to the maintenance of the institutional order and the symbolic universe it was based on.[57]

Maintenance of the institutional order and the symbolic universe is also a major preoccupation of the writers of Joshua–Kings, especially in so far as they are devoted to the Deuteronomic idea of worshiping YHWH, and YHWH alone, in one place only (Deut 12). When the high priest Hilkiah reports to have recovered the book of the law (*sēper hattôrâ*) in the temple, King Josiah orders him to inquire YHWH concerning the book, which, to all appearances, prohibits sacrifices to gods other than YHWH. Hilkiah, together with four high officials including the scribe Shaphan, go to Huldah, a female prophet who is said to be the wife of Shallum, keeper of the wardrobe, presumably of the temple of Jerusalem (2 Kgs 22). The narrative is interesting in many respects. The female gender of the prophet alone is noteworthy. Huldah is the last prophet in Joshua–Kings, Deborah being the first (Judg 4:4), and these are the only female prophets mentioned;[58] if anything, this indicates that the writers were familiar with the non-gender-specific nature of Near Eastern prophecy and did not hesitate to ascribe a divine word of paramount importance to the mediation of a female prophet who at least indirectly, through her husband, is affiliatied with the temple of Jerusalem. Moreover, the narrative presents an interesting case of interaction of divinatory methods: an authoritative text, itself a medium of the divine word, is being cross-checked with another divi-

---

56. Cf. Corinne Bonnet, "Dove vivono gli dei? Note sulla terminologia fenicio-punica dei luoghi di culto e sui modi di rappresentazione del mondo divino," in *Saturnia Tellus: Definizioni dello spazio consacrato in ambiente etrusco, italoci, fenicio-punico, iberico e celtico* (ed. Xavier Dupré Raventós, Sergio Ribichini, and Stéphanie Verger; Roma: Consiglio nazionale delle ricerche, 2008), 673–85, esp. 680.

57. For the machinery and social organization of "universe-maintenance," see Peter L. Berger and Thomas Luckmann, *The Social Construction of Reality: A Treatise in Sociology of Knowledge* (New York, Anchor Books, 1989 [orig. 1966]), 104–28. For the ideological background of the Neo-Assyrian prophetic texts, see Parpola, *Assyrian Prophecies*, xviii–xlviii.

58. Cf. H. G. M. Williamson, "Prophetesses in the Hebrew Bible," in *Prophecy and Prophets in Ancient Israel: Proceedings of the Oxford Old Testament Seminar* (ed. John Day; LHBOTS 531; London: T&T Clark, 2010), 65–80.

natory medium, prophecy.⁵⁹ The prophecy of Huldah does not give any cultic instructions, but it prompts Josiah to effectuate an unprecedented cultic reform, which adds Huldah's name to the inventory of Near Eastern prophets appearing as advocates of legitimate worship.

Even other prophets are given a crucial role in mediating the divine word concerning legitimate and illegitimate worship in Joshua–Kings. First Kings 13 is explicitly connected with the Josiah narrative, reporting the performance of an anonymous prophet (*'îš hā-'ĕlōhîm*) while King Jeroboam of Israel is sacrificing by the altar of the sanctuary of Bethel where he had erected the notorious golden calves: "O altar, altar, thus says the LORD: 'A son shall be born to the house of David, Josiah by name; and he shall sacrifice on you the priests of the high places who offer incense on you, and human bones shall be burned on you'" (1 Kgs 13:1–2). The prophecy is followed by the destruction of the altar as a sign of the illegitimacy of the cult in Bethel; once again, a prophet appears as an advocate of legitimate worship, albeit *per viam negationis*. The man of God and Huldah are placed in two ends of the narrative span, marking the beginning and the end of the phase of royal idolatry in the writers' scheme of the history of Israel.

It is not uncommon to find prophets in cult places or in their vicinity. The book of Joshua does not mention a single prophet but makes Joshua, the successor of Moses, a leader of people who does not need prophetic mediation to receive the divine word but plays the roles of the king, the priest, and the diviner at the same time. He performs divinatory and cultic acts upon God's direct orders, such as lot-casting (see above), circumcision (Josh 5:2–9), and building an altar (8:30–31). Samuel, the first male prophet mentioned by name in Joshua–Kings, is given to be dedicated to God as a little boy (1 Sam 1:24–28), hence having a role akin to that of the above-mentioned votaresses (*šēlūtu*) uttering prophecies in Assyrian temples. It is in the temple of Shiloh where God henceforth is said

---

59. Jonathan Ben-Dov ("Some Precedents for the Religion of the Book: Josiah's Book and Ancient Revelatory Literature," in Grabbe and Nissinen, *Constructs of Prophecy*, 43–62, esp. 50–51) suggests that *sēper hattôrāh* in the oldest, pre-Deuteronomistic version of the story refers to a written oracular document, and its equation with Deuteronomy as a *sēper habbĕrît* is due to Deuteronomistic editing. He finds a similar case of double-checking the divine message in the letter of Nur-Sin to Zimri-Lim (FM 7 39 = SBLWAW 12 1), in which oracles obtained from extispicy (*tērtum*, an Akkadian cognate of *tôrâ*) are immediately elaborated by prophets and reported to the king in a letter.

to reveal his word to Samuel (1 Sam 3:21). Samuel's roles and activities are manifold, and it is difficult to determine whether he should be called a prophet, a priest, or a judge in the first place. He is explicitly identified as a prophet, whether a *nābî'* (1 Sam 3:20), a *rō'ê* (1 Sam 9:11, 18–19), or an *'îš hā-'ĕlōhîm* (1 Sam 9:6, 10), but he also functions in priestly roles not usually associated with prophetic activities. Such a profusion of different functions of one and the same individual is probably due to textual growth; it has been assumed that Samuel's prophetic role is secondary to his more original priestly function.[60]

While Samuel's close affilitation to the temple of Shiloh, together with his cultic functions, may be due to his priestly past in the history of the narrative itself, there are several other prophets in Samuel–Kings appearing in temple contexts. The band of prophets whose prophetic frenzy Saul shares is located in the "hill of God" (*gib'at 'ĕlōhîm* 1 Sam 10:5; cf. v. 10). The encounter of the anonymous *'îš hā-'ĕlōhîm* with Eli (1 Sam 2:27–36) only makes sense within the context the temple of Shiloh, all the more because the explicit concern of the prophecy is the proper execution of the priestly office. The legacy of this temple is carried forward by the prophet Ahijah the Shilonite (1 Kgs 11:29–39), who continually lived in Shiloh and was consulted there by Jeroboam as if the ancient temple were still standing (1 Kgs 14:1–18). Even Isaiah seems to be located in the temple of Jerusalem; Hezekiah, when facing the threat from Assyria (2 Kgs 19:1–7; cf. Isa 37:1–7), goes to the temple wearing a sackcloth and sends his rep-

---

60. Recent studies on Samuel explain his different roles in different ways. Walter Dietrich ("Samuel—ein Prophet?" in *Prophets and Prophecy in Jewish and Early Christian Literature* [ed. Joseph Verheyden, Korinna Zamfir, and Tobias Nicklas; WUNT 2/286; Tübingen: Mohr Siebeck, 2010], 1–17) argues that the role of the historical Samuel was that of a judge, whereas his prophetic functions are the result of a literary development. According to Marvin Sweeney ("Samuel's Institutional Identity in the Deuteronomistic History," in Grabbe and Nissinen, *Constructs of Prophecy*, 165–74), the Deuteronomistic writer uses an earlier Samuel narrative in which he functions as a priest and turns him into a prophet; according to him, Samuel follows the Northern model of priest, where the firstborn functioned in this pre-Levitical role. Serge Frolov ("1 Samuel 1–8: The Prophet as Agent Provocateur," in Grabbe and Nissinen, *Constructs of Prophecy*, 77–85), on the other hand, argues that 1 Sam 1–8 in its entirety is polemically directed against the Deuteronomic and Deuteronomistic concept of prophecy, Samuel being introduced as an agent provocateur, commissioned by God to cause the people to bring a disaster upon themselves.

resentatives, also clothed with sackcloth, to Isaiah, as if the prophet was to be found there.⁶¹

According to 1 Kgs 18:21–40, Elijah slaughtered four hundred prophets of Baal and Asherah after demonstrating YHWH's superiority in a formidable sacrificial performance at an altar specifically constructed for this purpose on Mount Carmel. This account, apart from the Samuel narratives, is the only occasion in ancient Near Eastern literature where a prophet himself performs a sacrificial ritual, but it hardly gives any information concerning the prophets' cultic role. Nevertheless, a connection between prophets and altars in the writer's (and the implied reader's) mind is suggested also by Elijah's mention of the killing of prophets with sword in the same breath as throwing down the altars (1 Kgs 19:10, 14), as if all this was the result of a single act of violence against every type of idolatry.

In the ancient Near East, temples were divinely ordered centers of the mythological universe.⁶² Likewise in the Hebrew Bible, the temple of Jerusalem is the focal point of the identity of Israel, the establishment of which appears as a decisive act of the maintenance of the symbolic universe in Joshua–Kings. The prophet Nathan's oracle to King David combines the dynastic promise with the ordinance that David's son will build a temple for YHWH: "He shall build a house for my name, and I will establish the throne of his kingdom for ever. I will be a father to him, and he shall be a son to me" (2 Sam 7:13–14). As we saw earlier, the dynastic promise in Nathan's oracle can be read against a common Near Eastern royal ideology. A further Near Eastern feature in 2 Sam 7 is the expression of the divine initiative in temple-building and its placement in the mouth of a person who is called a prophet; however: "The dissociation of temple building and dynastic promise, as promulgated in 2 Sam 7, is unprecedented in the Ancient Near East."⁶³

---

61. According to Hans Wildberger, "the situation is purely political; the ministers … are sent to Isaiah, who is certainly not a temple prophet and is clearly not held in very high regard by the priestly circles at the temple" (*Isaiah 28–39: A Continental Commentary* [trans. Thomas H. Trapp; Minneapolis, Fortress, 2002], 400). This is consistent with Wildberger's image of the prophet Isaiah as closely related to the court but not to the temple (cf. ibid., p. 569–72), but not necessarily with Isa 37:1–7//2 Kgs 19:1–7, where the prophet seems to be consulted in the context of a mourning ritual.

62. See Beate Pongratz-Leisten, *Ina šulmi īrub: Die kulttopographische und ideologische Programmatik der akītu-Prozession in Babylonien und Assyrien im 1. Jahrtausend v.Chr.* (Baghdader Forschungen 16; Mainz: Philipp von Zabern, 1994), 20, 36.

63. Wolfgang Oswald, "Is There a Prohibition to Build a Temple in 2 Samuel 7?"

The Literary Portrayal of Prophets

We have seen above that prophecy, as presented in Joshua–Kings, is in many ways analogous to the image of prophecy that can be obtained from the ancient Near Eastern sources available to us. Prophecy fulfills the function of the divinatory *Herrschaftswissen* needed by the king and other leaders of the people; it is essentially connected to the kings' politics, warfare, and succession; and it has an affiliation with worship, which sometimes is its principal concern.

On the other hand, the portrayal of prophecy in Joshua–Kings has several features poorly represented or unknown in the extant Near Eastern sources. We have already noted above the fluidity of the boundary between prophecy and technical divination, for which there is very little evidence in the ancient Near East. Moreover, Samuel, immediately after Saul is proclaimed king, gives his farewell speech to the people presenting himself the following way (1 Sam 12:3):

> Here I am; testify against me before the LORD and before his anointed. Whose ox have I taken? Or whose donkey have I taken? Or whom have I defrauded? Whom have I oppressed? Or from whose hand have I taken a bribe to blind my eyes with it? Testify against me and I will restore it to you.

This corresponds in every respect to the ancient Near Eastern ideal of a just king also illustrated when the god Adad says to King Zimri-Lim: "When a wronged man or woman cries out to you, be there and judge their case. This only I have demanded from you."[64] The curious thing with Samuel is that, while having executed his office as a judge the way a just king does, he also acted as a prophet, diviner, and priest. Such a combination of diverse roles within one and the same person is unknown in Near Eastern documents of prophecy.

---

in *Thinking towards New Horizons: Collected Communications to the XIXth Congress of the International Organization for the Study of the Old Testament, Ljubljana 2007* (ed. Matthias Augustin and Hermann Michael Niemann; BEATAJ 55; Frankfurt: Lang, 2008), 85–89, esp. 88. For the literary development of theological ideas in 2 Sam 7, see also Thilo Alexander Rudnig, "König ohne Tempel: 2 Samuel 7 in Tradition und Redaktion," *VT* 61 (2011): 426–46.

64. FM 7 39 (= SBLWAW 12 1): 53–55; cf. FM 7 38 (= SBLWAW 12 2) r. 6–11.

In Joshua–Kings, there are many other prophets whose portrayal goes beyond the usual socioreligious repertoire of an ancient Near Eastern prophet as we know it from the available sources. Nathan, besides acting in a prophetic role in mediating the divine promise, also functions as the king's closest advisor executing considerable political power.[65] Deborah bears the title "prophetess," and she actually transmits divine words to Barak (Judg 4:6–9), but she also acts as a judge for the Israelites; one wonders if the combination of her roles as a diviner and a judge actually implies the idea of a divine judgment by means of technical divination performed under the palm tree named after her (Judg 4:4–5).[66]

Furthermore, unlike any prophet in the ancient Near Eastern sources, biblical prophets may perform miraculous deeds. Health, for instance, was an important concern of Near Eastern kings (Esarhaddon in particular[67]), but they usually seem to have consulted magicians and scholars rather than prophets in matters of healing. Neither do prophets perform healing rituals in the sources known to us, even though their presence in such a ritual is mentioned in one Neo-Assyrian text.[68] In the Hebrew Bible, Elijah and Elisha, both designated as "prophets" or "men of God," appear as powerful healers and resuscitators (1 Kgs 17:17–24; 2 Kgs 4:8–37; 5:1–19)— Elisha even after his death (2 Kgs 13:20–21). Isaiah also acts as the healer of King Hezekiah, performing another miracle: he cries to God who lets

---

65. Cf. Wolfgang Oswald, *Nathan der Prophet: Eine Untersuchung zu 2 Samuel 7 und 12 und 1 Könige 1* (AThANT 94; Zürich: Theologischer Verlag, 2008), 258: "Nathan ist von dem, was historisch plausibel gemacht werden kann, weit entfernt und kann nicht in die Geschichte der Prophetie der frühen Königszeit eingeordnet werden."

66. Klaas Spronk ("Deborah, a Prophetess: The Meaning and Background of Judges 4:4–5," in *The Elusive Prophet: The Prophet as a Historical Person, Literary Character and Anonymous Artist* [ed. Johannes C. de Moor; OTS 45; Leiden: Brill, 2001], 232–42) surmises that the figure of Deborah was originally that of a necromancer similar to the woman of En-Dor in 1 Sam 28. On the other hand, Yaakov Kupitz and Katell Berthelot ("Deborah and the Delphic Pythia: A New Interpretation of Judges 4:4–5," in *Images and Prophecy in the Ancient Eastern Mediterranean* [ed. Martti Nissinen and Charles E. Carter; FRLANT 233; Göttingen: Vandenhoeck & Ruprecht, 2009], 95–124) find intriguing similarities in the figures of Deborah and the Pythia of Delphi.

67. See, e.g., SAA 10 187; 201; 213; 241; 242; 243; 297; 299; 302; 309; 315; 318–327.

68. Ritual of Ištar and Dumuzi (SBLWAW 12 118), 31–32: "For the frenzied men and women (*zabbi zabbati*) and for the prophets and prophetesses (*mahhê u mahhūti*) you shall place seven pieces of bread. Then let the sick person recite the following to Ištar: (…)." It is unclear whether the prophecy of Irra-gamil concerning the death of a royal baby in ARM 26 222 (= SBLWAW 12 33) coincided with a healing ritual.

the shadow retreat ten intervals as a sign of Hezekiah's recovery from his illness (2 Kgs 20:1–11; cf. Isa 38:1–8).

Biblical prophets also sometimes control the weather. Samuel, having finished his farewell speech, calls upon God to send thunder and rain (1 Sam 12:17–18) and Elijah's contest with the prophets of Baal and Asherah, motivated by a draught declared by him, ends with a heavy rain (1 Kgs 18:38–45; cf. 17:1). The narratives on Elijah and Elisha include many other miracles performed by these two persons who in different ways control the forces of nature (2 Kgs 2:14, 19–22; 4:38–41; 6:1–7, 18–20), including a kind of clairvoyance (2 Kgs 6:8–17) and the multiplication of food (1 Kgs 17:7–16; 2 Kgs 4:1–7, 42–44). No such activities are reported with regard to ancient Near Eastern prophets in the sources at our disposal.

The differences between the biblical and ancient Near Eastern portrayals of prophecy may partly be due to different socioreligious circumstances on the historical scene. The amalgamation of the prophetic role with other socioreligious functions can, at least in theory, be explained by the small-scale and less differentiated structure of the Israelite/Judahite/Yehudite society, allowing an individual to assume a cluster of social roles not to be found in the more differentiated societies of ancient Mesopotamia. While this remains a possibility especially with regard to divinatory functions, it deserves attention that similar differences cannot be observed comparing sources coming from imperial Assyria and the city-state of Mari, despite all dissimilarities in the socioreligious structure of these societies.

The principal reason for the diverse portrayals of prophets is to be sought first and foremost in the difference in their emergence, transmission, and literary function. The information about prophets and prophecy in ancient Near Eastern sources comes from a variety of texts of different types: written oracles, letters, word-lists, ritual texts, administrative documents, and inscriptions, which were written, edited, and deposited in archives relatively soon after the events they describe. They do not usually have a long editorial history behind them; however, they are not neutral accounts either, but represent the interests of the writers and officials who have selected the material to be included in the archives.[69] The Assyrian

---

69. Cf., e.g., Jack M. Sasson, "The Posting of Letters with Divine Messages," in *Florilegium Marianum II: Recueil d'études à la mémoire de Maurice Birot* (ed. Dominique Charpin and Jean-Marie Durand; Mémoires de NABU 3; Paris: SEPOA, 1994), 299–316; Karel van der Toorn, "From the Oral to the Written: The Case of Old Babylonian Prophecy," in *Writings and Speech in Israelite and Ancient Near Eastern Prophecy*

prophecies, for example, represent an orthodox royal ideology, portraying the prophets accordingly.[70] The narratives, including prophetic performances in Joshua–Kings,[71] primarily function within the literary contexts of this multilayered composition scholars call the Deuteronomistic History, serving the narrative and ideological purposes of their multiple editors, and only occasionally informing about historical factualities. Therefore, any comparison between biblical and Near Eastern sources concerns the *constructs* of prophecy represented by the texts and it is to be expected that the construct is dependent on the agenda of the writers of each text, biblical or nonbiblical. It is no wonder that official royal documents from imperial Assyria and the post-586 writers of Joshua–Kings have very distinct views of the function of prophets, resulting in divergent constructs of prophecy.

The narratives in Joshua–Kings show what the (post-)Deuteronomistic writers living in the Second Temple communities[72] took for granted with regard to prophets and their activities in the times these literary compositions describe. It is reasonable to assume that a part of the image of the ancient prophets in these writings is based on older documents. This said, it is important to recognize that all this material is reread and adapted to a secondary context, and new layers of redaction have modified the image of the prophets and added new dimensions to their characteristics.

(ed. Ehud Ben Zvi and Michael H. Floyd; SBLSymS 10; Atlanta: Society of Biblical Literature, 2000), 219–234; Dominique Charpin, "The Writing, Sending and Reading of Letters in the Amorite World," in *The Babylonian World* (ed. Gwendolyn Leick; New York: Routledge, 2007), 400–417.

70. See Martti Nissinen, "Prophecy as Construct: Ancient and Modern," in *"Thus Speaks Ishtar of Arbela": Prophecy in Israel, Assyria and Egypt in the Neo-Assyrian Period* (ed. Robert P. Gordon and Hans M. Barstad; Winona Lake, Ind.: Eisenbrauns, 2013), 11–35.

71. For recent studies on prophets and prophecy in the Deuteronomistic History, see, e.g., Walter Dietrich, "Prophetie im deuteronomistischen Geschichtswerk," in *The Future of the Deuteronomistic History* (ed. Thomas Römer; BETL 147; Leuven: Peeters, 2000), 47–65; Ben Zvi, "The Prophets"; and the articles collected in *Past, Present, Future: The Deuteronomistic History and the Prophets* (ed. Johannes C. de Moor and Harry F. van Rooy; OTS 44; Leiden, Brill, 2000).

72. Recent thoroughgoing analyses of the emergence of Joshua–Kings include Kratz, *The Composition of the Narrative Books*; Jan Christian Gertz, "Tora und vordere Propheten," in *Grundinformation Altes Testament* (ed. Jan Christian Gertz; UTB 2745; Göttingen: Vandenhoeck & Ruprecht, 2006), 187–302, esp. 278–302; Römer, *The So-Called Deuteronomistic History*.

The stories about Elijah and Elisha, for example, belong primarily to their present literary contexts with a complex editorial history.[73] They may contain ancient elements, but they are not first-hand evidence of prophecy in the ninth-century northern kingdom. It is commonly assumed that the narratives are based on older traditions about miracle-workers who have only secondarily been given a prophetic designation.[74] On the other hand, it is noteworthy that "much of the Elijah material belongs to the genre of hagiography, and therefore it can be compared with, among other things, the Life of Anthony the Hermit by Athanasius, the rabbinic traditions about Hanina ben Dosa the Galilean wonder-worker, or the biographical memoir of the Pythagorian sage Apollonius of Tyana written by Philostratus";[75] this may imply a late rather than an early origin of some of the miracle stories in the Elijah-Elisha cycle.

The overwhelmingly positive attitude toward the king in ancient Near Eastern—especially Assyrian—prophecy, and the largely critical stance of the prophets toward the kings in Joshua-Kings both reflect the constructs of prophecy represented by each source material. In Assyria, and also at

---

73. The complicated literary history of the Elijah and Elisha narratives has been analyzed with varying results; for recent contributions, see, e.g., Susanne Otto, *Jehu, Elia und Elisa: Die Erzählung von der Jehu-Revolution und die Komposition der Elia-Elisa-Erzählungen* (BWANT 152; Stuttgart: Kohlhammer, 2001); Jyrki Keinänen, *Traditions in Collision: A Literary and Redaction-Critical Study on the Elijah Narratives 1 Kings 17-19* (Publications of the Finnish Exegetical Society 80: Helsinki: Finnish Exegetical Society and Göttingen: Vandenhoeck & Ruprecht, 2001); Bernhard Lehnart, *Prophet und König im Nordreich Israel: Studien zur sogenannten vorklassischen Prophetie im Nordreich Israel anhand der Samuel-, Elija- und Elischa-Überlieferungen* (VTSup 96; Leiden: Brill, 2003); Matthias Köckert, "Elia: Literarische und religionsgeschichtliche Probleme in 1Kön 17-18," in *Der Eine Gott und die Götter: Polytheismus und Monotheismus im antiken Israel* (ed. Manfred Oeming and Konrad Schmid; AThANT 82; Zürich: Theologischer Verlag, 2003), 111-44; Dagmar Pruin, *Geschichten und Geschichte: Isebel als literarische und historische Gestalt* (OBO 222; Fribourg: Academic Press and Göttingen, Vandenhoeck & Ruprecht, 2006). I would also like to refer to the forthcoming Göttingen dissertation of Ruth Sauerwein on Elisha in the context of Israelite and and Near Eastern history of religion.

74. Gertz, "Tora und die vorderen Propheten," 296: "Wie groß der Umfang der in die Zeit des Elija (Elischa) zurückgehenden Traditionen im Einzelnen auch immer zu bestimmen ist, am Anfang der Traditionsbildung scheint ein Wundertäter und Regenmacher gestanden zu haben, der erst im Zuge der dtr (oder: nach-dtr) Rezeptionsgeschichte zum Paradigma für einen Jhwh-Propheten wurde, dessen Wort in jedem Fall in Erfüllung ging."

75. Blenkinsopp, *A History of Prophecy in Israel*, 59.

Mari, the documentation of prophecy derives from the royal archives, and it comes up to every expectation that devastating criticism never ended up in these archives. The Assyrian collections of prophetic oracles in particular are intentionally designed to proclaim the Assyrian state religion and ideology.[76] The present composition of Joshua–Kings, on the other hand, represents the postmonarchichal, or post-586, view of the past kingdoms of Israel and Judah. Also the image of prophecy in this literature has been constructed with the destruction of Jerusalem belonging to the shared memory and this causes ideological subversions of royal prophecy, such as the reversal of the dynastic promise concerning the kingdom of Israel. The basic prophetic function of transmitting the *Herrschaftswissen* to the king remains the same as everywhere in the Near East, but the contents of the message proclaimed by the prophets is oriented toward the end of monarchy.[77]

In sum, the portrayals of prophets in Joshua–Kings bear enough resemblance to the images of ancient Near Eastern prophets known from the sources from Mari and Assyria to warrant the conclusion that the biblical narrators were familiar with the phenomenon as an ancient tradition, probably also as a contemporary practice. The prophetic phenomenon was probably not drastically different in Mesopotamia and the southern Levant. As in the Near East, the socioreligious foundation of prophecy in Joshua–Kings consists of the institutions of divination, kingship, and worship. It is evident that prophecy was a significant element in the symbolic world of the writers of the evolving historical narrative that eventually became the literary composition labeled by scholars as the Deuteronomistic History.

However, the biblical portrayal of prophets also often diverge from what is familiar to us from ancient Near Eastern sources. This may partially go back to culture-specific differences in divinatory functions and socioreligious positions of prophets in Israel, Judah, and Yehud, but the primary source of the discrepancies should be sought from the context-specific constructs of prophecy in different literary and ideological contexts.

---

76. Cf. Parpola, *Assyrian Prophecies*, XVIII–XLIV.

77. Reinhard G. Kratz, *Die Propheten Israels* (Munich: Beck, 2003), 35: "Das alles erinnert an die altorientalischen Zustände. Nur, daß das Verhältnis der Propheten zum Königtum in der biblischen Überlieferung von Anfang an gestört und das Ende der Monarchie vorprogrammiert ist."

Moses, Israel's First Prophet, and the Formation of the Deuteronomistic and Prophetic Libraries

Thomas C. Römer

"Is Moses also among the prophets?"—This question may sound astonishing, but when we look at the Hebrew Bible more closely, we see that he is very seldom identified as a *nābî'*. In fact, this title is attributed to him directly only in two or three passages of the Hebrew Bible. In Deut 18 he seems to inaugurate the prophetic office in Israel, since the text states that YHWH will from now on raise other prophets like Moses (18:15). In Deut 34:10–12 Moses is distinguished from the prophets that follow, who cannot compare with him ("Never since has there arisen a prophet in Israel like Moses, whom YHWH knew face to face"). Finally, Hos 12:14 mentions a nameless prophet who brought Israel up from Egypt and guarded it, a probable allusion to Moses. In Exod 3, Moses' call gives him a prophetic color of sorts, as we will see, but he is never explicitly depicted as a prophet. In the plague stories he is YHWH's representative facing Pharaoh. Interestingly in this context, and according to a priestly or post-priestly redactor, Moses himself becomes like a god (*'ĕlōhîm*), whereas his brother Aaron is designated as Moses' prophet: "YHWH said to Moses, 'See, I have made you God to Pharaoh, and your brother Aaron shall be your prophet'" (Exod 7:1). In the book of Numbers, Moses is twice related to the prophets, without being himself called a *nābî'*. In Num 11, after his spirit is put upon seventy elders and on two more people, they all prophesy without interruption.[1] And Moses, arguing against the concern of his servant Joshua, defends the idea of a democratization of prophecy: "But Moses said to him, 'Are you jealous for my sake? Would that all YHWH's

---

1. It seems more logical that the original text had the root *swp* ("they did not stop") and the Masoretes then vocalized in order to suggest the root *ysp* ("they did not continue"). See H. Holzinger, *Numeri* (KHC 4; Tübingen: Mohr Siebeck, 1903), 45.

people were prophets, and that YHWH would put his spirit on them!'"
(11:29). The story apparently indicates that Moses' spirit enables the elders
to prophesy. One could therefore argue that the author or redactor of Num
11 considers Moses as possessing a prophetic spirit that can be transmitted. On the other hand, the following chapter draws a clear distinction
between Moses and the prophets. Whereas YHWH speaks to the prophets
in visions (*mar'ōt*) and dreams (*ḥălōmôt*), this is not the case for Moses:
"Not so with my servant Moses; he is entrusted with all my house. With
him I speak face to face—clearly (*mar'eh*), not in riddles (*ḥidōt*); and he
beholds the form of YHWH" (12:8). Here Moses receives the title *'ebed
yhwh*, and this is also the way in which he is very often designated in the
books of the Former Prophets. Outside the Torah and the so-called Deuteronomistic History, Moses appears in Jer 15:1 together with Samuel as a
potential intercessor for Israel who is unable to prevent coming disaster.
In Mic 6:4 he is mentioned together with Aaron and Miriam. In this triad
Aaron represents the priests and Miriam the prophets, whereas Moses is
Israel's chief and guide.[2] This is also the case in Isa 63:11–14, Ps 77:21, Ps
105:25 (in both psalms he appears together with Aaron). At the end of the
prophetic corpus in Mal 3:22–24 ("Remember the teaching of my servant
Moses, the statutes and ordinances that I commanded him at Horeb for all
Israel. I will send you the prophet Elijah before the great and terrible day
of YHWH comes"), Moses appears together with Elijah. Here it is clearly
Elijah, who represents the prophets, whereas Moses refers to the Torah as
in many other texts, especially in the Deuteronomistic History (DtrH).
Here Moses is above all YHWH's servant, and mediator of the law. Why is
he then presented in Deut 18 as Israel's first prophet?

Deuteronomy 18:15–22 in the Context of Deuteronomy and the "Deuteronomistic Library"

The passage about the installation of the prophetic office concludes the
section of laws about figures of authority among the people (16:18–18:22).
The section starts with prescriptions concerning judges (*šōpĕṭîm*) and
state officers (*šōṭĕrîm*), followed by the laws about the king, the levitical
priests (*hakkōhănîm hallĕwiyyīm*), and finally the prophet. However, the
paragraph dealing with the prophet is preceded by a passage that enumer-

---

2. Interestingly, in Ps 99:6–7 Moses and Aaron are both called "priests."

ates illicit means of consulting the future or the gods, including different kinds of divination, augury, soothsaying, sortilege, and necromancy. In the ancient Near East, most of these practices are related to "prophetic" activity, whereas the authors of Deut 18 want to establish a clear differentiation by redefining the prophetic office in opposition to traditional investigations of the divine will.[3]

Deuteronomy 18:15-22 is apparently an attempt to redefine the role and function of a prophet. First, each prophet is a "new Moses" of sorts (v. 15: "YHWH your God will raise up for you a prophet like me"), and this indicates Israel's particularity in contrast to the people of the land who practice divination (*qsm*, v. 14). Interestingly, in some texts of the Hebrew Bible the *qōsēm* (diviner)[4] is associated with the Judean prophets (Isa 3:2; Jer 29:8; Ezek 13:1), and in other texts divination is a prophetic activity (Mic 3:11: "its prophets practice divination for money"). The author of Deut 18 wants to dissociate the prophet from divination, and locates the origin of the prophetic office in the divine revelation at Horeb (18:16-17). In the two versions of the Sinai/Horeb—revelation in Exod 19-20 and Deut 5 the people indeed ask for a mediator, but there is no mention that the mediation should be done by a succession of prophets.

> Exod 20:18-19: 18 When all the people witnessed the thunder and lightning, the sound of the trumpet, and the mountain smoking, they were afraid and trembled and stood at a distance, 19 and said to Moses, **"You speak to us, and we will listen**; but do not let God speak to us, or we will die."

> Deut 5:23-29: 23 When you heard the voice out of the darkness ... 24 and you said, "Look, YHWH our God has shown us his glory and greatness, and we have heard his voice out of the fire. ... 25 So now why should we die? For this great fire will consume us; if we hear the voice of YHWH our God any longer, we shall die. ... 27 Go near, you yourself, and hear all that the Lord our God will say. **Then tell us everything that YHWH our God tells you, and we will listen** and do it." 28 YHWH heard your words when you spoke to me, and YHWH said to me: "I have heard the

---

3. Thomas Römer, "Les interdits des pratiques magiques et divinatoires dans le livre du Deutéronome (Dt 18,9-13)," in *Magie et divination dans les cultures de l'Orient* (ed. Jean-Marie Durand and Antoine Jacquet; Cahiers de l'IPOA 3; Paris: Jean Maisonneuve, 2010), 73-85.

4. Römer, "Interdits," 78.

words of this people, which they have spoken to you; *they are right in all that they have spoken.* 29 If only they had such a mind as this, to fear me and to keep all my commandments always, so that it might go well with them and with their children forever!"

Deut 18:16-18: 16 This is what you requested of YHWH your God at Horeb on the day of the assembly when you said: "<u>If I hear the voice of YHWH my God any more, or ever again see this great fire, I will die.</u>" 17 Then YHWH replied to me: "*They are right in what they have said.* 18 I WILL RAISE UP FOR THEM A PROPHET LIKE YOU FROM AMONG THEIR OWN PEOPLE; I WILL PUT MY WORDS IN THE MOUTH OF THE PROPHET, WHO SHALL SPEAK TO THEM EVERYTHING THAT I COMMAND."

Apparently Deut 18 presupposes Exod 20:18-19 and Deut 5:23-29. The author of Deut 18:16-18 rewrites the older texts in order to root prophecy in the Horeb revelation. The prophet appears in Deut 18:18 as YHWH's spokesman who has to communicate the divine words to the people ("I will put my words in his mouth, and he shall speak to them everything that I command"); those who will not listen to the prophetic word,[5] YHWH will seek (*drš*) for judgment. The focus here is on the audience's reaction to the prophetic word: This "seeking" of the reluctant may be understood as referring to an individual (see in this sense Ps 10:13); in the context of the Deuteronomistic History this correlation may also serve to explain the destruction of Jerusalem and the exile; according to some texts, as we will see, this disaster happened because of the rejection of YHWH's prophets.

The last paragraph, Deut 18:20-22, deals with the problem of distinguishing between true and false prophets, and may be a later addition. The author of Deut 18 takes up the section about prophets in Deut 13:2-5, which is probably older than Deut 18, since it does not presuppose the Mosaic etiology of prophecy. In Deut 13 the "false" prophets (who are related to dreams and signs) are prophets who are promoting "other gods";[6] in Deut 18:20-22 this topic has become unproblematic (a prophet

---

5. The MT has "my words" (YHWH), whereas Samaritanus and most Greek manuscripts read "his [the prophet's] words."
6. Deut 13:2-6* has a parallel in the treaty of Esarhaddon (see Eckart Otto, *Das Deuteronomium: Politische Theologie und Rechtsreform in Juda und Assyrien* [BZAW 284; Berlin: de Gruyter, 1999], 57-87), and belongs to the first edition of Deuteronomy in the seventh century B.C.E.

invoking the authority of other gods is necessarily a false prophet); the concern is now on prophets, who speak in the name of YHWH. The "wait and see" solution that the redactor of these verses suggests (see especially v. 22: "If a prophet speaks in the name YHWH but the thing does not take place or prove true, it is a word that YHWH has not spoken") may point to rival viewpoints among prophets of YHWH, as reflected in the book of Jeremiah (see for instance the encounter between Jeremiah and Hananiah in chapter 28). Deuteronomy 18:10–22 was certainly added after the destruction of Jerusalem in order to legitimate in the context of the Deuteronomistic corpus prophets of doom instead of prophets of "salvation."[7]

---

7. Perhaps this addition was made in several steps. There is, however, no need to distinguish diachronically between vv. 14–15 and 16–18, as suggested sometimes. See, among others, Udo Rüterswörden, *Von der politischen Gemeinschaft zur Gemeinde: Studien zu Dt 16,18–18,22* (BBB 65; Frankfurt: Athenäum, 1987), 85 ; Sebastian Grätz, "'Einen Propheten wie mich wird dir der Herr, dein Gott, erwecken': Der Berufungsbericht Jeremias und seine Rückbindung an das Amt des Mose," in *Moses in Biblical and Extra-Biblical Traditions* (ed. Axel Graupner and Michael Wolter; BZAW 372; Berlin: de Gruyter, 2007), 61–77, here 63–64. Verse 18 is a "Wiederaufnahme," as is rightly observed by Carl Steuernagel (*Das Deuteronomium* [2nd ed.; HKAT; Göttingen: Vandenhoeck & Ruprecht, 1923], 121), but this is not an argument against the literary unity of vv. 14–18, since v. 18 legitimates, through a YHWH-speech, Moses' recapitulation in v. 15, as rightly observed by Steuernagel and recently by Christophe Nihan ("'Moses and the Prophets': Deuteronomy 18 and the Emergence of the Pentateuch as Torah," *SEÅ* 75 [2010]: 21–55, here 32–34). The case may be different in regard to vv. 21–22. These verses may constitute a later addition, as argued by Joseph Blenkinsopp in *Prophecy and Canon: A Contribution to the Study of Jewish Origins* (CSJCA 3; Notre Dame, Ind.: University of Notre Dame Press, 1977), 45–46; Fabrizio Foresti, "Storia della redazione di Dtn. 16, 18–18, 22 e le sue connessioni con l'opera storica deuteronomistica," *Teresianum* 39 (1988): 1–199, here 136–38; Matthias Köckert, "Zum literargeschichtlichen Ort des Prophetengesetzes Dtn 18 zwischen dem Jeremiabuch und Dtn 13," in *Liebe und Gebot: Studien zum Deuteronomium* (ed. Reinhard Gregor Kratz and Hermann Spieckermann; Göttingen: Vandenhoeck & Ruprecht, 2000), 80–100, here 94; and many others. Deuteronomy 18:21–22 introduces a new theme—how to recognize whether a prophet has spoken in the name of YHWH or not—whereas 18:14–20 concerns the definition and the functions of a true prophet of YHWH. As was already observed by Steuernagel (*Deuteronomium*, 123), vv. 21–22 concern predictions of future events, whereas vv. 19–20 present the prophet as the mediator or preacher of YHWH's commandments. The case is difficult to decide. One could also consider 18:14–22 a literary unit and argue that the author of this passage wants to gather different questions and topics about the prophets, as these have done: Christa Schäfer-Lichtenberger, *Josua und Salomo: Eine Studie zu Autorität und Legitimität des Nachfolgers im Alten Testament* (VTSup 58; Leiden: Brill,

The definition of the prophet as a "preacher" of the divine word, a preacher that calls to obedience to the divine law, creates a link with the book of Kings, but also with the book of Jeremiah. In both books, the prophets are labeled as YHWH's servants.

YHWH's Servants, the Prophets in the Books of Kings and Jeremiah

In the Hebrew Bible, the expression "YHWH's servants, the prophets" occurs sixteen times (either in the third person, "his servants the prophets," or in the first person, "my servants the prophets"[8]). Eleven of these occur in the books of Kings and Jeremiah, the other five are found in Ezek 38:17; Amos 3:7; Zech 1:6; Dan 9:6, 10; and Ezra 9:11. Most of these passages underwent Deuteronomistic redaction or display an ideology related to the Deuteronomistic History. In the book of Kings, the title "servant" is also used for individual prophetic figures: in 1 Kgs 14:18 for Ahijah, in 2 Kgs 14:25 for Jonah, and indirectly in 1 Kgs 18:36 for Elijah. The use of the title *'ăbādîm* for prophets may stem from Deut 18:14–22, where the prophets appear as Moses' successors. And, in the Hebrew Bible, Moses, together with David, is the *'ebed yhwh* par excellence.[9] Interestingly, in the Deuteronomistic History, prophets as *'ăbādîm* are only found in the book of Kings. This may strengthen the idea of some scholars who argue that Kings is the most "Deuteronomistic" book in the Former Prophets.[10] With the exception of Jonah ben Amittai, these prophets do not announce positive divine intervention: they are preachers of the law, admonishing the people and the kings to respect the divine prescriptions. Since their exhortations are not taken seriously, they are also prophets of doom, delivering oracles of destruction and exile. According to 2 Kgs 17:13–14, the

---

1995), 100–103; Harald Knobloch, *Die nachexilische Prophetentheorie des Jeremiabuches* (BZABR 12; Wiesbaden: Harrassowitz, 2009), 234–37; Nihan, "Moses and the Prophets"; and others.

8. The only exception is the second person in the prayer of Dan 9:6, "your servants the prophets."

9. Ingrid Riesener, *Der Stamm* עבד *im Alten Testament: Eine Wortuntersuchung unter Berücksichtigung neuerer sprachwissenschaftlicher Methoden* (BZAW 149; Berlin: de Gruyter, 1979).

10. Knauf, "Does 'Deuteronomistic Historiography' (DtrH) Exist?"; Kurt L. Noll, "Deuteronomistic History or Deuteronomistic Debate? (A Thought Experiment)," *JSOT* 31 (2007): 311–45.

fall of Samaria happened because of the unwillingness of the kings and the people to behave according to YHWH's law:

> YHWH solemnly warned Israel and Judah through all his prophets and all the seers: "Turn back from your evil ways; obey my commandments and rules that are recorded in the law. I ordered your ancestors to keep this law and sent my servants the prophets to remind you of its demands." But they did not pay attention and were as stubborn as their ancestors, who had not trusted YHWH their God.

The prophets also announce the fall of Judah in reaction to Manasseh's misbehavior:

> So YHWH announced through his servants the prophets: "King Manasseh of Judah has committed horrible sins.... So this is what YHWH God of Israel says, 'I am about to bring disaster on Jerusalem and Judah.... I will destroy Jerusalem the same way I did; I will wipe Jerusalem clean, just as one wipes a plate on both sides. I will abandon this last remaining tribe among my people and hand them over to their enemies ... because they have done evil in my sight and have angered me from the time their ancestors left Egypt right up to this very day!" (2 Kgs 21:10–15)[11]

And when the destruction of Jerusalem happens, the Deuteronomists insert a final reminder that this was done by YHWH according to the prophetic warnings (2 Kgs 24:2: "He sent them to destroy Judah, as he had warned he would do through his servants the prophets"). These mentions of the prophets are clearly related to Deut 18, and they present the Deuteronomistic concept of prophecy. As was already noted, "the servants the prophets" also play an important role in the book of Jeremiah. This confirms the idea that the book of Jeremiah is related somehow to the Deuteronomistic History, or—to speak more cautiously—to the books of Deuteronomy and Kings.

---

11. Probably a late Deuteronomistic addition, according to Konrad Schmid, "Manasse und der Untergang Judas: 'Golaorientierte' Theologie in den Königsbüchern?" *Bib* 78 (1997): 87–99.

Jeremiah as the Last Prophet Like Moses

The six passages in Jeremiah that mention anonymous prophets as YHWH's servants are set in a chronological framework covering the period of the last years of the monarchy until after the destruction of Jerusalem and the deportation to Babylon, as well as the exile in Egypt. Jeremiah 7:25–26 follows Jeremiah's announcement of the possible destruction of the temple. It is set in a context that extends the disapproval of an unethical temple cult to a general rejection of the sacrificial cult:

> On the day that I brought your fathers out of the land of Egypt, I did not speak to them or command them concerning burnt offerings and sacrifices. But this command I gave them: "Obey my voice, and I will be your God, and you shall be my people." (vv. 22–23).

This astonishing statement may reflect a situation where the non-Priestly (D or J) account of the exodus and the Sinai, which contains no laws on sacrifices, and the Priestly version of the exodus and the desert, which focuses on the revelation of the sacrificial cult, still existed as separate documents.[12] Jeremiah 7:25–26 speaks of YHWH's sending his servants the prophets ("since the day that your fathers came out of the land of Egypt unto this day"), taking over the Deuteronomistic idea of Moses as Israel's first prophet. The statement that the people did not listen (*lōʾ šāmʿû*) may also be related to the concept of the prophets as preachers of the law, because the appeal to listen appears frequently in the book of Deuteronomy. The same holds true for Jer 25:1–7, a passage that (in LXX as well as in MT) concludes the first half of the book. Again the addressees' stubbornness is paralleled with the refusal of their "fathers" to behave according to the prophetic exhortations. Interestingly, the appeals to conversion by "YHWH's servants the prophets" correspond to those of Jeremiah's temple

---

12. This view is, however, not prominent among scholars. Most commentators discuss whether this oracle is total or a partial rejection of the sacrificial cult; see the overview given by Georg Fischer (*Jeremia 1–25* [HTKAT; Freiburg: Herder, 2005], 311–12). He thinks that YHWH's statement in 7:22 לא דברתי may stem from Deut 18:21 (309). The best explanation can still be found in Bernhard Duhm, *Das Buch Jeremia* (KHC 11; Tübingen: Mohr Siebeck, 1901), 81–82, who shows that the author of the passage does not know the priestly laws or—could one add—that he does not like them.

sermon. This indicates that the redactors of these passages considered Jeremiah to be continuing the ministry of the foregoing prophets.

Jer 25	Jer 7
4: And YHWH had sent unto you all his servants the prophets, *rising up early and sending them*, but you have not listened, nor inclined your ear to hear,	
5: saying, Return you now every one from his evil way, and from the evil of your doings, and you will dwell in the land that YHWH had given to you and to your fathers, since eternity to eternity:	3: Thus says YHWH of hosts, the God of Israel, Amend your ways and your doings, and I will cause you to dwell in this place. 7: … in the land that I gave to your fathers, since eternity to eternity.
6: and go not after other gods to serve them, and to worship them, and provoke me not to anger with the work of your hands; and I will do you no hurt.	6: … neither go after other gods to your own hurt:
7: But you have not listened to me, says YHWH.	13: And now, because you have done all these deeds, says YHWH, and I spoke unto you, *rising up early and speaking*, but you did not listen.

The link between Jeremiah's temple speech and "YHWH's servants the prophets" is even strengthened in the "summary" of this speech in Jer 26, where, in contrast to Jer 7, the mention of YHWH's ongoing sending of the prophets is presented as constituting a part of Jeremiah's discourse announcing the destruction of the temple (Jer 26:5–6). A very similar formulation appears in Jer 35:15,[13] where the Rechabites, who are faith-

---

13. This confirms the idea that Jer 7, 25, and 35 are the pillars of a "Deuteronomistic" edition of the book of Jeremiah. For more details, see Thomas Römer, "How Did Jeremiah Become a Convert to Deuteronomistic Ideology?" in *Those Elusive Deuteronomists* (ed. Steven L. McKenzie and Linda S. Schaering; JSOTSup 268; Sheffield: Sheffield Academic Press, 1999), 189–99; Bernard Gosse, "Trois étapes de la rédaction du livre de Jérémie : La venue du malheur contre ce lieu (Jérusalem), puis contre toute chair (Juda et les nations), et enfin de nouveau contre ce lieu, mais identifié cette fois à Babylone," *ZAW* 111 (1999): 508–29.

ful Yahwists, are opposed to the Judeans, who constantly refuse to behave according to the divine will:

> I have sent to you all my servants the prophets, rising up early and sending them, saying, "Return now, everyone of you, from your evil way, and amend your doings, and do not go after other gods to serve them, and then you shall dwell in the land that I gave to you and your fathers." But you did not incline your ear or obey me.

In Jer 29:19, "YHWH's servants the prophets" appears in a somewhat difficult construction[14] in order to explain that YHWH will exterminate those who had not been deported after the events of 597, because they still behave like their stubborn ancestors. The condemnation of the non-deported population has its counterpart in the last mention of the sending of the prophets, which occurs in Jeremiah's invective against the Judeans who had fled to Egypt. He reminds them of the reasons for the collapse of Jerusalem and Judah:

> Yet I raised up early sending to you all my servants the prophets, saying, "I beg you not to do this abominable thing that I hate!" But they did not listen or incline their ear, to turn from their wickedness and make no offerings to other gods. So my wrath and my anger were poured out and kindled in the towns of Judah and in the streets of Jerusalem; and they became a waste and a desolation, as they still are today. (Jer 44:4–6)

The mention of "YHWH's servants, the prophets" occurs in the book of Jeremiah in passages that can be labeled "Deuteronomistic." It is difficult to decide whether they all stem from one redactor. The distribution of the passages and the network they constitute fosters, however, the probability of a coherent redaction activity.[15] There is an important difference

---

14. In the MT there is a quite difficult change from the third to the second person: "Because they have not listened to my words, says YHWH, wherewith I sent unto them my servants the prophets, rising up early and sending them; but you have not listened, says YHWH."

15. For the difficult question of how to understand the "Deuteronomistic" texts in Jeremiah, see Konrad Schmid (*Buchgestalten des Jeremiabuches: Untersuchungen zur Redaktions- und Rezeptionsgeschichte von Jer 30–33 im Kontext des Buches* [WMANT 72; Neukirchen-Vluyn: Neukirchener, 1996]), who argues that Deuteronomistic phraseology can very easily be imitated, and Christl Maier, *Jeremia als Lehrer der Tora: Soziale Gebote des Deuteronomiums in Fortschreibungen des Jeremiabuches* (FRLANT

from the passages in the book of Kings: each of the Jeremiah texts mentions YHWH's persistent sending of prophets, which is expressed through two absolute infinitives: *haškēm wěšālōaḥ*. This expression strengthens the idea of an ongoing chain of prophets. According to these texts, Jeremiah is the last of YHWH's prophets who were sent to warn the people. The opening chapter of the Jeremiah scroll insists on the parallels between Moses and Jeremiah, Israel's first and last prophet. It has often been observed that Jer 1 wants to relate Jeremiah to Moses.[16] First of all, the structure of Jeremiah's call (1:5–8) has a close parallel in Moses' call (Exod 3:10–12). But the installation of Jeremiah as YHWH's prophet also refers to Deut 18:

Deut 18:18	Jer 1
נתתי דברי בפניו	v. 9 נתתי דברי בפיך
ודבר אלהים את כל אשר אצונו	v. 7 ואת כל אשר אצוך תדבר

The author of this text wants to show that Jeremiah was the last of the prophets sent by YHWH to his people since the time of Moses. Jeremiah's message also fits the Deuteronomistic criteria of "true prophecy" in Deut 18:20, since his oracles of judgment become reality at the end of the book. For this reason, a redactor added at the very end of Jeremiah a kind of excerpt taken over from 2 Kgs 24–25, so that the book of Jeremiah ends with exile and diaspora. And the distinction between false and true prophets, which is at stake in Deut 18:20, is also a major issue in the book of Jeremiah (Jer 20 and 28). Indeed, the Deuteronomistic edition of

---

196; Göttingen: Vandenhoeck & Ruprecht, 2002), who nevertheless thinks that one can speak of several "Deuteronomistic" redactions in the book. This is also my view. See Thomas Römer, "The Formation of the Book of Jeremiah as a Supplement to the So-Called Deuteronomistic History," in *The Production of Prophecy: Constructing Prophecy and Prophets in Yehud* (ed. Diana Edelman and Ehud Ben Zvi; BibleWorld; London: Equinox, 2009), 168–83.

16. Werner H. Schmidt, "Jeremias Berufung: Aspekte der Erzählung Jer 1,4–9 und offene Fragen der Auslegung," in *Biblische Welten* (ed. Wolfgang Zwickel; OBO 123; Freiburg: Universitätsverlag, 1993), 183–98; Bernard Renaud, "Jér 1: Structure et théologie de la redaction," in *Le livre de Jérémie: Le prophète et son milieu: Les oracles et leur transmission* (ed. Pierre-Maurice Bogaert; BETL 54; Leuven: Peeters, 1997), 177–96; Carolyn J. Sharp, "The Call of Jeremiah and Diaspora Politics," *JBL* 119 (2000): 421–38; William H. Duke Jr., "Jeremiah 1:4–18," *Int* 59 (2005): 184–86.

Jeremiah shows that Jeremiah is, according to Deut 18, a true prophet of YHWH, since the doom he announced happened. Jeremiah is also a Deuteronomistic prophet in the sense that YHWH ordered him to exhort the Judeans to listen—and they did not listen. (Deut 18:18: "Anyone who does not listen to the words that the prophet shall speak in my name, I myself will hold accountable.")

The Deuteronomistic description of Jeremiah, portrayed as the last prophet of doom sent by YHWH according to the above-mentioned texts, does not cover all passages of the book. Jeremiah 30–33 opposes the Deuteronomistic vision by announcing a new covenant and a time of restoration, and Jer 37–43* depicts, contrary to Jer 29, a prophet who supports the people who remain in the land. This means that the final edition of Jeremiah integrated different conceptions of the prophet.[17] The same holds true for the prophets in the Deuteronomistic History, especially in the book of Kings.

The "Deuteronomistic" and the "Other" Prophets in the Book of Kings

In addition to the stereotypical phrase "YHWH's servants the prophets," the book of Kings also contains a pattern of prophetic oracles and fulfillment, which we will not discuss here (e.g., Ahijah's oracle against Jeroboam's house is fulfilled in Baasha's revolt, 1 Kgs 15:27–29).[18] This pattern matches the criteria of Deut 18 that the oracles of a true prophet of YHWH are always fulfilled. The prophetic narratives, however, especially those concerned with Elisha and Elijah, do not fit the Deuteronomistic ideology of prophecy. This is especially the case with Elisha, who is not much concerned about preaching the (Deuteronomistic) law, but who is a traditional soothsayer, operating in a trance (2 Kgs 3:15–16), behaving like a magician, and being able to raise the dead (2 Kgs 4), even when he himself is dead (2 Kgs 13:20–21); he can also use the name of YHWH to

---

17. Christopher R. Seitz, *Theology in Conflict: Reactions to the Exile in the Book of Jeremiah* (BZAW 176; Berlin: de Gruyter, 1989); Carolyn J. Sharp, *Prophecy and Ideology in Jeremiah: Struggle for Authority in the Deutero-Jeremianic Prose* (OTS; London: T&T Clark, 2003).

18. Gerhard von Rad, "Die deuteronomistische Geschichtstheologie in den Königsbüchern (1947)," in *Gesammelte Studien zum Alten Testament* (TB 8; Munich: Chr. Kaiser, 1958), 189–204; Dietrich, *Prophetie und Geschichte*.

curse boys who insult him, and who are then mauled by two she-bears (2 Kgs 2:23–24). He practices divination (belomancy; 2 Kgs 13:14–19), and has the ability to heal and provide food in miraculous ways (2 Kgs 4:38–5:27). This means that Elisha resembles some of the experts in magic and divination who in Deut 18 are condemned and contrasted to the true prophet of YHWH.

It is often acknowledged that some of the Elisha narratives provided the model after which some stories about Elijah as a miracle worker were elaborated (especially the miracles concerning food and resurrection in 1 Kgs 17).[19] Both Elijah and Elisha intervene in royal affairs, anointing or confronting kings. In contrast to Elisha, however, Elijah is also constructed in comparison and contrast to Moses. In 1 Kgs 19, he appears as a second Moses: He travels forty days and nights to Horeb, the mountain of God (1 Kgs 19), and like Moses in Exod 33 he is granted a private theophany—one that criticizes or corrects the Mosaic theophany. In 1 Kgs 18, Elijah acts quite in accordance with the idea of Deuteronomy concerning the eradication of other deities' worship. After YHWH has manifested himself through fire from heaven and consumed the sacrifices, Elijah orders the prophets of Baal to be killed (cf. Deut 13 or Deut 7). Whereas YHWH's revelation in 1 Kgs 18 corresponds to the Deuteronomistic concept of a theophany (see for instance Deut 5:22–27, in which YHWH manifests himself to Israel "out of the fire"; 9:10 etc.), the divine manifestation in 1 Kgs 19 seems to correct such a conception, since YHWH neither appears in a storm nor in an earthquake, nor in the fire, but in a "sound of sheer silence" (19:12). The contrast between 1 Kgs 18 and 1 Kgs 19 may suggest some redactional activity during the literary formation of the Elijah narratives.[20] In the end, Elijah surpasses Moses. The latter's death is more than remarkable, since he is buried by YHWH himself and his grave remains unknown (Deut 34:6).[21] Elijah, however,

---

19. See, among many others, Rofé, "Classes in the Prophetical Stories"; Erhard Blum, "Der Prophet und das Verderben Israels: Eine ganzheitliche historisch-kritische Lektüre von 1 Reg. xviii–xix," *VT* 47 (1997): 277–92.

20. According to many scholars, 1 Kgs 19 contains an older account that was later reworked. See the overview given in Lehnart, *Prophet und König*, 181–89, and his own analysis in 240–58.

21. Samuel Loewenstamm ("The Death of Moses," in *Studies on the Testament of Abraham* [ed. G. W. E. Nickelsburg Jr.; SBLSCS 6; Missoula, Mont.: Scholars Press, 1976], 185–211) has argued that Deut 34:6 wants to correct a tradition about Moses'

does not experience death, but ascends to heaven in a whirlwind (2 Kgs 2). The importance given to Elijah in the book of Kings prepares for the idea of his return, which is expressed at the end of the prophetic collection in Mal 3:22–24. The story about Elijah's ascent in 2 Kgs 2 seems to be an attempt to construct Elijah as surpassing Moses the prophet, and to introduce an eschatological perspective into the concept of prophecy. Before his ascent, Elijah behaves like Moses (Exod 14) and Joshua (Josh 3–4), parting the waters of the Jordan (2 Kgs 2:8). But then he appears as even more important, since he is taken directly into the divine sphere.

For different reasons, the Elisha and the Elijah narratives do not match the Deuteronomistic concept of the prophets as successors of Moses. It is therefore plausible to assume, with Steve McKenzie and others,[22] that these stories have been inserted at a later stage than the first or second Deuteronomistic edition of Kings. This does not mean that they were not composed earlier than the Persian period. They may have been transmitted independently—especially the Elisha narratives—before their integration into the books of Kings.[23] One may speculate that the construction of Elijah as a new Moses who surpassed the original was a reaction to the division of the book of Deuteronomy from the Former Prophets, and its subsequent new function as conclusion of the Torah. Since there was no longer an immediate link between Moses and the prophets, and since the books of Joshua–Kings were gathered with other prophetic books, Elijah became the new "patron" of the *něbî'îm* (see Mal 3:22–24).

The appearance of the prophet Isaiah in 2 Kgs 18–20 also pertains to a strategy for promoting the relation between Joshua–Kings and the collection of prophetic books. These chapters create a cross-reference with the scroll of (Proto-) Isaiah, since Isa 36–39 contains a parallel account of the prophet's activity under Hezekiah. In these chapters Isaiah appears above all as a prophet of salvation with medical or magical skills, thus preparing important themes of the "Latter Prophets."

---

ascension. This would bring Moses and Elijah in an even closer relation, but the thesis is quite speculative.

22. McKenzie, *Trouble with Kings*, 81–100; Otto, *Jehu, Elia, und Elisa*. For an presentation in English: Otto, "The Composition of the Elijah-Elisha Stories."

23. See the works of Otto and Lehnart and also Dany Nocquet, *Le livret noir de Baal : La polémique contre le dieu Baal dans la Bible hébraïque et dans l'ancien Israël* (Actes et Recherches; Genève: Labor et Fides, 2004), 231–63.

Moses, the "Second" Prophet, Surpassing All Other Prophets

When the book of Deuteronomy was separated from the corpus of the Former Prophets and constructed as the conclusion of the Pentateuch, it also became the conclusion of a "biography" of Moses that covers the books of Exodus (Exod 2:1–10: Moses' birth) to Deuteronomy (Deut 34: Moses' death). This Moses-Exodus story was combined at one stage of the Torah's formation with the patriarchal narratives. In European scholarship this literary link is now considered quite late, stemming perhaps from the Priestly writer or redactor (cf. Gen 17:1 and Exod 6:2)[24] or from a somewhat earlier redactor.[25] Some of the patriarchal narratives apparently react to or at least presuppose the exodus tradition. In Gen 20, which according to Blum and others is the latest of the three versions of the narrative of the patriarch presenting his wife as his sister,[26] Abraham is called a prophet, and intercedes for Abimelech (vv. 7 and 17), so that God may heal him from his illness (sterility or impotence?). Thus, in the context of the Torah, Gen 20 makes Abraham the first prophet,[27] and not Moses. Whereas

---

24. Thomas Römer, *Israels Väter: Untersuchungen zur Väterthematik im Deuteronomium und in der deuteronomistischen Tradition* (OBO 99; Freiburg: Universitätsverlag, 1990), 546–47; Jan Christian Gertz, "The Transition Between the Books of Genesis and Exodus," in *A Farewell to the Yahwist? The Composition of the Pentateuch in Recent European Interpretation* (ed. Thomas B. Dozeman and Konrad Schmid; SBLSymS 34; Atlanta: Society of Biblical Literature, 2006), 73–87; Albert de Pury, "P^g as the Absolute Beginning," in *Les dernières rédactions du Pentateuque, de l'Hexateuque et de l'Ennéateuque* (ed. Thomas Römer and Konrad Schmid; BETL 203; Leuven: Peeters University Press, 2007), 99–128; and especially Konrad Schmid, *Erzväter und Exodus: Untersuchungen zur doppelten Begründung der Ursprünge Israels innerhalb der Geschichtsbücher des Alten Testaments* (WMANT 81; Neukirchen-Vluyn: Neukirchener, 1999); English translation: *Genesis and the Moses Story: Israel's Dual Origins in the Hebrew Bible* (Siphrut 3; Winona Lake, Ind.: Eisenbrauns, 2010).

25. John Van Seters, "The Patriarchs and the Exodus: Bridging the Gap between Two Origin Traditions," in *The Interpretation of Exodus* (ed. Riemer Roukema; CBET 44; Leuven: Peeters, 2006), 1–15; Christoph Levin, "The Yahwist and the Redactional Link Between Genesis and Exodus," in *A Farewell to the Yahwist?*, 131–41.

26. Erhard Blum, *Die Komposition der Vätergeschichte* (WMANT 57; Neukirchen-Vluyn: Neukirchener, 1984), 405–10; Matthias Köckert, "Die Geschichte der Abrahamüberlieferung," in *Congress Volume Leiden 2004* (ed. André Lemaire; VTSup 109; Leiden: Brill, 2006), 103–28, here 125.

27. In a way Abraham is also depicted as a prophet in Gen 15, where he receives the divine word in the same way as Jeremiah or Ezekiel. See Thomas Römer, "Abraham

Moses intercedes in Exod 32 and Num 14 for his own people, Abraham prays in Gen 20 for a foreign king, who symbolizes a God-fearing pagan. In reaction to the attempt to present Abraham as the first prophet, some passages in the Pentateuch try to show that Moses is, in contrast to the assertion of Deut 18, more than a prophet. This is the case in Exod 7:1, mentioned earlier, in which Moses is presented as *'ĕlohîm*, whose prophet is his brother Aaron. The same phenomenon appears in Num 12:6–8, in which Moses also surpasses the regular prophets by dint of his immediate relationship with God. Finally, Moses appears as an incomparable mediator in the epitaph of Deut 34:10–12, which also distinguishes him from all the other prophets:

> Never since has there arisen a prophet in Israel like Moses, whom YHWH knew face to face. He was unequalled for all the signs and wonders that YHWH sent him to perform in the land of Egypt, against Pharaoh and all his servants and his entire land, and for all the mighty deeds and all the terrifying displays of power that Moses performed in the sight of all Israel.

This conclusion emphasizes that Moses is a "super-prophet," very close to the divine sphere: the signs and wonders that the author of 34:10–12 attributes to Moses are executed by YHWH himself in the exodus narrative. Therefore, in the context of the Torah, Moses is no longer Israel's first prophet, but more than a prophet, Israel's incomparable mediator.

Conclusion

In the context of the Deuteronomistic network composed by the books of Deuteronomy, Kings and Jeremiah, Moses is constructed as opening a series of YHWH's servants, the prophets, whose last representative is Jeremiah. The Deuteronomistic prophets are above all prophets of doom, and even more, preachers of the law. This conception of prophecy is revised through the insertion of the Elisha and Elijah narratives into the books of Kings. When Deuteronomy was attached to the Torah, Deut 18 came to stand after Gen 20, so that Abraham became Israel's first prophet. In

---

and the Law and the Prophets," in *The Reception and Remembrance of Abraham* (ed. Pernille Carstens and Niels Peter Lemche; PHSC 13; Piscataway, N.J.: Gorgias, 2011), 103–18.

reaction, the final redactors of the Pentateuch added Deut 34:10–12 and other texts in order to emphasize the fact that, although Moses is no longer Israel's first prophet, he surpasses all of them because of his close relationship to YHWH.

Samuel: A Prophet Like Moses or a Priest Like Moses?*

Mark Leuchter

In the late seventh or early sixth century B.C.E., the prophet Jeremiah lamented that he was completely unable to intercede on behalf of the nation to YHWH.[1] In a particularly dramatic manner, Jeremiah declared that Israel was past the point of no return: "Then YHWH said to me: "Even if Moses and Samuel stood before me, yet my mind could not be toward this people; cast them out of my sight, and let them go forth" (Jer 15:1). The Jeremiah tradition attests to efforts by the Judahite elite to elicit a positive oracle from the prophet in the face of impeding political doom (Jer 20:1–6; 21:1–2; 37–38). Jeremiah's response—that no positive oracle was forthcoming—is reinforced by the rhetorical weight of the aforemen-

---

* Some material in this essay is drawn from my monograph *Samuel and the Shaping of Tradition* (Oxford: Oxford University Press, 2013) and appears here with permission.

1. I accept as tenable the view that many oracles in Jer 1–25 may be traced back to the titular prophet himself in some form. I argued in my monograph *Josiah's Reform and Jeremiah's Scroll* (Sheffield: Sheffield Phoenix, 2006) that the book of Jeremiah preserves a memory of the prophet possessing scribal training. See also Jack R. Lundbom, "Baruch, Seraiah, and Expanded Colophons in the Book of Jeremiah," *JSOT* 36 (1986): 107–8. It is clear that much subsequent redaction may be sensed within these chapters deriving from later scribes writing in the prophet's name. I would suggest, however, that oracles that emphasize the Shiloh tradition may be more closely related to the prophet's own purview, given his roots at Anatoth and the Shilonite/Elide priestly line based in that village. See recently Sean D. McBride, "Jeremiah and the Levitical Priests of Anatoth," in *Thus Says the Lord: Essays on the Former and Latter Prophets in Honor of Robert R. Wilson* (ed. John J. Ahn and Stephen L. Cook; LHBOTS 502; London: T&T Clark, 2009), 179–96. Since the Moses/Samuel tradition is so deeply connected to the Shilonite circles, Jer 15:1 may justifiably be viewed as an authentic sentiment expressed by Jeremiah, even if it was committed to textual form by a later writer.

tioned verse. If neither Moses nor Samuel could sway divine opinion on the fate of Judah, Jeremiah's efforts to secure a favorable turn of events would be utterly futile.

Other texts within the book of Jeremiah have affinities with the Moses and Samuel traditions,[2] but Jer 15:1 is the most overt indication that, in the twilight of the preexilic period (and certainly by the exilic era), Moses and Samuel were regarded in some circles as parallel prophetic figures. That this view is presupposed in the book of Jeremiah may be explained by the latter's well-known reliance upon the Deuteronomistic History (DH) and the presentation of Samuel therein as the definitive prophet of his day, who followed in the footsteps of Moses in the book of Deuteronomy. In broad strokes, Samuel's prophetic function within the DH parallels that of Moses: both intercede between the nation and YHWH (Deut 5:4–5; 18:16; 1 Sam 7:3–14; 12:18–23), both convey prophecy through the divine word (Deut 18:18; 1 Sam 3:22), both institute legislation regarding kingship (Deut 17:14–20; 1 Sam 10:25), and both commission civil leaders who are to function within the parameters of their prophetic teachings and authority (Deut 31:14, 23; Josh 1:1ff.; 1 Sam 10:17–27; 12; 16:1–13). These parallels invariably contributed to Jeremiah's choice to set himself within a prophetic trajectory including Moses and Samuel.[3] Since Jer 1:9 overtly invokes the legislation in Deut 18:15–18 that YHWH will raise up prophets like Moses in successive generations,[4] there can be no doubt that Jeremiah saw himself as the holder of a prophetic office that Samuel occupied in an earlier time.

The Moses/Samuel parallel in the DH is part of the Deuteronomistic attempt to present the prophets of the past as a united front.[5] Prophetic

---

2. See my discussion of the early layers of Jeremiah's call narrative (Jer 1:4–5) in *Josiah's Reform and Jeremiah's Scroll*, 76–78.

3. It is noteworthy, too, that the Jeremiah tradition presents a similar characterization of the prophet, insofar as Jeremiah commissions a nonpriest/nonprophet—Baruch—to be the trustee of his legacy (Jer 45).

4. On this interpretation of Deut 18:18, see Wilson, *Prophecy and Society*, 162 n. 52.

5. Scholarship is divided, of course, on when such an attempt would have surfaced. For recent discussions representing diverse perspectives, see Römer, *So-Called Deuteronomistic History*, 154; Ben Zvi, "The Prophets"; Jeffrey C. Geoghegan, *The Time, Place, and Purpose of the Deuteronomistic History: The Evidence of "Until This Day"* (BJS 347; Providence, R.I.: Brown University Press, 2006), 152–60; Raymond F. Person Jr., *The Deuteronomic History and the Books of Chronicles: Scribal Works in an Oral World* (Atlanta: Society of Biblical Literature, 2010), 163; idem, "The Deutero-

speech in individual cases is highly stereotyped in the DH, and the redactors attempt to categorize history against an ostensibly consistent message that all the prophets communicated together time and time again (2 Kgs 9:7; 17:13, 23; 21:10; 24:2). Samuel is situated as the first of these prophetic types within the DH following the death of Moses. Though other prophets appear before him (Deborah, the anonymous prophets of Judg 6:8–10 and 1 Sam 2:27–36),[6] it is Samuel who shifts Israel from one epoch to the next (premonarchic to monarchic), just as Moses had helmed the nation during its transition from slavery in Egypt to would-be settlers of the land, and it is he who makes the law once again a central tenet of settled life (1 Sam 12:14–15, cf. also the Deuteronomistic terms in vv. 20–21).[7] Within the Deuteronomistic schema of history, Samuel "resets" the applicability of the Mosaic law and becomes its initiating exponent at the outset of the monarchy, thereby laying the foundations for the monarchic-era prophets who follow him.

The redactors of the DH have developed a carefully structured periodization of history, a learned trend in scribal circles found elsewhere in biblical historiography.[8] However, Samuel's resetting of Mosaic standards is not strictly a literary artifice deriving from the Deuteronomistic redactors. While the Moses/Samuel parallel in Jer 15:1 may have been influenced by the Deuteronomistic redaction of the Samuel material, it is not the Deuteronomists who established the parallels between these luminaries, but earlier tradents. The Moses/Samuel parallel is witnessed in Ps 99, a liturgical work of pre-Deuteronomistic origin:

Moses and Aaron among his priests [בכהניו],
and Samuel among them that call upon his name,
They called upon YHWH, and he answered them.... (Ps 99:6)

---

nomic History and the Books of Chronicles: Contemporary Competing Historiographies," *Reflection and Refraction: Studies in Biblical Historiography in Honour of A. Graeme Auld* (ed. Robert Rezetko et al., VTSup 113; Leiden: Brill, 2007), 315–36.

6. Despite the differences, the appearance of these prophets before Samuel is the result of Deuteronomistic rhetorical tactics. See further below.

7. On the admixture of pre-Deuteronomistic and Deuteronomistic traditions in this chapter, see Jeremy M. Hutton, *The Transjordanian Palimpsest: The Overwritten Texts of Personal Exile and Transformation in the Deuteronomistic History* (BZAW 396; Berlin: de Gruyter, 2009), 293, 304–5, 310–11.

8. Sara Japhet, *By The Rivers of Babylon to the Highlands of Judah: Collected Studies on the Restoration Period* (Winona Lake, Ind.: Eisenbrauns, 2006), 426–28.

The current form of Ps 99 possesses a redactional layer that harmonized its contents with the theology of the Jerusalem priesthood. This layer introduced language from the pentateuchal P source, along with the mention of Aaron. In its earlier form, however, Ps 99 equated Samuel with Moses alone, and the allusions to their similar conduct—"they called upon YHWH"—invoked the traditions preserved in 1 Sam 7:9 and Exod 19:16–19.[9] The rhetorical function of the Samuel/Moses parallel in Ps 99 is to legitimize the transfer of Shilonite iconography to Jerusalem, and to position Jerusalem as the inheritor of the Shiloh cult.[10] This must be viewed differently from traditions that cast Shiloh as a compromised institution and Jerusalem as a superseding cult center (e.g., Ps 78:60–66). Psalm 99 derives from an early period, before the Zion tradition developed an exclusionist attitude toward northern cultic heritage. As such, we have in Ps 99 a testament to the Moses/Samuel parallel predating the Deuteronomistic material, and it is significant that it is not as prophets but as priests (כהנים) that Samuel and Moses are set in tandem. This is consistent with the general picture of premonarchic religious leadership: though late texts like Deuteronomy distinguish between priestly and prophetic functions, prophetic/oracular duties were subsumed under priestly authority in an earlier period.[11] Even if Samuel rose to prominence through prophetic facility, the outstanding

---

9. See my discussion of this material in Mark Leuchter, "The Literary Strata and Narrative Sources in Psalm xcix," *VT* 55 (2005): 30–36. Similar language is never used to characterize Aaron.

10. Ibid, 34–36.

11. I would tentatively suggest that it is with the alienation of Levite groups from the state cults in the north and the south that the increased distinction between priestly and prophetic behavior finds its basis. As I will discuss further below, the Levite caste was formed to keep priestly families from abusing their cultic authority in the premonarchic period. However, the later monarchic support of priests would force Levites to adopt different forms of critical expression when older, premonarchic forms of protest were no longer effective and these elite priestly families could no longer be challenged or ousted from power. Prophecy would be a suitable vehicle for Levites incapable of stepping in to realign the state-run cult with agrarian covenantal concepts from the late tenth century onward (I am indebted to my colleague Jeremy Hutton for discussing this possibility with me; he will no doubt produce a detailed examination of this topic in due course). Before this time, though, we may view prophecy as a component of the cult, not an adversary to it. The overlap between priests and prophets survives in later periods as well, as Joachim Schaper has noted ("Exilic and Postexilic Prophecy and the Orality/Literacy Problem," *VT* 55 [2005]: 334); differentiation between groups as indicated by passages such as Jer 18:18 seems to me to be more a

feature of the text relating to his activity is his position vis-à-vis the challenges posed by kingship, and it was indeed the priesthood that had the most to lose with the rise of this new institution.[12]

The Deuteronomists thus developed a pre-Deuteronomistic Moses/Samuel parallel which initially emphasized their priestly stature. The roots of this parallel, I propose, are embedded within the pre-Deuteronomistic narratives that recount the beginning of Samuel's presence at Shiloh, cresting in his inaugural prophetic experience in 1 Sam 3. With regard to the Moses/Samuel parallel, these narratives shed light on an ancient struggle for priestly power that has been somewhat obscured through the text's incorporation into a Deuteronomistic macrostructure. To be more precise: the origins of the Moses/Samuel parallel are to be traced to Samuel's eclipse of the Elides, a priestly line that claimed descent from Moses, and whose dominant position over the priesthood was significantly compromised by the mid-eleventh century B.C.E.[13] In conceiving of how Samuel challenged this family for priestly supremacy, the originators of the narrative tap into a stream of Mosaic discourse that long predated the Deuteronomistic movement, but that survived into their own casting of Samuel as a Mosaic prophet. To better understand the manner in which Samuel's prophetic experience fits within this earlier tradition, we must consider the points of contact between 1 Sam 1–3 and the features of the premonarchic priestly culture, and in particular, the role Levites played in this culture.

Samuel as a Levite at Shiloh

The degree of historical veracity regarding Samuel at Shiloh is a contested matter. Some scholars see the narrative of 1 Sam 1–3 as a largely retrospective effort, in which a tradent took a well-known character from traditional lore (Samuel), and introduced him into remembered events regarding

---

question of the depth of an individual's engagement with spheres of conduct than of strict identification with one group to the exclusion of the other.

12. For a full treatment of this topic, see Baruch Halpern, "The Uneasy Compromise: Israel Between League and Monarchy," in *Traditions in Transformation: Turning Points in Biblical Faith* (ed. Baruch Halpern and Jon D. Levenson; Winona Lake, Ind.: Eisenbrauns, 1981), 59–96.

13. On the Elides as claimants to a genealogical connection to Moses, see the classic study by Frank M. Cross on the priestly houses in early Israel in *Canaanite Myth and Hebrew Epic* (Cambridge: Harvard University Press, 1973), 195–215.

the Elides and the twilight years of the Shiloh sanctuary.¹⁴ This has led to speculation that Samuel's connection to the Shiloh sanctuary was strictly a literary construct.¹⁵ However, there exists a good amount of incidental information in subsequent chapters that suggests that 1 Sam 1–3 contain some historically reliable data connecting Samuel to the sanctuary and to the Elides therein.¹⁶ Regardless of which position is adopted, embedded in the narrative regarding the dedication of Samuel to priestly service at Shiloh is information regarding the early development of the Levites. While Levites in late texts are characterized by genealogical qualifications, the Levite caste in premonarchic Israel was considerably more permeable.¹⁷ Priestly clans (such as the Elides) were responsible for maintaining order between disparate kinship groups that frequented the shrines and sanctuaries wherein they were stationed.¹⁸ These clans took on new devotees from these kinship groups given over to priestly service at their sanctuary, thereby reinforcing their influence over the populations whence these priestly adepts were drawn.¹⁹

As many scholars have noted, the etymological origins of the term לוי, "connected [to]," relates to the process whereby individuals became part of this Levite caste, enculturated in the doctrines and traditions of the priestly

---

14. See especially Robert K. Gnuse, "A Reconsideration of the Form-Critical Structure in I Samuel 3: An Ancient Near Eastern Dream Theophany," *ZAW* 94 (1982): 379–90.

15. Gnuse, "Reconsideration," 389.

16. Leuchter, *Josiah's Reform and Jeremiah's Scroll*, 19–23. The Moses/Samuel parallel in Ps 99 discussed above also factors into this evaluation, for it supports an early concept of the Shiloh-to-Jerusalem transition that factors Samuel directly into the equation.

17. The important recent studies by Jeremy M. Hutton of the early development of the Levite caste make a compelling case in this regard. See his essays "The Levitical Diaspora (I): A Sociological Comparison with Morocco's Ahansal," in *Exploring the Longue Durée: Essays in Honor of Lawrence E. Stager* (ed. J. David Schloen; Winona Lake, Ind.: Eisenbrauns, 2009), 229; idem, "All the King's Men: The Families of the Priests in Cross-Cultural Perspective," in *"Seitenblicke": Nebenfiguren im zweiten Samuelbuch* (ed. W. Dietrich; OBO; Freiburg: Universitätsverlag, 2011), 117–43. Hutton's work expands concepts first suggested by Lawrence E. Stager in his groundbreaking study of early Israelite settlement and kinship ("The Archaeology of the Family in Ancient Israel," *BASOR* 260 [1985]: 28).

18. Hutton, "Levitical Diaspora." 228–29.

19. Ibid.

clan dominating the major sanctuaries where they were trained.[20] Deuteronomy 33:9 is often cited as an example of Levites' severing ties with their biological kin in their capacity as priests, and is part of a more elaborate poetic meditation on priestly function as devotion to cultic rather than socioeconomic interests typical of lay agrarian life:

> Thy Thummim and thy Urim be with thy steadfast one [איש חסידך][21] whom thou didst prove at Massah, with whom thou didst strive at the waters of Meribah; *Who said of his father, and of his mother: 'I have not seen him'; neither did he acknowledge his brethren, nor knew he his own children; for they have observed thy word, and keep thy covenant....* (Deut 33:8–9)[22]

These verses foster an ideal to which a priest might aspire when faced with biases rooted in the interest of biological kinship. But utopian ideals do not obviate more practical realities. If the devotion of sons to priestly service as Levites was conducted as a matter of a family's socioeconomic survival,[23] then ongoing interaction with members of that family (via their frequenting of the regional shrine) would sustain a degree of kinship allegiance. If this is the case, then investiture of sons into the ranks of the priesthood carried an additional, ideological, dimension related to the egalitarian-agrarian ethic of early Israel. A hallmark of the social hierarchies of the late Bronze Age Egypto-Canaanite culture—the sociopolitical world that the early Israelite highlanders rejected—saw an intermingling of monarchic

---

20. On this definition of לוי, see Stager, "Archaeology of the Family," 27; Karel van der Toorn, *Family Religion in Babylonia, Syria, and Israel: Continuity and Change in the Forms of Religious Life* (Leiden: Brill, 1996), 304 (though van der Toorn dates the origination of the Levite caste to the monarchic era).

21. Cross and others have assumed that the "steadfast one" (איש חסידך) refers specifically to Moses (*Canaanite Myth*, 197–98) by virtue of the ensuing allusion to the Massah-Meribah event in Exod 17:1b–7. However, Joel S. Baden has recently argued convincingly that the investiture of the Levites currently found in Exod 32:26–29 was originally connected to the Massah-Meribah episode ("The Violent Origins of the Levites," in *Levites and Priests in Biblical History and Tradition* [ed. Mark Leuchter and Jeremy M. Hutton; Atlanta: Society of Biblical Literature, 2011], 103–16). As such, "steadfast one" seems more likely to apply to Levites in a general sense. Since Deut 33:9b refers to Levites in the plural, איש חסידך functions as a collective singular.

22. I have retained here the more archaic language from the JPS translation which, I think, is fitting for a highly stylized poem of antique origins.

23. Stager, "Archaeology of the Family," 28.

and cultic politics in which the peasant caste was relegated to a lowly and vulnerable position.[24] Indeed, the biblical authors nod several times to the close connection of priestly and royal status, implying the fine line separating the two and the possibility that sacral authority could be parlayed into royal authority, bringing with it the potential for the abuse of power.[25] The drawing of Levites from the local populations could function as a safeguard against this, with the traditions of hinterland families or clans represented at the shared sanctuaries by the individuals dedicated to priestly service and keeping the priestly faculty therein accountable to the public.[26]

The tension between hegemonic priestly misappropriation and egalitarian, hinterland clan values is woven into 1 Sam 1–2. Samuel is devoted to priestly service from a regional family who continually cast their allegiance to the Shiloh sanctuary (1 Sam 1:3), and with whom Samuel maintains close contact during his priestly training (1 Sam 2:11, 18–20). Running parallel to this are the details concerning the foibles of Eli (1 Sam 1:13–14) and the corruption of his sons (1 Sam 2:12–17), who abuse their power to the detriment of public sacral interest. The "manner of the priests" related in 1 Sam 2:13–17 reveals the sins of the sons; Eli's lack of punitive action (vv. 22–25) lays bare the sins of the father. Indeed, the narrative is clear that Eli presides over the cult at Shiloh from his "throne" (כסא) in 1 Sam 1:9 and 4:13,18, implying a dangerously close proximity between priestly and royal authority. It is clear from these passages that, despite their formidable priestly influence, the Elides have behaved in a manner that ignores the needs and values of the public to which they were

---

24. See the concise overview by Theodore J. Lewis, "Family, Household, and Local Religion in Late Bronze Age Ugarit," in *Household and Family Religion in Antiquity* (ed. John Boden and Saul M. Olyan; Malden: Blackwell, 2008), 72–77. On the nature of the Israelite rejection of these older cultural traits, see Mark Leuchter, "'Why Tarry The Wheels of His Chariot? (Judg 5,28)': Canaanite Chariots and Echoes of Egypt in the Song of Deborah," *Bib* 91 (2010): 256–68.

25. E.g., the legislation in Deuteronomy that a king could not lead the cult, but must take instruction from the priests (Deut 17:18–20); the memory of Gideon's taking up the role of chieftain/priest (Judg 8:27), which ultimately became the basis for a stab at a limited monarchy (attested by the name of his son Abimelech; Judg 8:31); the tensions between Samuel and Saul as the latter instituted cultic initiatives (1 Sam 14:35) and assumed priestly subordination and loyalty to the crown (1 Sam 22).

26. Indeed, the ancient poem in Exod 15 attests to this agrarian ethic as a central theme in the premonarchic cult. See Mark Leuchter, "Eisodus as Exodus: The Song of the Sea (Exod 15) Reconsidered," *Bib* 92 (2011): 321–46.

accountable. These emphases are not segregated into independent literary scenes (e.g., 1 Sam 1 dealing solely with Elkanah and Hannah; 1 Sam 2 dealing solely with the Elides), but intertwined to suggest that priestly conduct cannot be extracted from the hinterland family social context that gave rise to it.[27]

That the intertwining of emphases in 1 Sam 1–2 pertain to ethics rooted in agrarian kinship structures is reinforced by the oracle delivered by the anonymous prophet in 1 Sam 2:27–36. This speech is deeply indebted to the Deuteronomists, but it preserves some details that predate their redactional shaping, and that shed light on why, exactly, the Elides fell into a state of corruption over against more auspicious priestly ideals. The first few verses of the speech are especially revealing:

> Thus says YHWH: I indeed revealed myself unto the house of your father [בית אביך] when they were in Egypt in bondage to Pharaoh's house, and I chose him out of all the tribes of Israel to be my priest, to ascend my altar, to burn incense, to wear an ephod before me, and I gave to the house of your father [בית אביך] all the offerings of the children of Israel made by fire. Why, then, do you kick at my sacrifice and at my offering, which I have commanded in my habitation, and honor your sons above me, to make yourselves fat with the choicest of all the offerings of my people Israel? (1 Sam 2:27–29 following the LXX)

In these verses, the anonymous prophet identifies the root of Eli's complacency regarding his sons' misconduct: their claim of descent from an auspicious ancestor who served the interests of the public. Though the text is not explicit in identifying this ancestor, it appears to be Moses who is intended.[28] That the oracle heaves criticism upon the Elides by highlighting the differences between them and their ancestor suggests that it was conceived to counter an Elide claim to power based upon this genealogical connection. As studies into biblical genealogies reveal, claims to authority are often grounded in the rhetorical shaping of lineage details, a phenomenon that surfaces in comparative anthropological models regarding

---

27. For an insightful discussion of the parent/child motif paralleling the family of Samuel with the family of Eli, see Keith Bodner, *1 Samuel: A Narrative Commentary* (Sheffield: Sheffield Phoenix, 2009), 30–34, 42. The surrogate parent/child relationship between Eli and Samuel is made clear in 1 Sam 3:6, 16, where Eli refers to Samuel as his son (בני).

28. Cross, *Canaanite Myth*, 196–98 (citing earlier arguments made by Wellhausen).

priestly power claims as well.²⁹ It is not surprising, then, that a criticism of the Elides would incorporate tropes that they themselves used for apologetic purposes. The twice-mentioned בית אביך identifies this as the pivotal issue in the critique, referring not only to the ancestor in question but to the language and concept of lineage (namely, the "ancestral house" or בית אב) through which Israelite social order was structured.³⁰ The oracle thereby impugns the basis for Elide legitimacy by juxtaposing the Elides against their own ancestral legacy, as 1 Sam 2:29 makes clear, suggesting that it was this very legacy that they had touted for their own interests.

As the oracle continues, the abstraction and reapplication of Mosaic language becomes especially pointed: "And I will raise up for myself a faithful priest [כהן נאמן] … and I will build him a sure house [בית נאמן]" (1 Sam 2:35aα, bα).³¹ Embedded in this passage is an echo of the tradition currently found in Num 12:7 (see below) that identifies the unique qualities of Moses in comparison to other sacral types: "Not so with my servant Moses; he is trusted [נאמן] in all my house [בתי]." Once again, the oracle highlights the gulf between the Elides and Moses, going so far as to say that a non-Elide (a priest of a different "house") will inherit Mosaic qualities. However, this only increases the likelihood that the Elides were themselves using traditions regarding their ancestor to reify their power. In this case, the rhetoric of the oracle deflates the efficacy of the Elide strategy. Laying claim to the traditions of their ancestor Moses is futile: for YHWH a non-Elide will be characterized by those Mosaic traditions and typologies irrespective of biological descent.

First Samuel 2:27–36 is obviously an *ex eventu* composition. It knows not only that Eli's sons will die, but that the surviving Elides will be demoted to a client status (v. 36). This could support a Deuteronomistic provenance for the entire oracle in relation to the house of Zadok's replacing the Elides at Solomon's ascent to the throne (1 Kgs 2:26–27). How-

---

29. Hutton, "Levitical Diaspora," 229.

30. Van der Toorn, *Family Religion*, 194–98; Stager, "Archaeology of the Family," 20–22.

31. *Pace* Menahem Haran (*Temples and Temple-Service in Ancient Israel* [Oxford: Clarendon, 1978], 98 n. 18), the remainder of the verse contains secondary clauses with Deuteronomistic language, and reflects the hand of a later redactor. See Mark Leuchter, "Something Old, Something Older: Reconsidering 1 Samuel 2:27–36," in *Perspectives on Hebrew Scriptures* (ed. Ehud Ben Zvi; Piscataway, N.J.: Gorgias, 2006), 533–40.

ever, its references to Moses and its use of Mosaic rhetoric means that it also knows that the "faithful priest" who replaced the Elides was regarded as Mosaic in typology, a quality that is nowhere else applied to Zadok, the Zadokites or the Aaronides more generally.[32] The oracle thus more likely relates to a different challenger to Elide priestly dominance. Given the ensuing events in 1 Samuel and the Moses/Samuel parallel in Ps 99, Samuel stands out as the prime candidate. The retrospective content of the oracle points to its origin among Samuel's supporters, characterizing the rise of their scion as divinely mandated over against the priestly clan to which he was entrusted.

Here, however, we encounter a potential problem: according to both textual and anthropological evidence, a Levite derives priestly authority through the numinous power of the priests under whom he received training.[33] Yet it is clear from 1 Sam 1–2 that the Elides are no saints in terms of their commitment to sacral order, public welfare, or connection to the realm of the divine. In effect, Samuel's priestly training under the Elides yields no real sacral trump card to justify his authority, and is in fact a potential liability.[34] This, in fact, weighs in favor of a genuine historical connection between Samuel and the Elides at Shiloh. A pro-Samuel writer would hardly fashion a narrative so heavily critical of the Elides, on the one hand, and then depict Samuel's priestly enculturation under that same flawed family, on the other; the narrative must therefore reflect the memory of Samuel's actual training at Shiloh.[35] But in order for Samuel to supersede the Elides and claim the mantle of Mosaic leadership, a new encounter with the divine was needed to authenticate his leadership as saintly and numinous, one that could rival—and sideline—the Elides' genealogical claims of descent from Moses.

---

32. Even the later P recasting of the inauguration of the priesthood establishes a typological disconnection between Moses and Aaron. Aaron receives vestments to initiate his office that are never given to Moses (Exod 39), and takes on instructional authority regarding divine will that rivals Moses' own (Lev 10:11, 19–20).

33. Hutton, "Levitical Diaspora," 227, 229.

34. This is elucidated further in the careful examination by George W. Savran, *Encountering the Divine: Theophany in Biblical Narrative* (London: Continuum, 2005), 41–46.

35. Pace Gnuse, "Reconsideration," 388–89.

1 Samuel 3 and Samuel's Priestly Credentials

The narrative of 1 Samuel 3 provides the details regarding just such an encounter. In this episode, Samuel moves from priestly adept to prophet via his nighttime encounter with YHWH in the crypt containing the ark, in which YHWH informs him that the Elides will be punished for their abuse of power (vv. 11–14). Many scholars have argued that this is an account of a dream theophany akin to other dream theophanies within and beyond the Hebrew Bible.³⁶ This conclusion is understandable and even defensible, since revelation in a dream state is a common fixture of ancient prophecy. Moreover, as Choon-Leong Seow has demonstrated, the Shiloh sanctuary fostered remnants of an old El cult, and the Ugaritic literature is clear that El often makes his will known through dreams.³⁷ Given this setting, and taking into consideration the El theophoric in both Samuel's own name and that of his father (שמואל; אלקנה), it is reasonable to conclude that the narrative presents the contents of the divine revelation as a dream vision concomitant with the predilections of the El traditions. However, a closer look at the events within the episode suggests a different set of circumstances.

> And YHWH called Samuel; and he said: "Here am I [הנני]." And he ran to Eli, and said: "Here am I; for you called me." And he said: "I called not; lie down again." And he went and lay down. And YHWH called Samuel yet again. And Samuel arose and went to Eli, and said: "Here am I; for you called me." And he answered: "I called not, my son; lie down again." Now Samuel did not yet know YHWH, and the word of YHWH was not yet revealed to him. And YHWH called Samuel again a third time. And he arose and went to Eli, and said: "Here am I; for you called me." And Eli perceived that YHWH was calling the child. Therefore Eli said to Samuel: "Go, lie down; and it shall be, if you are called, that you will say: Speak, YHWH; for your servant [עבדך] hears." So Samuel went and lay down in his place. And YHWH came, and stood [ויבא ה׳ ויתיצב], and called as at other times: "Samuel, Samuel." Then Samuel said: "Speak; for your servant [עבדך] hears." (1 Sam 3:4–10)

---

36. Gnuse, "Reconsideration"; Choon-Leong Seow, *Myth, Drama, and the Politics of David's Dance* (HSM 44; Atlanta: Scholars Press, 1989), 30–31; *TDOT* 4:428.

37. Seow, *David's Dance*, 11–54.

In this passage, the divine voice calling Samuel rouses him from his slumber; Samuel is awake as he runs to Eli in response to the voice that he hears. The implication is that just as he is awake when he runs to Eli, Samuel is awake as he finally answers YHWH's call. Robert Gnuse notes that the awakening of the dreamer is a common feature of the dream theophany, at which point the deity shows the awakened dreamer a vision.[38] However, Samuel does *not* receive a vision in 1 Sam 3—there is no vision report offered or imagery described, only the relating of divine intention and the subsequent account of Samuel's conveying the divine word to Eli (v. 18). Indeed, it is the divine word (דבר ה'), not dreams or visions, that receives repeated emphasis throughout the narrative. The narrator makes clear that it is the divine word that YHWH reveals to Samuel (v. 7). This reflects a phenomenology rather different from visionary experience as attested in other prophetic contexts.[39] It may be that the author, aware of the El tradition fostered at Shiloh, flavored the narrative with a setting suggestive of a dream theophany for the sake of formal authenticity.[40] But even while including the familiar elements of dream theophanies, the account deliberately makes a *distinction* between the type of dream theophany the audience might expect at the outset of the narrative and what Samuel ultimately experiences. The end result of the narrative creates distance between Samuel and the Elides, as his experience stands apart from what is presented as business-as-usual under their tutelage, a challenge to Elide dominance that saturates the larger narrative.[41]

---

38. Gnuse, "Reconsideration," 383.

39. The דבר in prophetic texts is usually not connected to dream or vision reports, but constitutes the impulse empowering a coherent diatribe or critique (e.g., Amos 3–5; Mic 1; Hos 1:1-2; 4:1-19; Jer 7:1-2; 11:1; 25:1). The Jeremiah material is especially significant insofar as Jeremiah's visions (1:13-19; 24) are not classified under the rubric of the divine דבר. The *locus classicus* for the distinction between dreams/visions and direct divine communication is Num 12:6-8, which will be discussed below. Nowhere in the narratives regarding Samuel is he depicted as receiving visions, nor is he called a visionary (חוזה) at any point.

40. See here Gnuse's observations regarding the form-critical features of the narrative ("Reconsideration," 382–88). See also P. Kyle McCarter (*1 Samuel* [AB; Garden City, N.Y.: Doubleday, 1980], 98), who notes that the time of day conforms to ancient expectations regarding the reception of revelation.

41. Savran, *Encountering the Divine*, 46; Lyle Eslinger, *Kingship of God in Crisis: A Close Reading of 1 Samuel 1-12*. (Decatur, Ga.: Almond, 1985), 45–146.

The unexpected turns in the narrative have much in common with the traditions about YHWH's relationship with Moses. Parallels between Samuel's encounter with YHWH and that of Moses in Exod 3 have long been noted: both receive a call that repeats their name (1 Sam 3:10; Exod 3:4), both respond with הנני (1 Sam 3:4–5, 8; Exod 3:4), the divine appears before both (1 Sam 3:7; Exod 3:6). In Exod 3:6 Moses hides his face to avoid seeing the divine countenance; in 1 Sam 3:7 Samuel receives a revelation (יגלה) akin to YHWH's earlier revelation to Moses as spoken by the anonymous prophet in the previous chapter (הנגלה נגלתי in 1 Sam 2:27).[42] However, the episode in Num 12 noted above is especially pertinent to the Moses/Samuel parallel. A look at the larger passage is instructive:

> Hear now my words:
> If there be a prophet among you,
> I YHWH make myself known to him in a vision,
> I speak with him in a dream.
> Not so with my servant [עבדי] Moses;
> He is trusted in all my house;
> With him do I speak mouth to mouth [פה אל פה],
> directly, and not in dark speeches;
> And he beholds the similitude of YHWH [ותמנת ה']. (Num 12:6–8)

In this passage Moses is categorized as completely different from other divine intermediaries. The hallmark of his uniqueness is the very clear statement that YHWH appears in person to Moses, who sees the divine presence (ותמנת ה'), and with whom he speaks directly (פה אל פה). The redactor of Numbers has drawn these verses from an ancient source (evidenced in part by their poetic structure),[43] and the antiquity of the tradition behind this source is supported not only by the passage in Exod 3:6, but by the persistence of this same idea in different strata of the Pentateuch (Exod

---

42. On this last point, see Roy L. Heller, *Power, Politics, and Prophecy: The Character of Samuel and the Deuteronomistic Evaluation of Prophecy* (LHBOTS 440; London: T&T Clark, 2006), 67, though Heller does not specify that the ancestor in question is indeed Moses. On further connections between Moses and Samuel, see Rolf Rendtorff, "Samuel the Prophet: A Link between Moses and the Kings," in *The Quest for Context and Meaning: Studies in Biblical Intertextuality in Honor of James A. Sanders* (ed. Craig A. Evans and Shemaryahu Talmon; Leiden: Brill, 1997), 30–32, 34–36.

43. Cross, *Canaanite Myth*, 203 n. 35. The possible origin of this source is suggested below.

33:11; Deut 34:10). Evidently, the concept of the deity's speaking directly to Moses was too firmly entrenched for later biblical writers and redactors to ignore or curb, even in the face of later ideologies that had increasingly abstracted the divine presence and rendered it transcendent rather than immanent. When we consider that Samuel, like Moses, is identified as YHWH's עֶבֶד, that the revelation to him is conveyed in the waking state, and that the deity literally appears before him (ויבא ה' ויתיצב in v. 10), the parallels between the Moses tradition in Num 12:6–8 and 1 Sam 3 become even more concrete.

In attempting to identify a *Sitz im Leben* for the origination of Num 12:6–8, I would suggest that an early form of this tradition—or at least the concept behind it—obtained among the Elides at Shiloh. Pursuant to the El traditions that persisted at that sanctuary (as identified by Seow), dream theophanies are accepted as legitimate in these verses.[44] Nevertheless, Moses is held above those who receive them, and this would support Elide claims to superiority over potential challengers to their priestly authority: descent from Moses, the man with whom YHWH spoke directly, trumps other numinous claims. This also sheds some light on why Samuel is asleep in the sacred crypt at the outset of 1 Sam 3. If the suggestion of some commentators is correct that the young Samuel sleeps in the sacred crypt for the purpose of incubating a dream theophany,[45] then the Elides may have attempted to assert control over who could experience dream theophanies by working that phenomenon into the cult that they helmed.[46] This could support their priestly primacy at the sanctuary, insofar as it confirms the distinction that Mosaic authority harnessed by the Elides was higher and mightier than visions or dreams secured by others, and should therefore supervise or oversee these subsidiary forms of revelation.

What eventually unfolds, however, is a rather dramatic turn of events that accomplishes two things simultaneously. First, it contributes to the

---

44. Seow, *David's Dance*, 31.

45. On incubation, see Thomas H. McAlpine, *Sleep, Divine and Human in the Old Testament* (JSOTSup 38; Sheffield: JSOT, 1987), 158–59. For 1 Sam 3 as an incubation scene, see Steven von Wyrick, "El," *Eerdman's Dictionary of the Bible* (ed. David Noel Freedman; Grand Rapids: Eerdmans, 2000), 385; Blenkinsopp, *History of Prophecy in Israel*, 52.

46. If, as Seow has argued, the Shiloh cult retained devotion to El, then such dream incubation may have been an inherited feature of the tradition at Shiloh at the time the Elides came to power over the site.

sense throughout the narrative of 1 Sam 1–3 that the standards and practices of the Elides were ineffective, dream incubation included (as suggested by the opening note אין חזון נפרץ). Samuel's revelation is a unique event, something that does not occur under the aegis of Elide strategy. Second, and building upon the first, it declares that Samuel has the very same experience that is elsewhere attributed to Moses—i.e., YHWH speaking directly to him in a waking state. As we have seen, this is reinforced by the words of the anonymous prophet in 1 Sam 2:35 who claims that the new priestly house that is to eclipse the Elides was to be founded by a figure who will himself carry Mosaic qualities similar to those in Num 12:6–8.

I have suggested elsewhere that, before the Deuteronomists redacted the material currently found in 1 Samuel 1–3, much of the contents of this oracle was once part of the message received by Samuel in 1 Sam 3.[47] By being placed in the mouth of an anonymous prophet before Samuel's own experience in the crypt, 1 Sam 2:35 is removed from any tradition of Samuel's rise to priestly power and is then applied to the removal of the Elide Abiathar and the rise of the house of Zadok under Solomon (1 Kgs 2:26). However, in its pre-Deuteronomistic state, the oracle likely rested within the recounting of revelation given to Samuel in the crypt, consistent as it is with the Mosaic overtones pervading 1 Sam 3. The entire episode, then, rendered Samuel the recipient of an unmitigated divine encounter, one that follows a Mosaic paradigm and thereby fulfills its own prediction of a "faithful priest"—Samuel—rising up to replace the Elides in Mosaic fashion.

In the early Samuel narratives we thus find the origin of the Moses/Samuel parallel. The revelation to Samuel in 1 Sam 3 becomes the basis for a claim against the Elides that descent from Moses was enough to maintain priestly hegemony at Shiloh in the face of otherwise compromising qualities. Rather, Mosaic typology was just that—a typology of sacral status that could be granted by YHWH to a fitting substitute not bound by biological

---

47. Leuchter, "Something Old, Something Older," 539–40. See also the comment by Heller, who notes that the oracle in 1 Sam 2:27–36 lacks the expected reaction from Eli (*Power, Politics, and Prophecy*, 46). 1 Sam 3:16–18, however, *does* contain the expected reaction in response to Samuel's relating the contents of his revelation to Eli, suggesting that in an earlier form, material in the anonymous prophet's oracle in the previous chapter was part of the episode involving Samuel and Eli. This and other points of contact (such as the גלה terminology applied both to Samuel and to Moses in the anonymous prophet's oracle) suggest the original unity of the material.

lineage to the Mushite line. This included the ability not only to communicate with the divine (a quality of which the Elides are bereft in 1 Sam 1–3), but also to maintain social order. If Moses was entrusted with the entirety of the divine "house" (בכל בתי in Num 12:8), this surely included the social structures of the hinterland that YHWH had planted therein (Exod 15:13, 17).[48] Here the egalitarian dynamic mentioned above comes into play: Samuel's towering stature in subsequent chapters and his influence in the earliest days of the monarchy retains the perception that as a priest he indeed represented the interests of the public and repaired the injuries to the socio-sacral order perpetrated by the Elides. To be a faithful priest, a priest like Moses, required a commitment to hinterland life and values alongside ritual authority and oracular ability. The Samuel traditions highlight these traits alongside Samuel's oracular and priestly qualities—Elkanah's good clan-based lineage and highland residence, Hannah's devotion to the ethic of procreation,[49] Samuel's ongoing interaction with his family while in priestly training, and later Samuel's commitment to maintaining juridical standards throughout the hinterland—making clear that his fitness for cultic leadership was rooted in agrarian society and its value system.[50]

Conclusion

The ascription of Mosaic qualities to Samuel via his prophetic experience provides a window into how, as Karel van der Toorn has put it, Moses

---

48. Leuchter, "Eisodus as Exodus."
49. On procreation as a sacral charge fostered among the pioneer families in early Israel, see Carol Meyers, *Discovering Eve: Ancient Israelite Women in Context* (New York; Oxford University Press, 1988), 95–121.
50. This same agrarian value system underlies Samuel's rebuke of kingship in 1 Sam 8. Though the chapter's current form results from a Deuteronomistic scribal hand (Mark Leuchter, "A King Like All the Nations: The Composition of I Sam 8,11–18," *ZAW* 117 [2005]: 543–58), its sentiments preserve the agrarian, antimonarchic ethic that characterized earliest Israelite rebukes of Canaanite-style monarchies. See the classic study by I. Mendelsohn, "Samuel's Denunciation of Kingship in Light of the Akkadian Documents from Ugarit," *BASOR* 143 (1956): 17–22. I would adjust my earlier view that Samuel's rebuke is entirely Deuteronomistic, and suggest that while a Deuteronomist adjusted the particulars of the rebuke to align with Neo-Assyrian imperial experiences, the concept behind the rebuke itself is entirely appropriate in the context of a Levitical-priestly critique of early kingship.

became a patron saint to the Levites.[51] Through appealing to Moses as a standard, an ideal type over and above the strictures of genealogical lineage, Levites were empowered to step forward as priestly stewards of the cult when more established cultic authorities lost the confidence of the public. That Mushites (such as the Elides) were themselves eventually subsumed within the Levite genealogies suggests that Moses' typological characteristics—such as those applied to Samuel—overshadowed his importance as the progenitor of the Mushite priestly line. The tradents who originated the Samuel narratives where this takes place did so, no doubt, to support their own religious and social interests, but it is difficult to determine when this took place. Some scholars suggest a fairly late reworking of the sources.[52] This is theoretically possible, since the Elide circles appear to have persisted down to the late seventh century B.C.E. (Jer 1:1; 11:21–23), and a contemporaneous competing group could have shaped the Samuel traditions at that time or shortly thereafter. But this seems unlikely if the purpose of the Samuel traditions discussed above was to challenge Elide claims to priestly prominence, since this claim could not be made from the late tenth century onward. Solomon had seen to it that any priests associated with Shiloh would have no part in his state cult (1 Kgs 2:26; see also Ps 78:60–66), and Jeroboam would later do the same in the north.[53] Though descendants of the Elide house may have found a way back in to the cult during the Josianic era, Deuteronomy's leveling of all priestly lines as "Levite" suggests that they were not special in any way in pursuing such ends. In essence, the late preexilic period does not see a context where a pro-Samuel, anti-Elide polemic would have taken root, and there is little to indicate that exilic or postexilic conditions would have seen this either.

By contrast, the tenth century B.C.E. provides a suitable background for the origins of the tradition on the oral level and, perhaps, some textual

---

51. Van der Toorn, *Family Religion*, 304.

52. Blenkinsopp, *History of Prophecy in Israel*, 52; Römer, *So-Called Deuteronomistic History*, 138, 147, 152.

53. Baruch Halpern, "Levitic Participation in the Reform Cult of Jeroboam I," *JBL* 95 (1976): 38–41. The passage in Ps 78:60–66 reflects a Jerusalemite critique that is informed by the politics of Solomon. I have argued that the psalm originated in Solomon's reign as a propagandistic reframing of history (Mark Leuchter, "The Reference to Shiloh in Psalm 78," *HUCA* 77 [2006]: 1–31). But even if one wished to date the psalm to a later era, the anti-Shilonite ideology that characterized Solomon's court policies is still encoded therein.

alloform.[54] Since Abiathar maintained an important place in the priestly caste of both Saul's and David's day, it is possible that circles who followed Samuel may have constructed these traditions to carve out a sacral niche for themselves in the earliest days of the monarchy over against the influence of Abiathar and his own supporters. In vying for a place in the fledgling monarchic cult and administration, various cases were invariably advanced for the fitness of one priestly house over another.[55] Though Abiathar and the Elides would later suffer during Solomon's reign, they seem to have emerged the victors as the priestly line deemed most fit to represent the northern tribes during David's rise to the throne. Given David's own deference to Samuel's sacral authority (1 Sam 16:1–13; 19:18),[56] it is likely that some *rapprochement* between Abiathar's circle and the supporters of Samuel was eventually negotiated as northern priestly/Levite groups formed coalitions in support of David over Saul

---

54. David M. Gunn has examined texts in proximate settings both literary and, ostensibly, temporal, and highlighted their oral provenance, or at least the oral style emulated in these works ("Narrative Patterns and Oral Tradition in Judges and Samuel," VT 24 [1974]: 286–317). The oral traditions incorporated into these works, however, would have emerged alongside the rudimentary formation of written materials as the early monarchic state emerged; see Hutton, *Transjordanian Palimpsest*, 173–74. In an environment where textuality was recruited to legitimize developing state systems, similar strategies are not beyond the pale of possibility with regard to the legitimization of priestly claims within those systems. Considering both the priestly predilection toward oral instruction and, at the same time, the recurring characterization of priests as literate throughout the biblical record (Ian M. Young, "Israelite Literacy: Interpreting the Evidence," VT 48 [1998]: 239–53, 408–22), it seems possible to posit both the oral composition of narratives regarding Samuel and the brief written formation of complementary traditions, both of which were subsequently combined into a composite text.

55. The importance of priestly groups in solidifying the monarchy, especially in David's day, is discussed by Saul M. Olyan, "Zadok's Origins and the Tribal Politics of David," *JBL* 101 (1982): 190–93.

56. Hutton identifies 1 Sam 16:1–13 as part of a later redactional stratum added to the book of Samuel emphasizing Samuel's prophetic authority (*Transjordanian Palimpsest*, 250–51). But even if this is the case, the account preserves dynamics that support traditional rural social structures and presupposes a pre-Hezekian provenance. For instance, the cultic prerogatives of the elders, which would have suffered during the Hezekian urbanization program, are still in place in 1 Sam 16:5. Levites would have retained a significant socioreligious role overseeing local, clan-based religious events (e.g., Samuel arriving to conduct a local sacrifice, even if it is simply a pretext in the drama of the narrative).

and his descendants.[57] In any case, an early form of the tradition must have been in place by the time the initial stratum in Ps 99 was composed, which we have seen presupposes a very early point in the development of the Zion tradition.

The Deuteronomists who inherited this complex of tradition reworked it to fit their needs and vision.[58] The encounter originally meant to solidify Samuel's priestly status became the inaugural event in a prophetic career, which heralded successive prophets who arose after him to continue speaking on behalf of YHWH. It is through the divine word (דבר ה׳) that these prophets communicate divine will, and it is this same divine word that Samuel's inaugural experience reestablishes among Israel at Shiloh. A difference, however, should be noted. The lexical formula characterizing most of the experience of prophets in the DH beyond Samuel is [PN] ויהי דבר ה׳ אל (e.g., 2 Sam 7:4; 24:11; 1 Kgs 13:20; 17:2, 8; 18:1; 21:17, 28; 2 Kgs 20:4), and indeed this formula is applied to Samuel in a Deuteronomistic passage as well (1 Sam 15:10).[59] However, it does not appear at all in 1 Sam 3. Rather, the author of 1 Sam 3 informs us that before he was prepared to accept the divine word, it was not yet "revealed" to him (וטרם יגלה אליו דבר ה׳, v. 7), that YHWH was himself revealed to Samuel through the divine word (אל שמואל בשלו בדבר ה׳ כי נגלה ה׳, v. 21) and that this was the basis of his renown as a prophet (v. 20). The דבר language in this episode has much in common with the דבר language in the rest of the DH as the vehicle for prophetic experience, but does not conform to it. It may therefore have contributed to the subsequent appli-

---

57. Hutton, "All the King's Men," 127–42, with regard to priestly affiliation with David over later threats to his monarchic authority, which certainly included Saulide descendants.

58. Note, for example, the correspondence between 1 Sam 3:18 and Deut 13:1 (Heller, *Power, Politics, and Prophecy*, 69). Heller further notes that the opening clause of 1 Sam 4:1—the conclusion to the Deuteronomistic narrative of 1 Sam 3—equates the divine word with the word of Samuel and sees this as a problematic passage, viewing it as a potential semantic equation of the prophet with the deity (69–70). However, this too is characteristic of Deuteronomistic thought, since Deut 5:4–5 identifies prophetic intercession as the conduit to direct contact with the deity. The statement is not problematic in the manner addressed by Heller but is consistent with Deuteronomistic attempts to present the prophetic word in a hypostatic sense.

59. This, however, is only a brief Deuteronomistic incursion into an earlier source. See Hutton, *Transjordanian Palimpsest*, 311 n. 57.

cation of the דבר language to prophets beyond Shiloh who followed in Samuel's footsteps.[60]

It is thus Samuel's experience that set the terms of qualification as a Mosaic prophet in Deuteronomistic consciousness, despite the fact that the account of that experience originated as an argument for priestly primacy. The Mosaic qualifications he obtained in the account of his rise to power as a priest were transferred to his role as a prophet via the דבר phenomenology that empowered subsequent prophets in the DH. This, no doubt, was conditioned by the weight of the prophetic movement of the eighth century B.C.E., in which nonpriests such as Amos, Micah, and Isaiah made an enormous impact on Israel's sacral traditions. Deuteronomy accounts for this by legislating distinctions between priests (Deut 18:1–8) and prophets (Deut 18:15–22), and the redactors of the DH follow suit by situating Samuel within a larger spectrum of prophecy both preceding his inaugural experience (Judg 4:4–5; 6:8–10; 1 Sam 2:27–36) and, of course, following it. In this way, Samuel was subsumed within the Deuteronomistic declaration that YHWH had worked through an ongoing, consistent stream of voices termed "[his] servants, the prophets," first working within cultic structures and eventually in opposition to them.

Some wisps of the pre-Deuteronomistic Samuel tradition survived in the memory of later biblical writers: Ps 99 was expanded and canonized into the Psalter,[61] preserving the priestly equation between Moses and Samuel (though throwing Aaron into the mix), and the Chronicler not only identified Samuel as a Levite but credited him with participation in planning the roles for Levites in the Jerusalem temple (1 Chr 9:22).[62] But the dominant image of Samuel both within and beyond the Hebrew Bible conforms to the Deuteronomistic recasting of him as a prototypical

---

60. The linguistic affinities lend credence to the shaping of this narrative before its inclusion into the DH by a prophetic circle who influenced the Deuteronomists. This supports the theory of a Prophetic Record as a major stop along the way toward the canonical shape of Samuel–Kings, and is consistent with the Deuteronomists' interests in northern prophetic tradition; see Hutton, *Transjordanian Palimpsest*; Geoghegan, *Time, Place and Purpose*, 149.

61. Leuchter, "Psalm xcix," 25–26, 29, 37–38.

62. The dual attribution of this responsibility to both David and Samuel may echo, mnemo-historically, the traditions regarding Samuel's leadership of the Levite priesthood and the transition of that priesthood under Abiathar to David's hegemony following the move to Jerusalem in 2 Sam 5–6. On the Levites' connection to David, see again Hutton, "All the King's Men," 133–38.

prophet,⁶³ and this is fitting. Samuel's prophetic encounter with YHWH at Shiloh is a response to the social and cultic abuses of the Elides, and the Deuteronomists present the critiques of the prophets as a response to the social and cultic abuses of the kings and their subjects. The prophets became the inheritors of the ideology that was built into the institution of the Levite caste, promoting what the Deuteronomists believed to be the genuine interests of the people against the inclinations of the corrupt by calling them to adhere to the law.⁶⁴ This was ultimately what it meant to be a prophet like Moses, who initially brokered Israel's relationship with the divine and who, through Deuteronomistic ideology, provided them with the means to preserve it.

---

63. Such is implied by the Chronicler's emphasis on Samuel's prophetic pedigree even after acknowledging the traditions regarding his status as a Levite. See the insightful discussion concerning Samuel's importance to the Chronicler by Sara Japhet, *I and II Chronicles* (OTL; Louisville: Westminster John Knox, 1993), 1054–55. See also the evidence in Ben Sira, who regards Samuel first and foremost as a prophet (Sir 46:13–20).

64. This, perhaps, accounts for why parallels between the prophets and the Levites are encountered throughout the historiographic materials in Samuel–Kings. See van der Toorn, *Family Religion*, 314–15.

Prophetic Stories Making a Story of Prophecy

Mark O'Brien

The aim of this essay is quite straightforward: to examine how ancient Israelite authors did what all authors seek to do; how they made creative use of limited literary resources in order to give meaning to experience. Its focus is specific: the portrayal of prophets and their preaching in a selection of prophetic stories in the books of Samuel and Kings.[1] Its premise is self-evident: all literary forms are, to a greater or lesser degree, limited. Each provides an opportunity to communicate something in a creative way, but also imposes limitations. Hence, societies in all ages have found it necessary to develop a repertoire of literary forms to enhance their communicative capacity. Every society engages in the ongoing quest to make sense of the vagaries of experience, at both the individual and the collective levels. In order to do so, each draws on its repertoire of forms, both large and small, and utilizes them in ways that reveal creativity and expose limitation.

Despite occasional evidence to the contrary, human beings, thankfully, tend to hoard rather than discard. Even though most things we make have a use-by date, they provide a basis and a stimulus for making new things. Hence, one can trace the relationship between literary limitation and creativity, between old and new, by examining how forms are shaped and reshaped, and how different versions of the same form, or even new forms, are produced. This is the case both at the micro-level of phrases

---

[1]. This essay assumes the hypothesis of a Deuteronomistic History (DH), including the considerable complexity associated with it. See Antony F. Campbell and Mark A. O'Brien, *Unfolding the Deuteronomistic History: Origins, Upgrades, Present Text* (Minneapolis: Fortress, 2000). The term "prophetic stories" is used in a general sense for narratives about prophets that have a beginning and end and that unfold a plot via the interaction of characters.

and sentences and at the macro-level of stories, songs, or law codes. The ongoing need to make sense of experience, the utilization of various literary forms, and the creation of new ones, the work of all authors and audiences/readers leaves traces in the literature that is produced. These traces are themselves parts of the story of this or that literary form, of this or that body of literature. The term "story" can thus be applied in two senses. The first refers to the characters in a story and their interaction; the second to the authors and editors/redactors who produced it.

Given the prominence of stories about prophets in the books of Samuel and Kings, it is reasonable to presume that one will find evidence there of these two senses of the term, in particular at the level of a larger "story of prophecy." An indication that Samuel and Kings tell such a story is the recurring prophecy-fulfillment schema, which provides a link between individual prophetic stories and embraces them within a larger whole. Granted that biblical and ancient Near Eastern texts were in time often reworked and reshaped, it is likely that this story of prophecy will also tell us something of the story or history of those involved in such a process.[2] Another way of expressing the dynamic and at times tense relationship between creativity and limitation is Michael Fishbane's distinction between the "traditum" (the content of what is transmitted) and the "traditio" (the ongoing process of transmission that can involve revision and reshaping).[3] An essay such as this does not of course provide the scope for constructing a credible story or account of the relationship between "traditum" and "traditio."[4] What is undertaken here is of a more preliminary nature—that is, to identify textual traces that could be utilized, along with other evidence, in the construction of such a story.

Many of the prophetic stories in the books of Samuel and Kings are about encounters between prophets and kings. Both are authority figures that cooperate or clash over the destiny of the kingdom and its people. In

---

2. For evidence of the reworking of biblical and other ancient Near Eastern texts, see Jeffrey H. Tigay, *Empirical Models of Biblical Criticism* (Philadelphia: University of Pennsylvania Press, 1985).

3. Michael Fishbane, *Biblical Interpretation in Ancient Israel* (Oxford: Clarendon, 1985), 6 (for his understanding of these terms), 414–18 (for their application to narrative).

4. Some may prefer to speak of "reconstructing the history of the relationship." But, given the paucity of independent corroborative evidence, it seems to me more a case of constructing or imagining a reasonable and credible scenario.

the hypothesis of a Deuteronomistic Historian, prophetic stories became key building blocks in the construction of the story of Israel's monarchy, first as the united kingdom under David and Solomon, and subsequently as the divided kingdoms of Israel and Judah. Although commentators debate whether the Deuteronomistic History was composed in the preexilic or exilic periods, and in one or more stages, most would agree that the authority of prophecy was invoked to promote the Deuteronomistic Historian's agenda at strategic points. One can in a real sense speak of the Deuteronomistic History as a story of prophecy and fulfillment. Moses is cast as the paradigm prophet, obedience to the deuteronomic law is the core of his message, and the subsequent story of Israel unfolds the fulfillment of his prophecy. Even if one does not accept the Deuteronomistic History hypothesis, the fact that Joshua, Judges, Samuel, and Kings are known in Jewish tradition as "The Former Prophets" testifies to the importance of prophecy in this part of the canon.

CREATIVITY IN THE COMPOSITION AND USE OF PROPHETIC STORIES

Without the creative impulse of authors, there would of course be no story to listen to or to read. I will therefore begin with an exploration of creativity in the composition and use of prophetic stories, and then consider some of the limitations that emerge. This section of the essay will focus on the Elijah–Elisha narrative in 1 Kgs 17–2 Kgs 10*, followed by 1 Kgs 19 and 1 Sam 8.

On an initial reading, the Elijah–Elisha narrative looks like a classic example of the popular story plot—"overcoming the monster" or "the battle against evil"—made up of a number of "chapters" or "episodes."[5] There is the customary cast of heroes and villains, including even a "wicked witch" figure in Jezebel, and the story reaches a resounding climax with Jehu wiping out Baal worship in Israel (2 Kgs 10:28). The unfolding of the plot is marked at a number of points by prophecy-fulfillment schemas that give a sense of unity and purpose to the narrative. However, historical-critical analysis claims to have uncovered evidence of a complex narrative compiled by many hands over a considerable period of time.[6] Existing stories about Elijah and Elisha have been reshaped, while other stories about

---

5. Following the classification of Christopher Booker, *The Seven Basic Plots: Why We Tell Stories* (London: Continuum, 2004).

6. Historical-critical studies of the narrative are too numerous to be reviewed

them, as well as about other unnamed and named prophets have been added (1 Kgs 20, 22). One should find evidence here of creativity in the joining and reshaping of a variety of parts to advance the overall plot. In an attempt to illustrate this, I will examine a selection of texts about Elisha.

Second Kings 8:1–6 brings together the principal characters who feature in the preceding stories and anecdotes about Elisha. There is the prophet himself, the fickle king Joram, the wealthy woman of Shunem and her son whom Elisha resuscitated, and Gehazi, Elisha's servant. The prominence of Gehazi in 8:1–6 suggests a link not only with the woman of Shunem in 4:8–37 but also with Naaman the Aramean, who is healed in 2 Kgs 5. Within the context, the king's request in 8:4 to hear "all the great things that Elisha has done" can be taken to refer to all the preceding accounts of Elisha's activities. Second Kings 8:1–6 effectively functions as the goal or horizon of the preceding stories and anecdotes about Elisha. All those in Israel who have benefited from him reappear here in a kind of "all's well that ends well" finale to the collection (except of course Naaman, who is in Aram). Even Gehazi, punished with leprosy for deceiving Naaman, is rehabilitated by being cast as a preacher of the good news about Elisha to the king. The king's request also casts him in a favorable light, in contrast to his conduct in some of the preceding stories.

This rather sunny scene seems a world away from the story of Jehu's coup that follows. In 2 Kgs 9:21–26 Jehu accuses Joram of promoting the evil policies of his mother Jezebel; he kills him and orders his body to be thrown onto Naboth's plot to fulfill a prophecy uttered against his father Ahab. This is the first step in Jehu's execution of the brief given him by Elisha's disciple in 9:6–10. Within the larger context, his version of the prophecy refers to 1 Kgs 21:19–24, in which Elijah pronounces doom for the house of Ahab. How does the good king Joram of 8:1–6 become the bad king Joram, deserving of capital punishment? The only text that seems to provide some information is 8:18–19. It is not part of a prophetic story, but a judgment formula, a component of the so-called "regnal framework" that structures the account of each king's reign. The formula refers to Jehoram, son of Jehoshaphat of Judah. It assesses him negatively by accusing him of acting like "the kings of Israel, as the house of Ahab had done." The charge is that because Jehoram's wife was the daughter of Ahab (Athaliah),

---

here. Recent examples are Otto, *Jehu, Elia, und Elisa*; idem, "The Composition of the Elijah-Elisha Stories"; and Lehnart, *Prophet und König*.

he followed the policies of Ahab's house. Since Jehoram is a member of the Davidic dynasty ruling in Jerusalem, the accusation of walking in the "way of the kings of Israel" cannot refer to Jeroboam's establishment of an illegitimate rival cult to the Jerusalem temple. The accompanying phrase "as the house of Ahab had done" indicates that it refers to the cult of Baal initiated by Ahab and Jezebel. Although the judgment formula does not state this explicitly, it does allow one to assume that the reigning Israelite king, Joram, had reneged on his earlier reform against the Baal cult (3:2) and resumed the practices of Ahab and Jezebel. Second Kings 8:18–19 can thus provide a narrative context for Jehu's accusation against Joram and his execution as an apostate.

A number of commentators argue that the collection of stories about Elisha in 2 Kgs 4–8, or part of it, is a later addition.[7] If this is the case, the one or ones responsible for the addition, presumably followers of the Elisha tradition, were able to locate it so that it did not create conflict with the prophecy of Elijah and its fulfillment in the story of Jehu's coup. In fact, one can argue that they were able to enhance the impact of this prophecy-fulfillment story by heightening the contrast between good and bad Joram. The king who heard all the good things that Elisha and done and who personally benefited from his interventions, but who subsequently promoted the apostasy of his father Ahab, thoroughly deserved his demise. In short, two prophetic stories with their respective limited horizons were utilized to good effect by locating them strategically within the narrative sequence. Granted that 2 Kgs 8:1–6 is a later addition, it has been formulated and located in a way that enhances the larger story of prophecy and fulfillment.

Another, more subtle example of literary creativity is the critical portrayal of the prophet. There are two examples of this in the Elisha narrative, and they are both strategically located. The first occurs in the story of Elijah's assumption and the transfer of his spirit to Elisha (2 Kgs 2:1–18). Elisha requests a double share of the master's spirit, and is told that if he sees Elijah being taken he will receive it, but, if he does not, he will not. The report of Elijah's assumption leaves the reader (and Elisha) uncertain of what he saw, the departure of his master or the chariot and horsemen. The ambiguity of the Hebrew pronominal suffixes, coupled with Elisha's

---

7. For example, Otto identifies the earliest narrative sequence about Elisha in 2 Kgs 2* (the succession story) and 9–10*. This was incorporated into the Deuteronomistic History. The bulk of the "Elisha biography" (2 Kgs 4:1–6:3) is a late addition (*Jehu, Elia, und Elisa*, 241–46, 263).

cry "Father, father, the chariot of Israel and its horsemen," incline me to the latter.[8] This is supported by two further incidents in the story. On returning to the Jordan, Elisha asks "Where is the God of Elijah?"—which would be odd if he had received a double share of the master's spirit. He then strikes the river twice with Elijah's mantle—suggesting that the spirit does not rest on him. An allusion to doubting Moses striking the rock twice in Num 20:11 is difficult to deny. The company of prophets watching at a distance proclaims—from that distance—that "the spirit of Elijah rests on Elisha." But when they approach Elisha and bow to him, he is unable to assert authority and caves in to their demand to send a search party for Elijah. This is an unlikely portrait of one who is supposed to have a double share of Elijah's spirit. It is only when Elisha successfully responds to a request in 2:19–22 that he can be sure he has what he requested, or at least something of it. The message of 2 Kgs 2 seems to be that no one, least of all a prophet, can pin down when, where, and how the prophetic charism is bestowed. This is a subtle but powerful caveat at the beginning of the narrative about Elisha.

The second example is the story of the wealthy woman of Shunem (4:8–37), an important one in the collection, since Elisha raises her dead son. At first glance, Elisha seems to emulate his master Elijah, who raised a widow's son in 1 Kgs 17:17–24. However, the story subtly undermines this impression. Elisha initially bungles things by instructing Gehazi to do the job with his staff, which does not work. At this point the woman is cast as the one gifted with prophetic insight rather than the prophet. Her words, "As the Lord lives, and as you yourself live, I will not leave you," repeat the words spoken three times by Elisha to Elijah in 2:2–6. In a neat reversal of the earlier story, in which those words expressed the devotion or tenacity of the disciple in relation to the master, here they act as a prophetic word that Elisha must obey. As 4:30b states, "he rose up and followed her" to her house.[9]

---

8. For a more detailed analysis, see my "The Portrayal of Prophets in 2 Kings 2," *AusBR* 46 (1998): 1–16.

9. I agree with Rofé, *Prophetical Stories*, 29; Mary E. Shields, "Subverting a Man of God, Elevating a Woman: Role and Power Reversals in 2 Kings 4," *JSOT* 58 (1993): 59–69; Mark Roncace, "Elisha and the Woman of Shunem: 2 Kings 4:8–37 and 8:1–6," *JSOT* 91 (2000): 109–27. I disagree with Wesley J. Bergen, *Elisha and the End of Prophetism* (JSOTSup 286; Sheffield: Sheffield Academic Press, 1999), 62–66, and Otto, *Jehu, Elia, und Elisa*, 241–42.

One might think this story exalts Elijah at the expense of Elisha, but the master himself is portrayed in a critical way in 1 Kgs 19.[10] The prophet who has, in the narrative sequence, experienced the power of prophetic prayer on Mount Carmel, and triumphed over the prophets of Baal, flees in fear when threatened by Jezebel, and despairs of his life. When questioned by God at Horeb, he claims to be the only remaining faithful Israelite. In reply, God informs him that not only is there one other faithful Israelite whom he is to anoint as his successor (Elisha), but that there are seven thousand others who have not bowed to Baal. Elijah is instructed to anoint Hazael king over Aram and Jehu king over Israel. Neither of these does he get to do. His successor Elisha does. He does not even anoint Elisha his successor as instructed. Instead, Elisha becomes his servant. But how obedient and attentive a servant of the Lord is Elijah in this chapter?

Two additional prophetic stories cast a critical eye over prophets. One is the encounter between the man of God from Judah and the aged prophet of Bethel in 1 Kgs 13. The man of God is disobedient and the prophet of Bethel is a liar, yet both pronounce prophecies that are fulfilled and therefore true. In the final scene, the aged prophet instructs his sons to bury him beside the disobedient prophet who has been struck down by God because "the saying that he proclaimed by the word of the Lord … shall surely come to pass" (1 Kgs 13:32). The manner of the man of God's death validates the prophet of Bethel's pronouncement that he would not be buried in his ancestral tomb and, thereby, the truth of his prophecy against the altar at Bethel.

A second and perhaps less clear example can be identified in the story of Samuel. According to 1 Sam 4:1 the word of Samuel came to all Israel; he is the authoritative prophetic figure. Yet there are two subsequent episodes that seem to undermine him to a degree. The first is his installation of his sons as judges. This move proves a failure, and the people demand a different form of leadership, a king (1 Sam 8:1–5). The second concerns his execution of God's instructions in 8:7–9. He is told to listen to their voice—their demand for a king—but also to warn them and show them the ways of a king. In the subsequent text, Samuel only tells the people about the ways of a king. When instructed a second time by God to listen

---

10. See William J. Dumbrell, "What Are You Doing Here? Elijah at Horeb," *Crux* 22 (1986): 12–19.

to the people's voice and set a king over them (8:22), he dismisses the assembly. First Samuel 8 is a complex text and the repeated sequence of divine instruction, prophetic speech, and people's rejection may well be structural devices that enable editors to expand a base text. Is the present text meant to be read as a combination of varying viewpoints about monarchy, or as a critique of Samuel the prophet, even a critique of prophecy itself, or both?[11]

Whatever the case for the Samuel text, there is sufficient evidence in the other prophetic stories of a phenomenon that one also finds in the Pentateuch. According to Num 20:12 Moses and Aaron fail to trust God at the waters of Meribah, and are sentenced to die outside the land. Yet the words of Moses and the priestly actions of Aaron retain their divine authority. Deuteronomy has to acknowledge the tradition that Moses died outside the land, but it does not repeat or recall the Numbers text. Instead, it seems to appeal to the notion of corporate identity: a leader cannot completely escape the baneful impact of wicked subjects.[12] Moses says of the people's rebellion at Kadesh-barnea, "Even with me the Lord was angry on your account" (1:37). Moses requests the Lord to reconsider the ban on entering the land in 3:26, but to no avail, and 4:22 indicates that he accepts this is to be his fate. A further reference to his death outside the land occurs in 31:2; the overall effect is to shift attention from the person of Moses to his words. He is to die outside the land, but his words will endure as a torah for life in the land. They have divine authority and, according to 12:32 (MT 13:1), are not to be tampered with in any way.

There are a number of likely reasons for this focus on prophetic word at the expense of prophetic persona. An initial one emerges from the critical stance identified above in a number of prophetic stories. Being a prophet is not the same as holding an office such as kingship or priesthood. God bestows the prophetic spirit as and when God wills. Without it a prophet is just another fallible human being, and his or her words (and deeds) have no more authority or impact than anyone else's. Awareness of a prophet's complete dependence on the spirit to speak a prophetic word

---

11. For a study of the portrait of Samuel, see Heller, *Power, Politics, and Prophecy*. He concludes that "the Deuteronomistic stories of Samuel are, therefore, critical of prophecy" (145).

12. The different reason for Moses' death outside the land in Deut 32:48–52 is a later addition, substantially repeating what is generally regarded as a priestly text in Num 27:12–14 (Campbell and O'Brien, *Unfolding the Deuteronomistic History*, 96).

heightens the authority of that word. A second reason is the multiplicity of prophets and the need to sort the genuine from the fake. The perceived fulfillment of a prophet's word seems to have been regarded, at least in deuteronomic circles (18:20–22), as a reliable sign. By the same token, Jer 23:9–40 indicates that its author or authors realized that certainty in this area was not attainable. A third likely reason is the fear that a cult would develop around a prophet that, in Deuteronomistic eyes, could deflect attention and devotion from the Jerusalem temple.

Prophets were revered because they were bearers of God's word. But some stories about them were shaped to instruct readers and listeners that this did not mean they were supermen or women. Like all human beings, they had their limitations and flaws. It is probably not without significance that the gravesites of prophets are not recorded in the Deuteronomistic History, nor is there any mention that their graves became pilgrimage sites. Second Kings 13:20–21 tells of a completely unsolicited resuscitation at the grave of Elisha, but its location is not given. The same goes for the common grave of the Judean man of God and the Bethel prophet in 1 Kgs 13. Deuteronomy 34:6 asserts that no one knows the grave of Moses, while for Elijah, of course, there is no grave.[13]

One further factor driving the focus on words and deeds is the need for an authority to resolve disputes. A common way of explaining experience, and one that is employed extensively in the Bible, is the so-called act-consequence construct or connection.[14] Good acts are believed to have good consequences, while bad acts have bad ones. It is an ethical version of the physical law of cause and effect. But, unlike the laws of physics, it cannot be proved. Disputes inevitably arise at times and, in order to resolve them in religious societies, appeal is often made to the highest recognized authority, God. Rather like the TV umpire in contemporary sports, God is believed to see the whole field of play, and so can provide the definitive

---

13. In contrast, Scott D. Hill reports that for Muslim saints and sanctuaries in Palestine "seventy percent … were on hill tops (the biblical 'high places'), and sixty percent were accompanied by holy trees, much like the descriptions of popular worship found throughout the Bible (e.g., Deut 12:21; 16:21; 1 Kgs 14:23; Jer 3:6–9, 17:2–3; Ezek 20:28)"; see "The Local Hero in Palestine in Comparative Perspective," in *Elijah and Elisha in Socioliterary Perspective* (ed. Robert B. Coote; Semeia Studies; Atlanta: Scholars Press, 1992), 37–73, here 42.

14. Klaus Koch, "Is There a Doctrine of Retribution in the Old Testament?" in *Theodicy in the Old Testament* (ed. James L. Crenshaw; IRT 4; Philadelphia: Fortress, 1983), 57–87.

judgment via a prophet or some other reliable intermediary. (Sometimes this takes the form of a ritual.) A prophetic word that is believed to have come true assumes authority, and can be appealed to for resolving disputes in analogous situations. It can also be utilized by later figures claiming to be prophets. Considerable variety and even rivalry can emerge. This may not be troublesome when the various groups are independent of one another, but when they start to have an impact on national well-being, their relationship, or lack of it, will need to be addressed. One can imagine such a process behind the formation of the Elijah–Elisha narrative or a part of it. According to Antony Campbell's hypothesis of a "Prophetic Record," many prophets across a period of history are portrayed preaching a unified account of the prophetic guidance of Israel's monarchy, from its origins under Samuel, to the condemnation of the house of Ahab for promoting the cult of Baal, to the elimination of both by Jehu (cf. 2 Kgs 10:28). A recurring prophecy-fulfillment schema enhanced the unity of the Record. This was accepted as an authentic explanation of the course of Israel's history by later tradition, and became an integral part of the larger Deuteronomistic History.[15]

Given the emphasis on the prophetic word in the Prophetic Record and the Deuteronomistic History, particularly as expressed in the prophecy-fulfillment schema, why do these extensive narratives preserve accounts of the deeds and wonders of prophets such as Elijah and Elisha? Unlike words that live on, particularly written ones, deeds and wonders occur in the past. Two reasons can be offered. One is that the wonders or miracles are often about individuals or the common people. The overarching prophecy-fulfillment schema traces the realization of God's word in the national and international arenas, but the miracles affirm that God is just as concerned for the ordinary folk at the local level. In a word, the combination serves to focus attention on a God who is transcendent and immanent. A second reason draws on a characteristic prophetic phenomenon: signs are meant to confirm the divine origin of the words, while the words spell out the divine meaning of the signs. This would seem to be the function of the report about Moses' past "signs and wonders" in Deut 34:11. By these, in combination with the words pronounced by Moses in the body

---

15. Antony F. Campbell, *Of Prophets and Kings: A Late Ninth-Century Document (1 Samuel 1–2 Kings 10)* (CBQMS 17; Washington, D.C.: Catholic Biblical Association of America, 1986). According to Lehnart, the prophecy-fulfillment schema is a Deuteronomistic creation (*Prophet und König*, 285).

of the book, the reader receives double assurance that God was with him. By remembering both, the reader is attuned to God's purpose "that you may know that I am the Lord your God" (cf. Deut 8; 29:2–9 [MT 29:1–8]).

In Deut 18:15, Moses promises that God will raise up "a prophet like me," and says that the people are to heed such a prophet. The phrase "a prophet like me" can be read in two ways. One can appeal to 12:32 (MT 13:1) to show that it means one who preaches what Moses preached without addition or alteration. This meaning can embrace 34:10, which states there has never been another prophet "like Moses." It can also be traced in the prophecies that permeate the text of the Deuteronomistic History. According to one's understanding of the Deuteronomistic History hypothesis, these are either Deuteronomistic compositions or existing texts that were tweaked by Deuteronomistic editors to bring them into line with the Mosaic torah.[16] As Heller points out, such a move is an indirect acknowledgement of the authority of the prophetic tradition.[17]

But Deut 18:15 can also refer to a prophet who will be like Moses in the sense of being unique as he was unique. Deuteronomy 34:10 does not rule out the possibility of this kind of prophet. Also, God says in Deut 18:18 that "I will put my words in the mouth of the prophet who shall speak to them everything that I command." These may well be new words beyond those God spoke to Moses. One may combine both readings to assert that, for Deuteronomy, the sign that a post-Moses prophet is the genuine article will be his/her loyalty to the Mosaic torah. But this will in turn act as a sign that such a prophet may also be the bearer of new revelation. On this reading, Deuteronomistic theology was as ready to welcome a new prophetic word as it was loyal to the Mosaic torah.[18] The fact that no text in the Deuteronomistic History claims that a prophet, unique as Moses was unique, arose during Israel's life in the land may also be a sign of this Deuteronomistic attitude.

---

16. See Ben Zvi, "Prophets and Prophecy"; and more recently Barstad, "Some Remarks."

17. Heller, *Power, Politics, and Prophecy*, 141, 150.

18. Stephen B. Chapman (*The Law and the Prophets: A Study in Old Testament Canon Formation* [FAT 27; Tübingen: Mohr Siebeck, 2000]) argues that prophecy and torah enjoyed equal authority in the process of canon formation, as distinct from the differing traditions of canon reception.

Limitations of Prophetic Stories Leading to Another Stage in the Story of Prophecy

Thus far I have been exploring evidence of the creative shaping of prophetic stories to help explain the vicissitudes of Israel's experience. I would now like to present three examples in which this kind of creativity seems to have met its limits, but in whih this in turn acted as a catalyst for new forms of conveying prophetic theology. The three examples are: the contrasting assessments of Jehu in 2 Kgs 9–10 and in Hos 1:4, the clash between the prophetic condemnation of the house of Ahab and the promise of an everlasting dynasty for David (2 Kgs 8:19), and Huldah's promise to Josiah (2 Kgs 22:18–20).

The story of Jehu's coup in 2 Kgs 9–10 is a masterly example of the Israelite art of reticence in storytelling. There is ambiguity or uncertainty about the characterization of the main players, Jehu, Elisha and his disciple, and the people. These characterizations in turn raise questions about the author's intention and purpose.[19] Historical-critical analysis has sought to answer some of these questions by pointing to evidence of reworking at strategic points in the story.[20] What is clear, however, is that at the end of the story God tells Jehu that he has "done well in carrying out what I consider right" by eliminating the house of Ahab, and he is promised dynastic rule for four generations (10:30). This text may well be a later addition, but its interpretation of the story is clear. The one sin for which the text explicitly censures Jehu is his failure to turn from the sins of Jeroboam. The censure against Jehu is less severe than for earlier kings of Israel, who are accused of "walking in the way of Jeroboam."[21] In short, the assessment

---

19. Two recent studies of the narrative reflect this ambiguity. Lissa M. Wray Beal (*The Deuteronomist's Prophet: Narrative Control of Approval and Disapproval in the Story of Jehu [2 Kings 9 and 10]* [LHBOTS 478; New York: T&T Clark, 2007]) judges that, despite a level of approval, Jehu is censured for doing something unique among kings—usurping the prophetic role in a way contrary to the Deuteronomistic view. On the other hand, David T. Lamb (*Righteous Jehu and His Evil Heirs: The Deuteronomist's Negative Perspective on Dynastic Succession* [OTM; Oxford: Oxford University Press, 2007]) sees Deuteronomistic approval of Jehu in the prophecy-fulfillment schema and in Jehu's obedience to the prophetic word.

20. These are reviewed in Wray Beal, *Deuteronomist's Prophet*, 29–41.

21. Among earlier northern kings, only Joram is not accused of walking in the way of Jeroboam. Nevertheless, he too receives a more severe censure than Jehu because, as well as being like him in not "turning" (NRSV: "depart") from the sin of Jeroboam, he

of Jehu in 2 Kgs 10 stands in sharp contrast to that in Hos 1:4, where God vows that "in a little while I will punish the house of Jehu for the blood shed in Jezreel." Although formulated somewhat differently, the Hosean text is a pronouncement of doom over the house of Jehu similar to those in the Deuteronomistic History over the "houses" of northern dynasties, especially the "house of Ahab." Moreover, the reason for the pronouncement—the shedding of blood in Jezreel—refers to Jehu's violence, and therefore disagrees sharply with the prophecy of Elisha's disciple and God's approval of Jehu in 2 Kgs 10:30.[22] According to these, God commissioned him to eliminate Baal worship, and for doing so he was rewarded.

From a logical point of view, the rival Hosean theology could not be incorporated within the Deuteronomistic History storyline. But rather than discard one view in favor of the other, Israelite tradition retained both, and linked them by creating a new literary form, the prophetic book of Hosea, and attaching it via a superscription to a strategic point in the story of the two kingdoms. Hosea 1:1 informs the reader that the prophet preached in the reign of Jeroboam son of Joash, the second to last member of the Jehu dynasty (cf. 2 Kgs 14:23–29), and that he continued preaching after the exile of Israel, as the references to the Judean kings in the superscription indicate. Thus Hosea "saw" the fulfillment of his prophecy against the house of Jehu, when it came to a violent end in the assassination of Jeroboam's successor Zechariah (15:8–12). The relevant texts in 2 Kings provide indirect confirmation of Hosea's prophecy for the reader. In this way, the two views about the house of Jehu can play their respective roles in the story of the kings of Israel, even though they could not be included in the same narrative. One might even suggest that Hosea and/or his disciples did not see 1:4 as a contradiction of 2 Kgs 10:30. Jehu was rewarded for eliminating Baal, but in the process he shed much blood. Violence reaps violence (act-consequence), and Hosea proclaimed the judgment of the heavenly umpire that the consequences of Jehu's violence ultimately fell on his house in the assassination of Zechariah. In relation to

---

also "clung" to it. Northern kings after Jehu, except the last king Hoshea, receive the same censure as Jehu. Jehoahaz (2 Kgs 13:2) and Jehoash (13:11) are accused also of walking in the sins of Jeroboam.

22. In agreement with Lamb (*Righteous Jehu*, 86–88), and against Francis I. Andersen and David Noel Freedman, who argue that Hos 1:4 is not about why the house of Jehu is to be punished, but rather how it is to be punished (*Hosea* [AB; Garden City: Doubleday, 1980], 196).

this, it is worth noting that Hos 1:4 speaks of visiting/appointing (*pqd*) the blood of Jezreel on the house of Jehu, whereas the Deuteronomistic History generally speaks of cutting off every male of the northern dynasties.

The book of Hosea and the Deuteronomistic History combine in a more direct way to explain the fate of the northern kingdom. Hosea 1:4 includes a prophecy that God "will put an end to the kingdom of the house of Israel," and the Deuteronomistic History narrates how this came about. In the peroration on the northern kingdom in 2 Kgs 17:14–20, a reader can include Hosea among "his servants the prophets" who foretold its demise. Determining whether the book of Hosea was the first of its kind to appear in ancient Israel would involve detailed comparison with other prophetic books and is beyond the scope of this essay. As with most historical-critical reconstructions, no hypothesis is likely to satisfy everyone. What we can say, however, is that if the above outline reflects something of the development of Israelite tradition, it indicates how prophetic books like Hosea were included in the overall story of Israelite prophecy.

A second point of tension within the Deuteronomistic History is the impact of the condemnation of the house of Ahab on the promise to David of an enduring dynasty. The point of connection between the two, and the source of conflict, is the report in 2 Kgs 8:18 that Athaliah, the daughter of Ahab, became the wife of Jehoram of Judah, a member of the Davidic dynasty. A Jezebel-like influence is attributed to her in 8:26–27, which states how her son and Jehoram's successor Ahaziah "walked in the way of the house of Ahab … for he was son-in-law to the house of Ahab." A dynastic connection is forged via Athaliah between the house of David and the house of Omri and Ahab. According to 10:17, Jehu eliminates "all who were left to Ahab in Samaria," and this fulfilled the prophecy spoken by Elijah in 1 Kgs 21:20–24. Yet 2 Kgs 11:1 informs the reader that there were other children of Ahaziah in Jerusalem whom his mother sought to destroy. One is, however, preserved by king Joram's daughter and becomes the next Davidic king—Joash/Jehoash, son of Zibiah (2 Kgs 12).

Marvin Sweeney notes, "From the time of Joash on, the entire house of David is also descended from the house of Omri."[23] According to Sweeney, this made it subject to the prophecy of Elijah against the house of Omri and Ahab in 1 Kgs 21:20–24, and it ultimately suffered the same

---

23. Sweeney, *I and II Kings*, 12.

fate. While I agree with his first comment, the text of the Deuteronomistic History does not support the second and third. For example, 2 Kgs 8:19 implies that the promise of a lamp (or dominion) for David "all the days" (cf. 1 Kgs 11:36) trumps Elijah's proclamation of doom for all members of the house of Omri and Ahab.[24] I also doubt whether one can go so far as Sweeney in asserting that Manasseh "is explicitly compared to his ancestor King Ahab of Israel" in 2 Kgs 21:3.[25] Even though Manasseh's cultic policies made him responsible for the exile of Judah (cf. 21:10–15; 23:26) the judgment formula against him does not refer to "his father Ahab," as one might expect if an explicit comparison was meant to be drawn.[26] Moreover, there is no text that proclaims the end of the Davidic dynasty, and no corresponding fulfillment notice, as for the house of Omri and Ahab.

This evidence suggests that the Deuteronomistic redactors either favored the promise to David over the prophecy of Elijah or could not resolve their relationship within the narrative framework with which they operated. It may also reflect their Judean bias or convictions about the Davidic dynasty, perhaps influenced by the unresolved situation of the exiled king Jehoiachin, as reported in 25:27–30. Is there a hint here of a future return for Jehoiachin or his descendants, or is the intention to draw a parallel with Mephibosheth, the last member of the house of Saul? In arranging for Mephibosheth to eat always at the royal table, David is able to keep him powerless under surveillance (2 Sam 9:1–13; 19:24–30). Chronicles is able to avoid the difficulty by constructing a new narrative that does not include the prophecy of Elijah. In my judgment, 2 Chr 36 hints at the future of the Davidic dynasty beyond the exile, and these hints are made explicit in Ezra 1–3. That is, Jehoiachin/Jeconiah was taken to Babylon along with the sacred vessels from the temple (2 Chr 36:10), there to beget Shealtiel, who in turn begot Zerubbabel (1 Chr 3:16–19). After the fulfillment of Jeremiah's prophecy on the duration of the exile, Cyrus decreed that the exiles could return and build God's house in Jerusalem (2 Chr 36:22–23). According to Ezra 2:1–2; 3:8, Zerubbabel joined the returnees who brought back the sacred vessels. Because of the close connection forged between the Davidic

---

24. Following *THAT* 1:718, I take the term "all the days" (*kol-hayyāmîm*) to mean forever or for all time.

25. Sweeney, *I and II Kings*, 343.

26. The judgment formulas for Judean kings consistently compare them with their ancestor David.

dynasty and the Jerusalem temple in Chronicles, the renewal of temple worship would, ipso facto, include the restoration of the dynasty's rule.[27]

If the story of the house of David and the house of Omri and Ahab created a conflict between competing prophecies in the Deuteronomistic History, the story of Josiah in 2 Kgs 22–23 created a conflict between prophecy and deuteronomic law. The prophecy of Huldah in 2 Kgs 22:15–20, particularly the reference to Josiah's death and burial in verses 18–20, is complex and much debated. Whether one judges that the prophecy was composed as a *vaticinium ex eventu* or that an earlier version was revised to incorporate Josiah's untimely death, the present text of 2 Kgs 22:18–20 conflicts with Deuteronomy's reward-punishment theology (act-consequence connection).[28] Deuteronomy repeatedly insists that obedience to its commands will ensure a long, prosperous, and peaceful life in the land. According to the Deuteronomistic History, Josiah acted blamelessly, secured centrality of worship in accord with Deuteronomy, and carried out an extensive reform that was in accord with deuteronomic requirements. Yet he died a violent death at the hands of Pharaoh Neco. The corresponding version of Josiah's death in 2 Chr 35:20–27 also exposes the inadequacy of the text in Kings. The Chronicler, apparently borrowing elements from the story of Ahab in 2 Chr 18 (cf. 1 Kgs 22), constructed an account in accord with the act-consequence connection.

The case of Josiah allows for a final brief comment on two other texts that point to a similar limitation in the Deuteronomistic History. One is the narrative of Solomon's infidelities and Ahijah of Shiloh's announcement of the division of his kingdom. The Deuteronomistic History accounts for the historical fact that the schism did not occur in Solomon's day by having Ahijah proclaim the "delay" as a reward for David's loyalty (1 Kgs 11:34; also 11:12). However, 1 Kgs 11:14–25 indicates that a later hand thought this was inadequate, and so prefaced the story of Jeroboam's

---

27. Sara Japhet discerns a reticence in Chronicles about the fate of the dynasty that "may point to one of his most compelling convictions; an expectation of a renewal of the Davidic monarchy" (*I and II Chronicles*, 1072).

28. For the former, see Michael Putsch, "Prophetess of Doom: Hermeneutical Reflections on the Huldah Oracle (2 Kings 22)," in *Soundings in Kings: Perspectives and Methods in Contemporary Scholarship* (ed. Mark Leuchter and Klaus-Peter Adam; Minneapolis: Fortress, 2010), 71–80. For the latter, see Campbell and O'Brien *Unfolding the Deuteronomistic History*, 458–61.

rise with reports of trouble in the days of Solomon.[29] The act-consequence connection could be applied to Solomon, but at the price of some conflict with God's speech in 1 Kgs 11:9–13 and Ahijah's prophecy in 11:31–39. The other is the story of the prophet Micaiah ben Imlah and Ahab in 1 Kgs 22. The king's violent death puts the story in conflict with the preceding prophecy of Elijah and the "other" report of Ahab's death in 1 Kgs 22:40. According to the former (1 Kgs 21:27–29), God rewarded Ahab's repentance by delaying the punishment pronounced against him until his son's days (cf. Solomon and Rehoboam). For its part, the latter is the standard Deuteronomistic History reference to a king's peaceful death and is thus in keeping with Elijah's prophecy.[30]

What is interesting about the above examples is that, like the texts with which they clash, they make use of the prophecy-fulfillment schema in order to lend authority to their presentation of deuteronomic torah theology. Both employ the same or similar form but the result stretches the narrative form of the Deuteronomistic History to the point where it is in danger of no longer being an ongoing story but parallel or competing stories. The particular narrative form constructed by the Deuteronomistic editors had reached its limits. Nevertheless, this provided a stimulus for further creativity, in which good use was made of the existing narrative. One example is 1–2 Chronicles, a new narrative that was constructed with a focus that enabled it to avoid the conflicts within the Deuteronomistic History. Another is the prophetic book that developed various forms of prophetic speech, enabling its authors to explore and incorporate in one book more theological territory than the narrative form. Prophetic story and the prophecy-fulfillment schema are used selectively in prophetic books to enhance the prophetic word rather than to provide the setting for a prophetic word, as in the Deuteronomistic History, and thereby to impose limitations on its scope. Examples of this are the "biography" of Hosea in Hos 1–3, the story of Assyrian crisis in Isa 36–39 (cf. 2 Kgs 18–20) and the

---

29. See Campbell and O'Brien, *Unfolding the Deuteronomistic History*, 369.

30. The LXX arrangement of 1 Kgs 20–22 solves one of these problems. The story of Naboth's vineyard (MT 1 Kgs 21), in which Ahab sins, is sentenced, and then repents and receives a reprieve, is placed first. It is then followed by the LXX version of MT 1 Kgs 20, in which Ahab sins (again) and receives a sentence, but remains unrepentant. The story of his punishment by death in 1 Kgs 22 forms the logical conclusion to this sequence. This still leaves the clash with Ahab's death notice. Such a rearrangement could not be made in the cases of Josiah and Solomon.

so-called "passion of Jeremiah" in Jer 37–44. Another more important connection with the Deuteronomistic History is the way most of the prophetic books are linked via superscriptions to the reigns of respective kings. In this way, as was argued earlier for the book of Hosea, they become part of the ongoing story of Israel.[31] Prophetic stories and prophetic books thus combine to form a larger story of prophecy. The story is limited because literary forms are limited, as are the prophets, their support groups, the Deuteronomists, and others who shaped and reshaped them. The story is somewhat uneven in places, with evidence of disagreements and issues unresolved, once again because of human limitations and our inability to explain all the vicissitudes of history within a given framework. It is also unfinished because it is part of the ongoing story of Israel and humanity.

---

31. Ehud Ben Zvi points as well to textual and thematic connections ("The Prophets").

Prophets in the Deuteronomic History and the Book of Chronicles: A Reassessment

Raymond F. Person Jr.

The current consensus model states that the relationship between the Deuteronomistic History and the book of Chronicles is sequential, with the Deuteronomistic History preserving preexilic and exilic materials, using standard biblical Hebrew, serving as the primary source for the later book of Chronicles, which is a major postexilic revision of Samuel–Kings and other sources in the language of late biblical Hebrew. Thus, any place where the book of Chronicles lacks material found in Samuel–Kings must be a deliberate omission of the earlier material, any place with unique material must be an addition, and any place where the wording in parallel passages differs must be a deliberate substitution of the earlier material, all of which betray the distinctive theology of the Chronicler.

In *The Deuteronomic History and the Book of Chronicles: Scribal Works in an Oral World*, I directly challenge this consensus, concluding rather that the Deuteronomic History and the book of Chronicles are contemporary historiographies that were produced by different scribal guilds that nevertheless have a common institutional ancestor in the Deuteronomic school of the Babylonian exile.[1] The split occurred when the Deuteronomic school returned to Jerusalem with Zerubbabel to provide scribal support for the rebuilding of the temple and its cult, leaving what became the Chronistic school in Babylon. These two schools continued to interpret their common source in ways that are quite similar to the ways oral traditions develop, with multiformity as a characteristic, thereby producing the two contemporary historiographies. Then the two schools with

---

1. Raymond F. Person Jr., *The Deuteronomic History and the Book of Chronicles: Scribal Works in an Oral World* (SBLAIL 6; Atlanta: Society of Biblical Literature, 2010).

their different historiographies came into contact later, when Ezra and other Chronistic scribes returned to Jerusalem.[2]

As is evident from the study of oral traditions, what from our modern, highly literate perspective may seem to constitute theological and historical differences may be understood from the perspective of the ancient Israelites as remaining within the boundaries of the broader theological tradition.[3] Such multiformity is a characteristic of oral traditions and literatures with roots in primarily oral societies such as ancient Israel and, therefore, does not require us to postulate significantly conflicting theologies between the Deuteronomic and the Chronistic schools. In fact, such multiformity is widely accepted as a characteristic of the Hebrew Bible's textual history. Rather than demonstrating conflicting theologies, the literature of both these schools—that is, the Deuteronomic History and the book of Chronicles—may best be understood as two instantiations of the broader tradition of which they both remain faithful, yet incomplete, representations. In *The Deuteronomic School and the Book of Chronicles* I provide discussions of numerous passages, both synoptic and nonsynoptic, in which I contrast my reading of the passages as faithful representations of this tradition with readings based on the consensus model.[4]

In this essay, I extend the arguments made in my monograph by applying them to the portrayal of prophecy in these two literary works. The consensus model leads to conclusions that the portrayal of prophecy in these works differs significantly, based on the assumption that the deliberate changes made by the Chronicler to Samuel–Kings as his source reflect his different theological stance towards prophecy. Below I will explore the implications of my own approach to the question of the portrayal of prophecy in these two historiographies. I will demonstrate that it is quite possible that from the perspective of the ancient Israelites the portrayal of prophecy in these works does not require the interpretation that the respective scribal schools had significantly variant understandings of prophecy and its role in ancient Israel.

---

2. Person, *Deuteronomic History*.

3. In *Deuteronomic History*, I drew extensively from the Parry/Lord approach to oral traditions. For an excellent introduction to this approach as applied to ancient epics, see especially John Miles Foley, "Analogues: Modern Oral Epic," in *A Companion to Ancient Epic* (ed. John Miles Foley; Oxford: Blackwell, 2005), 196–212.

4. My conclusion is quite similar to that of Ehud Ben Zvi. See his "Are There Any Bridges Out There?"

Prophets in the Deuteronom(ist)ic History and the Book of Chronicles: Previous Studies

I will critique four recent studies by Yairah Amit, William Schniedewind, Pancratius Beentjes, and Gary Knoppers, all of whom assume the consensus model of the relationship of the Deuteronomistic History and the book of Chronicles.[5] Although there are subtle differences between them, they all conclude that the literary portrayal of prophets in Chronicles diverges from the understanding of classical prophecy as portrayed in Samuel–Kings, reflecting a postexilic understanding of prophecy. This divergent understanding includes a more expansive understanding of prophecy beyond what Schniedewind calls "traditional prophets" and what Amit and Knoppers call "professional prophets." Amit concludes, "By depriving the prophets of their exclusive mediation in the Deuteronomistic manner, the Chronicler was able to extend it to any devout person."[6] Schniedewind concludes, "Chr also allows for a new kind of prophecy, a prophecy not by prophets, but by ad hoc inspired messengers, who come not only from the cultic ranks but also include a military officer and a foreign king."[7] Beentjes concludes, "The majority of the prophets and inspired messengers we met in the book of Chronicles have been 'invented' by the Chronicler and should therefore be characterized as 'literary personages' rather than historical persons."[8] Knoppers concludes, "Professional prophets do not enjoy a monopoly on divine revelation."[9]

In their attempt to contrast the portrayals of prophets and prophecy, they identify various elements that together build up to their conclusions. Below I will carefully critique two of these elements—that is, (1) that Chronicles does not include prophets working miracles, and (2) that Chronicles does not include references to groups or schools of prophets—demonstrating that these contrasts actually depend on material that is

---

5. Amit, "Role of Prophecy"; Schniedewind, "Prophets and Prophecy"; Pancratius Beentjes, "Prophets in the Book of Chronicles," in *The Elusive Prophet: The Prophet as a Historical Person, Literary Character, and Anonymous Artist* (ed. Johannes C. de Moor; Leiden: Brill, 2001), 45–53; and Gary N. Knoppers, "Democratizing Revelation? Prophets, Seers, and Visionaries in Chronicles," in *Prophecy and Prophets in Ancient Israel* (ed. John Day; London: Continuum, 2010), 391–409.

6. Amit, "Role of Prophecy," 95.
7. Schniedewind, "Prophets and Prophecy," 222.
8. Beentjes, "Prophets," 53.
9. Knoppers, "Democratizing Revelation?" 398.

unique to Samuel–Kings. I will then explore further their basic conclusion concerning the expansive definition of prophecy in Chronicles, and show that their conclusions also apply to the Deuteronomic History, so that the contrast that they strive to maintain is based on a selective reading of the Deuteronomic History.

No Miracles or Signs

Amit concludes, "In creating his new image of the prophet, the Chronicler removed ... the prophet's ability to perform miracles."[10] Similarly Beentjes concludes, "Whereas in the Book of Kings the narrative on Ahijah, Elijah, Elisha and others commonly included miraculous elements ... in the Book of Chronicles the ministry of the prophets is nowhere described in terms of ecstasy, miracles or political dimensions."[11] Similarly, Knoppers concludes, "Unlike Elijah and Elisha in the Book of Kings, seers in Chronicles do not initiate any miracles.... The Chronicler's own prophets perform no signs, wonders, symbolic actions or portents."[12]

These conclusions clearly demonstrate their assumptions based on the consensus model, for the material that they are contrasting with Chronicles is unique to Kings. Although Ahijah is mentioned in both Kings and Chronicles in a fulfillment citation (1 Kgs 12:15//2 Chr 10:15), the contrast they draw regarding Ahijah only pertains to the unique material found in 1 Kgs 11:29–39; 14:1–20.[13] Although Chronicles includes a reference to Elijah in some of its unique material (2 Chr 21:12–15), the contrast they draw regarding Elijah only pertains to the unique material found in 1 Kgs 17–19; 21; 2 Kgs 1–2. Since Elisha is not mentioned at all in Chronicles, this contrast only concerns unique material in 2 Kgs 3–8; 13.[14]

---

10. Amit, "Role of Prophecy," 92.
11. Beentjes, "Prophets," 45.
12. Knoppers, "Democratizing Revelation?" 401.
13. For my fuller discussion of 1 Kgs 14:1–20, see Person, *Deuteronomic History*, 140–44.
14. For a fuller discussion of the Elijah and Elisha narratives in the context of 1 Kgs 16:23–2 Kgs 14:16, see Julio C. Trebolle, "The Different Textual Forms of MT and LXX in Kings and the Deuteronomistic Composition and Redaction of These Books," paper presented at the annual meeting of the Society of Biblical Literature, New Orleans, November 2009. For my own brief discussion based on Trebolle, see Person, *Deuteronomic History*, 115–21.

Obviously, Amit, Beentjes, and Knoppers are assuming that the Chronicler omitted this material. Another perspective could be the approach advocated by Graeme Auld—that is, that material unique in both Samuel-Kings and Chronicles was added to a common source.[15] If one takes this tack, then one might conclude that the later redactors of Kings added material emphasizing the roles of prophets working miracles, and that Chronicles' portrayal therefore remains closer to that of the common source.[16]

In my opinion, both of the above perspectives—that is, that of Amit, Beentjes, and Knoppers, and the hypothetical approach similar to Auld's—make the same mistake by assuming a unilinear process of textual development that is completely removed from its primarily oral context. When one understands that every text in the ancient world was necessarily an imperfect instantiation of a broader tradition preserved in the interplay of all of the texts recording that tradition and, more importantly, the tradition as preserved in the collective memory of the community, one must allow for a range of multiformity within that broader tradition. This multiformity will be evident between any two texts that record that tradition, even if they are understood to be faithful representations from the perspective of the ancients. Therefore, for example, one should not conclude that the Chronistic school rejected the portrayal of Elijah and other prophets working miracles, simply because it did not record that part of the tradition. The Chronistic school certainly was aware of the Elijah tradition (2 Chr 21:12-15) and may have had no problem with the idea of prophets working miracles. Likewise, one should not conclude that the Deuteronomic school emphasized Elijah's miracles (and therefore those of other prophets) by adding something unique to the text at a later time. Such "additions" may have existed in the broader tradition preserved in

---

15. My own approach to the Deuteronomic History and the book of Chronicles builds upon Auld's approach but, as I will explain below, there are significant differences based on my understanding of the important role of multiformity in the broader tradition. For his most expansive presentation of his argument, see A. Graeme Auld, *Kings without Privilege: David and Moses in the Story of the Bible's Kings* (Edinburgh: T&T Clark, 1994). For a more recent contribution that most directly relates to the topic of this essay, see A. Graeme Auld, "Prophets Shared—But Recycled," in *The Future of the Deuteronomistic History* (ed. Thomas Römer; BETL 147; Leuven: Leuven University Press, 2000), 19–28.

16. Interestingly, Auld himself does not reach this conclusion in his "Prophets Shared—But Recycled." Rather, he reaches a similar conclusion to the one I give below.

the collective memory of the community for a long time. Therefore, from the perspective of the ancients, they may have been in no way "additions," but simply written recordings of things that had been a part of the tradition for a long time. Therefore, although from our modern perspective it may be tempting to conclude that such multiformity in the tradition necessarily represents conflicting theological understandings of the prophets and prophecy, we should not do so too readily.

No Prophetic Schools/Groups

Amit concludes, "The professional bands of 'sons of prophets' or the institution of court prophets, which feature in the Deuteronomistic sources, are absent from the book of Chronicles."[17] Likewise, Knoppers concludes, "Chronicles does not normally speak of schools of prophets, professional prophetic training, prophetic membership within a certain Israelite tribe or of prophetic bloodlines within a given tribal phratry."[18] Although Amit does not provide references, Knoppers footnotes his comment by saying, "Groups of בני נביאים do not appear (cf. 1 Kgs 20.35; 2 Kgs 2.5,7,15; 4.1,38; 5.22; 6.1; 9.1)."[19]

Since all of these references refer to material that is unique to Kings, we can once again see that Amit and Knoppers are simply assuming that the Chronicler omitted this material due to his theological position, and that the opposite conclusion based on an approach similar to that advocated by Auld could be made—that is, that the Deuteronomic school added this material for its own theological purposes. As I argued above, however, these are not the only two positions. In fact, the preferred response would be to accept that such multiformity was a characteristic of the broader tradition, so that these "additions" in Kings are not really "additions" to the tradition itself, but simply the writing down of earlier material preserved in the tradition. Furthermore, what may appear to be a conflict between Kings and Chronicles is not necessarily one, since the tradition valued multiformity.

---

17. Amit, "Role of Prophecy," 85.
18. Knoppers, "Democratizing Revelation?" 399–400.
19. Ibid., 400 n. 29.

The Expansive Definition of Prophecy

Above I provided quotes from all four scholars when appropriate. Here I will simply quote Knoppers more fully, because I think his position incorporates the perspective of the earlier scholars' work. Knoppers concludes as follows:[20]

> Chronicles depicts a wide variety of prophets, prophetesses, seers, men of God and visionaries at work in Israelite history. The prophetic work includes both delivering oracles and writing compositions. Many are prophets by vocation, but others are *pro tem* prophets, who speak on behalf of God to address a need on a certain occasion. These include priests, Levites, a layperson and even foreign monarchs. Professional prophets do not enjoy a monopoly on divine revelation.

Although this characterization of Chronicles is certainly accurate, its rhetorical force sets up what is from my perspective a false contrast between Chronicles and the Deuteronomic History. All four of these scholars are interested in demonstrating how, in Amit's words, the Chronicler has "creat[ed] his new image of the prophet"[21] or how, in Beentjes' words, the prophets "have been 'invented' by the Chronicler."[22] In contrast, I want to take Knoppers's own words in this conclusion and demonstrate how his words also apply to the Deuteronomic History, thereby undercutting the rhetorical force of the contrastive aspect of the conclusion.

"*Chronicles depicts a wide variety of prophets, prophetesses, seers, men of God and visionaries at work in Israelite history.*" In contrast to the other three, Knoppers is more explicit about the similarities between Chronicles and Deuteronomy; in fact, he concludes that "the [Chronicler's] presentation of prophecy is, in some respects, closer to Deuteronomy than is the presentation of Samuel–Kings."[23] He writes as follows:[24]

> First, the Chronicler endorses the Deuteronomic reaction against some traditional forms of prophetic activity, which are deemed abhorrent to Yahweh. Secondly, he adopts the Deuteronomic definition of a prophet

---

20. Ibid., 398.
21. Amit, "Role of Prophecy," 92.
22. Beentjes, "Prophets," 53.
23. Knoppers, "Democratizing Revelation?" 399.
24. Ibid., 393.

as a mouthpiece of God. Thirdly, he takes quite seriously the promise of Moses that Yahweh would raise up prophets like Moses to follow him.

However, the rhetorical force of "a wide variety of prophets, prophetesses, seers, men of God and visionaries" could give the false impression that a similar wide variety does not exist in the Deuteronomic History. The Deuteronomic History also includes prophets (Nathan in 1 Kgs 1:8), prophetesses (Deborah in Jdgs 4:4; Huldah in 2 Kgs 22:14), seers (Gad in 2 Sam 24:11), men of God (Shemaiah in 1 Kgs 12:22), and visionaries (Nathan in 2 Sam 7:17). In fact, both the Deuteronomic History and the book of Chronicles include the full range of Hebrew terms for intermediation.[25] Thus, such "wide variety" actually demonstrates their similarities, not their differences.

"*The prophetic work includes both delivering oracles and writing compositions.*" The one example to illustrate this conclusion is given by Knoppers: "When Elijah prophesies in Chronicles, he writes a letter."[26] He then notes that "Willi, Fishbane, Day, Mason and others have commented on the intertextual nature of much post-exilic prophecy."[27] This observation is consistent with the consensus model that assumes that the Chronicler is reinterpreting scripture, especially Samuel–Kings, but that the Deuteronomistic History is early enough that such a description is anachronistic.[28] Thus, a contrast is drawn between the Deuteronomistic History and the book of Chronicles, suggesting that writing as a medium is more important in Chronicles than in the earlier Deuteronomistic History.

I address this false dichotomy more fully in *The Deuteronomic History and the Book of Chronicles*.[29] Here I will note first the primarily oral nature of prophecy, then where this dichotomy requires one to overlook the role of written texts within the Deuteronomic History. I agree with Martti Nissinen that prophecy is a strictly oral phenomenon: "From the point of view of the process of communication … the communication was considered finished when the message was received and heard."[30]

---

25. Similarly, Auld, "Prophets Shared—But Recycled," 26.
26. Knoppers, "Democratizing Revelation?" 401.
27. Ibid., 402.
28. See also Schniedewind, "Prophets and Prophecy," 221; Beentjes, "Prophets," 51.
29. See Person, *Deuteronomic History*, especially ch. 2.
30. Nissinen, "How Prophecy Became Literature," 169.

Anything beyond the original oral message must be considered interpretation of that prophecy.[31]

> The physical restrictions alone—the writing speed, the dimensions of the writing material, etc.—prevented the verbatim memorization of the spoken words of the prophet, and this was not even attempted. Hence, and according to the usual laws of communication, the interpretation began immediately when the word came out of the prophet's mouth.

Thus, Nissinen rejects the notion of literate prophets—at least as a general phenomenon—and suggests that such portrayals of prophets should be understood as scribal interpretations of an oral phenomenon. Of course, he is well aware of the use of writing as a means of conveying a prophetic message long distances (for example, the Mari letters). However, he argues that when writing was involved in conveying prophetic messages, professional scribes would have written the messages rather than the prophets themselves, as is illustrated in Jeremiah's dictation of the letter to the exiles to the scribe Baruch (Jer 36).

If prophecy is a strictly oral phenomenon, then both the Deuteronomic History and the book of Chronicles vary from that reality in their portrayals. Both understand Moses as prophet and writer. Moreover, the Deuteronomic History portrays Samuel the prophet as writing a book (1 Sam 10:25). Both also associate Huldah the prophetess with the authentication of the lawbook (2 Kgs 22–23//2 Chr 34–35).[32] However, I am unconvinced that either work portrays Elijah as literate, although I can see why someone might conclude otherwise. In 1 Kgs 18:18, Elijah makes a reference to "the commandments of the Lord," clearly referring to the law of Moses. In 1 Chr 21:12–13, Jehoram receives a "letter from Elijah the prophet." Both of these passages could be interpreted so that Elijah is a literate prophet who reads the law of Moses and writes his own letters. However, this interpretation is not necessary.[33] In my opinion, a better interpretation would be that Elijah's knowledge of the law of Moses would not

---

31. Ibid.

32. For a fuller discussion of 2 Kgs 22–23//2 Chr 34–35, see Person, *Deuteronomic History*, 121–25.

33. This interpretation is suggested by Schniedewind in his reading of Chronicles. For example, he argues that Zechariah's reference to the "commandments of the Lord" (2 Chr 24:20) indicates a reference to the written law ("Prophets and Prophecy," 221). However, since he wishes to draw a contrast between Chronicles and the Deu-

necessarily require reading abilities, since he could have become familiar with its public recitation or had some direct knowledge of it as a prophet, and since Elijah's prophetic message was recorded in a letter that was sent to Jehoram (much like Jeremiah's letter to the exiles in Jer 36). But no matter which interpretation of Elijah one favors, both the Deuteronomic History and the book of Chronicles portray some prophets as having some relationship to written texts, as authors, readers, or authenticators. Thus, I find no significant contrast here between them.

"*Many are prophets by vocation, but others are pro tem prophets, who speak on behalf of God to address a need on a certain occasion. These include priests, Levites, a layperson and even foreign monarchs.*" Although the Deuteronomic History may not have the exact same list of pro tem prophets, it nevertheless has what Schniedewind called "ad hoc messengers." Although Schniedewind insists that the Chronicler made "a sharp distinction between traditional prophets and the ad hoc inspired figures or 'messengers,'"[34] Knoppers more carefully avoids such distinctions in favor of arguing as follows:[35] "The point is not that priests, Levites and laypersons are all prophets. Rather, it is that characters who are not prophets may be employed by Yahweh to fulfill (temporarily) the role of prophet for the larger good of the people, if the occasion warrants it." In my opinion, it is quite difficult to categorize all of those called "prophets" (and related terms) into one of these two categories—professional prophet and ad hoc/pro tem prophet—on the basis of the information given. Let me provide two examples to illustrate this difficulty, both of which are found in synoptic materials. We know virtually nothing about "Shemaiah the man of God" (1 Kgs 12:22//2 Chr 12:5,15) and "Huldah the prophetess" (2 Kgs 22:14//2 Chr 34:22). Based on such little information, how can we conclude that they necessarily are "professional prophets" and not "ad hoc prophets?" But even if we conclude that all who are called "prophets" (and related terms) in the Deuteronomic History are "professional prophets," we can still find those who serve prophetic functions who must be understood as "ad hoc prophets." Schniedewind draws a distinction between "traditional prophets," whose titles are "prophet," "seer," and "man of God" and the "ad hoc prophets" who lack the prophetic titles but are identified

---

teronomistic History, he does not provide any reference to Elijah making the same reference in Kings.

34. Schniedewind, "Prophets and Prophecy," 204.
35. Knoppers, "Democratizing Revelation?" 397–98.

by the "possession formula"—that is, "the 'spirit (רוח)' moving upon an individual and inspiring that individual to prophesy."[36] If this is an acceptable definition of an "ad hoc prophet," then the Deuteronomic History also includes such "ad hoc prophets," including Saul's messengers (1 Sam 19:20), Saul himself (1 Sam 19:23), and David (2 Sam 23:2). In fact, Knoppers argues that in Chronicles both Necho (2 Chr 35:20-22) and Cyrus (2 Chr 36:22-23) function as temporary prophets.[37] But in the same way, Sennacherib may be understood as a temporary prophet in Kings, because of the possession formula: "I myself will put a spirit in him [Sennacherib], so that he shall hear a rumor and return to his own land" (2 Kgs 19:7). Thus, even though the lists of ad hoc prophets in the Deuteronomic History and the book of Chronicles contain different laypersons and foreign monarchs, both works contain a similar range of prophets, both professional and temporary. Thus, Knoppers's conclusion—"*Professional prophets do not enjoy a monopoly on divine revelation*"—applies equally well to the Deuteronomic History and to Chronicles.

Historiographical Writing as Prophecy

As an extension of their arguments that the Chronicler expanded the understanding of prophecy, Amit, Schniedewind, and Knoppers also suggest that the Chronicler's own self-understanding may have been related to prophecy as a written phenomenon. Amit concludes, "His [the Chronicler's] method of treating the prophets' visions and teachings as important historical sources indicates his intention of endowing his work with prophetic authority."[38] Schniedewind concludes, "It is quite possible that Chr saw himself in a role similar to his inspired messengers."[39] Knoppers concludes:

> The inspired exposition and explication of scripture also appears as a form of prophecy. God may speak through the exegesis and application of a written word by an authoritative interpreter. God continues to deliver his word, but does so employing a variety of speakers, contexts,

---

36. Schniedewind, "Prophets and Prophecy," 216.
37. Knoppers, "Democratizing Revelation?" 398.
38. Amit, "Role of Prophecy," 96.
39. Schniedewind, "Prophets and Prophecy," 222.

and forms. Indeed, the Chronicler may have thought of his own writing as participating in this larger interpretative prophetic tradition.[40]

In "How Prophecy Became Literature," Nissinen makes a distinction between "ancient Hebrew prophecy" and "biblical prophecy," respectively, a distinction between the strictly oral phenomenon behind the text and the interpretive portrayal of prophecy in biblical texts.[41] Although the prophetic messages in "ancient Hebrew prophecy" could be written down, as illustrated by Jeremiah's or Elijah's letters ("written prophecy"), "biblical prophecy" is a form of "literary prophecy"—that is, "literature that reinterprets earlier written records of prophecy, transcending the original proclamation situations and recontextualizing them in other contexts."[42]

If my interpretation of the Deuteronomic History in the context of a postexilic Deuteronomic school is accurate, then the Deuteronomic History, like Chronicles, is "literary prophecy." That is, both literary works reinterpret their sources, including prophetic narratives, for the new context of the Second Temple. Even if my interpretation is inaccurate, the consensus model's understanding of the redaction history of the Deuteronomistic History (whether Dtr[1] and Dtr[2] or DtrG, DtrP, and DtrN) also understands the later redactions as updating the source materials for a new context. Hence, I do not see a reason to conclude that "the Chronicler may have thought of his own writing as participating in this larger interpretative prophetic tradition," but not the Deuteronomist(s). From what I have presented above, the various contrasts that Amit, Schniedewind, Beentkes, and Knoppers strive to draw between the Deuteronomic History and the book of Chronicles do not stand up to close scrutiny once one no longer accepts the consensus model's assumptions about such a contrast and once one takes seriously the important role of multiformity in oral traditions and in texts produced in primarily oral societies like ancient Israel. Thus, both the Deuteronomic History and the book of Chronicles are best understood as two instantiations of a broader tradition in which ancient Hebrew prophecy was reinterpreted within competing scribal guilds, but that their portrayals of prophecy are both faithful rep-

---

40. Knoppers, "Democratizing Revelation?" 405.
41. Nissinen, "How Prophecy Became Literature," 166.
42. Martti Nissinen, "Comparing Prophetic Sources: Principles and a Test Case." in *Prophecy and Prophets in Ancient Israel* (ed. John Day; London: Continuum, 2010), 19.

resentations of the broader traditions' interpretation of the importance of prophets and prophecy in the monarchic period and in their own time.

Thus I conclude, paraphrasing closely Knoppers's conclusion, but expanding it to include both works: the Deuteronomic History and the book of Chronicles depict a wide variety of prophets, prophetesses, seers, men of God, and visionaries at work in Israelite history. The prophetic work includes both delivered oracles and written compositions. Many are prophets by vocation, but others are pro tem prophets, who speak on behalf of God to address a need on a certain occasion. These include various laypersons and possibly even foreign monarchs. Professional prophets do not enjoy a monopoly on divine revelation.

Bibliography

Ackerman, James S. "Prophecy and Warfare in Early Israel: A Study of the Deborah-Barak Story." *BASOR* 220 (1975): 5–13.

Amit, Yairah. *The Book of Judges: The Art of Editing*. Translated from Hebrew by J. Chipman. BibIntSer 38. Leiden: Brill, 1999.

———. "The Role of Prophecy and Prophets in the Chronicler's World." Pages 80–101 in *Prophets, Prophecy, and Prophetic Texts in Second Temple Judaism*. Edited by Michael H. Floyd and Robert D. Haak. LHBOTS, 427. London: T&T Clark, 2006.

Andersen, Francis I., and David Noel Freedman. *Hosea*. AB 24. Garden City: Doubleday, 1980.

Auld, A. Graeme. "The Deuteronomist and the Former Prophets, or 'What Makes the Former Prophets Deuteronomistic'?" Pages 116–26 in *Those Elusive Deuteronomists: The Phenomenon of Pan-Deuteronomism*. Edited by Linda S. Schearing and Steven L. McKenzie. JSOTSup 268. Sheffield: Sheffield Academic Press, 1999.

———. *Kings without Privilege: David and Moses in the Story of the Bible's Kings*. Edinburgh: T&T Clark, 1994.

———. "Prophets Shared—But Recycled." Pages 19–28 in *The Future of the Deuteronomistic History*. Edited by Thomas Römer. BETL 147. Leuven: Leuven University Press, 2000.

———. "Prophets through the Looking Glass: Between Writing and Moses." *JSOT* 2 (1983): 3–23.

Avioz, Michael. *Nathan's Oracle (2 Samuel 7) and Its Interpreters*. Bible in History. Bern: Peter Lang, 2005.

Baden, Joel S. "The Violent Origins of the Levites." Pages 103–16 in *Levites and Priests in Biblical History and Tradition*. Edited by Mark Leuchter and Jeremy M. Hutton. SBLAIL 9. Atlanta: Society of Biblical Literature, 2011.

Barstad, Hans M. "*Comparere necesse est?* Ancient Israelite and Ancient Near Eastern Prophecy in a Comparative Perspective." Pages 3–11 in *Prophecy in Its Ancient Near Eastern Context: Mesopotamian, Biblical, Arabian*

Perspectives. Edited by Martti Nissinen. SBLSymS 13. Atlanta: Society of Biblical Literature, 2000.

———. "Some Remarks on Prophets and Prophecy in 'The Deuteronomistic History." Pages 300–15 in *Houses Full of All Good Things: Essays in Memory of Timo Veijola*. Edited by Juha Pakkala and Martti Nissinen. PFES 95. Göttingen: Vandenhoeck & Ruprecht, 2008.

———. "The Understanding of the Prophets in Deuteronomy." *SJOT* 8 (1994): 236–51.

Barton, John. *Joel and Obadiah: A Commentary*. OTL. Louisville: Westminster John Knox, 2001.

Becker, Uwe. *Richterzeit und Königtum: Redaktionsgeschichtliche Studien zum Richterbuch*. BZAW 192. Berlin: de Gruyter, 1990.

Beentjes, Pancratius. "Prophets in the Book of Chronicles." Pages 45–53 in *The Elusive Prophet: The Prophet as a Historical Person, Literary Character and Anonymous Artist*. Edited by Johannes C. de Moor. Leiden: Brill, 2001.

Begg, Christopher. "The Non-Mention of Amos, Hosea, and Micah in the Deuteronomistic History." *BN* 32 (1986): 41–53.

Bellinger, William H. Jr. *Psalmody and Prophecy*. JSOTSup 27. Sheffield: JSOT Press, 1984.

Ben Zvi, Ehud. "Are There Any Bridges Out There? How Wide Was the Conceptual Gap between the Deuteronomistic History and Chronicles?" Pages 59–86 in *Community Identity in Judean Historiography: Biblical and Comparative Perspectives*. Edited by Gary N. Knoppers and Kenneth A. Ristau. Winona Lake, Ind.: Eisenbrauns, 2009.

———. "Chronicles and Its Reshaping of Memories of Monarchic Period Prophets: Some Observations." In *Prophets and Prophecy in Ancient Israelite Historiography*. Edited by Mark Boda and Lissa Wray Beale. Winona Lake, Ind.: Eisenbrauns, 2013.

———. "Exploring the Memory of Moses the Prophet in Late Persian/Early Hellenistic Period Yehud/Judah." In *Remembering Biblical Figures in the Late Persian and Early Hellenistic Periods: Social Memory and Imagination*. Edited by Diana Edelman and Ehud Ben Zvi. Oxford: Oxford University Press, 2013.

———. "The Generic Prophets and Their Role in the Construction of the Image of the 'Prophets of Old' within the Postmonarchic Readership(s) of the Book of Kings." Pages 387–99 in *The Books of Kings: Sources, Composition, Historiography and Reception*. Edited by Baruch Levine and André Lemaire. VTSup 129. Leiden: Brill, 2010.

———. *A Historical-Critical Study of The Book of Obadiah*. BZAW 242. Berlin: de Gruyter, 1996.

———. *Hosea*. FOTL 21a.1. Grand Rapids: Eerdmans, 2005.

———. "Imagining Josiah's Book and the Implications of Imagining It in Early Persian Yehud." Pages 193–212 in *Berührungspunkte: Studien zur Sozial- und Religionsgeschichte Israels und seiner Umwelt*. Edited by R. Schmitt, I. Kottsieper, and J. Wöhrle. AOAT 250. Münster: Ugarit, 2008.

———. "Josiah and the Prophetic Books: Some Observations." Pages 47–64 in *Good Kings and Bad Kings*. Edited by Lester L. Grabbe. LHBOTS 393. EABS 5. London: T&T Clark, 2005.

———. "Observations on Lines of Thought Concerning the Concepts of Prophecy and Prophets in Yehud, with an Emphasis on Deuteronomy–2 Kings and Chronicles." Pages 1–19 in *Words, Ideas, Worlds: Biblical Essays in Honour of Yairah Amit*. Edited by Athalya Brenner and Frank H. Polak. Sheffield: Sheffield Phoenix, 2012.

———. "The Prophetic Book: A Key Form of Prophetic Literature." Pages 276–97 in *The Changing Face of Form Criticism for the Twenty-First Century*. Edited by Marvin A. Sweeney and Ehud Ben Zvi. Grand Rapids: Eerdmans, 2003.

———. "Prophets and Prophecy in the Compositional and Redactional Notes in I–II Kings." *ZAW* 105 (1993): 331–51.

———. " 'The Prophets'—Generic Prophets and their Role in the Construction of the Image of 'Prophets of the Old' within the Postmonarchic Readership/s of the Book of Kings." *ZAW* 116 (2004): 555–67.

———. " 'The Prophets'—References to Generic Prophets and their Role in the Construction of the Image of the 'Prophets of Old' within the Postmonarchic Readership(s) of the Book of Kings" Pages 387–99 in *The Books of Kings: Sources, Composition, Historiography and Reception*. Edited by Baruch Levine and André Lemaire. VTSup 129. Leiden: Brill, 2010.

———. *Signs of Jonah: Reading and Rereading in Ancient Yehud*. JSOTSup 367. Sheffield: Sheffield Academic Press, 2003.

———. "Who Knew What? The Construction of the Monarchic Past in Chronicles and Implications for the Intellectual Setting of Chronicles." Pages 349–60 in *Judah and the Judeans in the Fourth Century B.C.E.* Edited by Oded Lipschits, Gary N. Knoppers, and Rainer Albertz. Winona Lake, Ind.: Eisenbrauns, 2007.

Ben Zvi, Ehud, and Michael H. Floyd, ed. *Writings and Speech in Israelite and Ancient Near Eastern Prophecy*. SBLSymS 10. Atlanta: Society of Biblical Literature, 2000.

Ben-Dov, Jonathan. "Some Precedents for the Religion of the Book: Josiah's Book and Ancient Revelatory Literature." Pages 43–62 in *Constructs of Prophecy in the Former and Latter Prophets and Other Texts*. Edited by Lester L. Grabbe and Martti Nissinen. SBLANEM 4. Atlanta: Society of Biblical Literature, 2011.

Bergen, Wesley J. *Elisha and the End of Prophetism*. JSOTSup 286. Sheffield: Sheffield Academic Press, 1999.

Berger, Peter L., and Thomas Luckmann. *The Social Construction of Reality: A Treatise in Sociology of Knowledge*. New York: Anchor, 1989.

Blenkinsopp, Joseph. *A History of Prophecy in Israel*. Rev. ed. Louisville: Westminster John Knox, 1996.

Blenkinsopp, Joseph, ed. *Prophecy and Canon: A Contribution to the Study of Jewish Origins*. CSJCA 3. Notre Dame: University of Notre Dame Press, 1977.

Blum, Erhard. *Die Komposition der Vätergeschichte*. WMANT 57. Neukirchen-Vluyn: Neukirchener, 1984.

———. "Der Prophet und das Verderben Israels: Eine ganzheitliche historisch-kritische Lektüre von 1 Reg. xviii–xix." *VT* 47 (1997): 277–92.

Boda, Mark J., and Lissa M. Wray Beal, eds. *Prophets, Prophecy, and Ancient Israelite Historiography*. Winona Lake, Ind.: Eisenbrauns, 2013.

Bodner, Keith. *1 Samuel: A Narrative Commentary*. Sheffield: Sheffield Phoenix, 2009.

Boling, Robert G. *Judges*. AB 6A. Garden City: Doubleday, 1975.

Bonnet, Corinne. "Dove vivono gli dei? Note sulla terminologia fenicio-punica dei luoghi di culto e sui modi di rappresentazione del mondo divino." Pages 673–85 in *Saturnia Tellus: Definizioni dello spazio consacrato in ambiente etrusco, italoci, fenicio-punico, iberico e celtico*. Edited by Xavier Dupré Raventós, Sergio Ribichini, and Stéphanie Verger. Roma: Consiglio nazionale delle ricerche, 2008.

Booker, Christopher. *The Seven Basic Plots: Why We Tell Stories*. London: Continuum, 2004.

Breytenbach, Andries. "Who Is Behind the Samuel Narrative?" Pages 50–61 in *Past, Present, Future: The Deuteronomistic History and the Prophets*. Edited by Johannes C. de Moor and Herrie F. van Rooy. OTS 44. Leiden: Brill, 2000.

Bronner, Leah L. *The Stories of Elijah and Elisha as Polemics against Baal Worship*. POS 6. Leiden: Brill, 1968.

Bunnens, Guy, John David Hawkins, and Isabelle Leirens, eds. *A New Luwian Stele and the Cult of the Storm-God at Til Barsib-Masuwari*. Tell Ahmar 2. Leuven: Peeters, 2006.

Buss, Martin J. "The Place of Israelite Prophecy in Human History." Pages 325–341 in *Israel's Prophets and Israel's Past: Essays on the Relationship of Prophetic Texts and Israelite History in Honor of John H. Hayes*. Edited by Brad E. Kelle and Megan Bishop Moore. LHBOTS 446. New York: T&T Clark, 2006.

Campbell, Antony F. *Of Prophets and Kings: A Late Ninth-Century Document (1 Samuel 12 Kings 10)*. CBQMS 17. Washington, D.C.: The Catholic Biblical Association of America, 1986.
Campbell, Antony F., and Mark A. O'Brien. *Unfolding the Deuteronomistic History: Origins, Upgrades, Present Text*. Minneapolis: Fortress, 2000.
Chapman, Stephen B. *The Law and the Prophets: A Study in Old Testament Canon Formation*. FAT 27. Tübingen: Mohr Siebeck, 2000.
Charpin, Dominique. "The Writing, Sending, and Reading of Letters in the Amorite World." Pages 400–417 in *The Babylonian World*. Edited by Gwendolyn Leick. New York: Routledge, 2007.
Charpin, Dominique, Francis Joannès, Sylvie Lackenbacher, and Bertrand Lafont, eds. *Archives épistolaires de Mari I/2*. ARM 26/2. Paris: Éditions Recherche sur les Civilisations, 1988.
Conrad, Edgar W. "The End of Prophecy and the Appearance of Angels/Messengers in the Book of the Twelve." *JSOT* 73 (1997): 65–79.
Cooley, Jeffrey L. "The Story of Saul's Election (1 Samuel 9–10) in the Light of Mantic Practice in Ancient Iraq." *JBL* 130 (2011): 247–61.
Cross, Frank M. *Canaanite Myth and Hebrew Epic*. Cambridge: Harvard University Press, 1973.
Cryer, Frederick H. *Divination in Ancient Israel and Its Near Eastern Environment: A Socio-Historical Investigation*. JSOTSup 142. Sheffield: Sheffield Academic Press, 1994.
Davies, T. Witton. *Magic, Divination, and Demonology among the Hebrews and their Neighbors*. London: James Clarde, 1898.
Dietrich, Walter. "Prophetie im deuteronomistischen Geschichtswerk." Pages 47–65 in *The Future of the Deuteronomistic History*. Edited by Thomas Römer. BETL 147. Leuven: Peeters, 2000.
———. *Prophetie und Geschichte*. FRLANT 108. Göttingen: Vandenhoeck & Ruprecht, 1972.
———. "Samuel—ein Prophet?" Pages 1–17 in *Prophets and Prophecy in Jewish and Early Christian Literature*. Edited by Joseph Verheyden, Korinna Zamfir, and Tobias Nicklas. WUNT 2/286. Tübingen: Mohr Siebeck, 2010.
Dozeman, Thomas B., Konrad Schmid, and Thomas Römer, eds. *Pentateuch, Hexateuch, or Enneateuch? Identifying Literary Works in Genesis through Kings*. SBLAIL 8. Atlanta: Society of Biblical Literature, 2011.
Duhm, Bernhard. *Das Buch Jeremia*. KHC 11. Tübingen: Mohr Siebeck, 1901.
———. *Israels Propheten*. Tübingen: Mohr, 1916.
———. *Die Theologie der Propheten als Grundlage für die innere Entwicklungsgeschichte der israelitischen Religion*. Bonn: Adolph Marcus, 1975.
Duke, William H. Jr., "Jeremiah 1:4–18." *Int* 59 (2005): 184–86.

Dumbrell, William J. "What Are You Doing Here? Elijah at Horeb." *Crux* 22 (1986): 12–19.

Durand, Jean-Marie. *Archives épistolaires de Mari I/1*. ARM 26/1. Paris: Éditions Recherche sur les Civilisations, 1988.

———. "Le *kispum* dans les traditions amorrites." Pages 33–52 in *Les vivants et leurs morts: Actes du colloque organisé par le Collège de France, Paris, les 14–15 avril 2010*. Edited by Jean-Marie Durand, Thomas Römer, and Jürg Hutzli. OBO 257. Fribourg: Academic Press; Göttingen: Vandenhoeck & Ruprecht, 2012.

———. "Mari." Pages 163–631 in vol. 1 of *Mythologie et religion des sémites occidentaux*. Edited by Gregorio del Olmo Lete. OLA 162. Dudley, Mass.: Leuven University Press, 2008.

Durand, Jean-Marie, and Michaël Guichard. "Les rituels de Mari." Pages 19–78 in *Florilegium Marianum 3: Recueil d'études à la mémoire d'André Parrot*. Edited by Dominique Charpin and Jean-Marie Durand. Mémoires de NABU 7. Paris: SEPOA, 1997.

Dutcher-Walls, Patricia. "The Circumscription of the King: Deuteronomy 17:16–17 in Its Ancient Social Context." *JBL* 121 (2002): 601–16.

Edelman, Diana. "From Prophets to Prophetic Books: The Fixing of the Divine Word." Pages 29–54 in *The Production of Prophecy: Construing Prophecy and Prophets in Yehud*. Edited by Diana Edelman and Ehud Ben Zvi. Bible World. London: Equinox, 2009.

———. "The Iconography of Wisdom." Pages 149–52 in *Essays on Ancient Israel in Its Near Eastern Context: A Tribute to Nadav Na'aman*. Edited by Y. Amit et al. Winona Lake, Ind.: Eisenbrauns, 2006.

———. "Taking the Torah out of Moses: Moses' Claim to Fame before He Became the Quintessential Law-Giver." Pages 13–42 in *La construction de la figure de Moïse/The Construction of the Figure of Moses*. Edited by Thomas Römer. Transeuphratène Supplément 13. Paris: Gabalda, 2007.

Eidinow, Esther. *Oracles, Curses, and Risk among the Ancient Greeks*. Oxford: Oxford University Press, 2007.

Ellis, Maria deJong. "The Goddess Kititum Speaks to King Ibalpiel: Oracle Texts from Ishchali." *MARI* 5 (1987): 235–66.

Eslinger, Lyle. *Kingship of God in Crisis: A Close Reading of 1 Samuel 1–12*. Decatur, Ga.: Almond, 1985.

Fischer, Georg. *Jeremia 1–25*. HTKAT. Freiburg: Herder, 2005.

Fishbane, Michael. *Biblical Interpretation in Ancient Israel*. Oxford: Clarendon, 1985.

Fleming, Daniel E. "Prophets and Temple Personnel in the Mari Archives." Pages 44–64 in *The Priests in the Prophets: The Portrayal of Priests, Prophets, and Other Religious Specialists in the Latter Prophets*. Edited by Lester

L. Grabbe and Alice Ogden Bellis. JSOTSup 408. London: T&T Clark, 2004.
Flint, Peter W. "The Prophet David at Qumran." Pages 158–67 in *Biblical Interpretation at Qumran*. Edited by Matthias Henze. SDSRL. Grand Rapids: Eerdmans, 2005.
Flower, Michael Attyah. *The Seer in Ancient Greece*. Berkeley: University of California Press, 2008.
Fohrer, Georg. *Elia*. ATANT 53. Zurich: Zwingli, 1968.
———. "Prophetie und Magie." *ZAW* 78 (1966): 25–47.
Foley, John Miles. "Analogues: Modern Oral Epic." Pages 196–212 in *A Companion to Ancient Epic*. Edited by John Miles Foley. Oxford: Blackwell, 2005.
Foresti, Fabrizio. "Storia della redazione di Dtn. 16, 18–18, 22 e le sue connessioni con l'opera storica deuteronomistica." *Teresianum* 39 (1988): 1–199.
Frolov, Serge. "1 Samuel 1–8: The Prophet as Agent Provocateur." Pages 77–85 in *Constructs of Prophecy in the Former and Latter Prophets and Other Texts*. Edited by Lester L. Grabbe and Martti Nissinen. SBLANEM 4. Atlanta: Society of Biblical Literature, 2011.
Geoghegan, Jeffrey C. *The Time, Place, and Purpose of the Deuteronomistic History: The Evidence of "Until This Day."* BJS 347. Providence, R.I.: Brown University Press, 2006.
Gerleman, Gillis, and Eberhard Ruprecht, "דרש, *drš*, fragen nach." *THAT* 1, cols. 460–67.
Gertz, Jan Christian. "Tora und vordere Propheten." Pages 187–302 in *Grundinformation Altes Testament*. Edited by Jan Christian Gertz. UTB 2745. Göttingen: Vandenhoeck & Ruprecht, 2006.
———. "The Transition Between the Books of Genesis and Exodus." Pages 73–87 in *A Farewell to the Yahwist? The Composition of the Pentateuch in Recent European Interpretation*. Edited by Thomas B. Dozeman and Konrad Schmid. SBLSymS 34. Atlanta: Society of Biblical Literature, 2006.
Gnuse, Robert K. "A Reconsideration of the Form-Critical Structure in I Samuel 3: An Ancient Near Eastern Dream Theophany." *ZAW* 94 (1982): 379–90.
Goffman, Erving. *Frame Analysis: An Essay on the Organization of Experience*. New York: Harper & Row, 1974.
Gosse, Bernard. "Trois étapes de la rédaction du livre de Jérémie: La venue du malheur contre ce lieu (Jérusalem), puis contre toute chair (Juda et les nations), et enfin de nouveau contre ce lieu, mais identifié cette fois à Babylone." *ZAW* 111 (1999): 508–29.
Grabbe, Lester L. *Priests, Prophets, Diviners, Sages: A Socio-Historical Study of Religious Specialists in Ancient Israel*. Valley Forge, Penn.: Trinity, 1995.

Grabbe, Lester L., and Martti Nissinen, eds. *Constructs of Prophecy in the Former and Latter Prophets and Other Texts.* SBLANEM 4. Atlanta: Society of Biblical Literature, 2011.

Grätz, Sebastian. "'Einen Propheten wie mich wird dir der Herr, dein Gott, erwecken': Der Berufungsbericht Jeremias und seine Rückbindung an das Amt des Mose." Pages 61–77 in *Moses in Biblical and Extra-Biblical Traditions.* Edited by Axel Graupner and Michael Wolter. BZAW 372. Berlin: de Gruyter, 2007.

Gray, John. *I and II Kings: A Commentary.* OTL. Philadelphia: Westminster, 1970.

Guillame, Alfred. *Prophecy and Divination among the Hebrews and other Semites.* London: Hodder & Stoughton, 1938.

Gunn, David M. "Narrative Patterns and Oral Tradition in Judges and Samuel." *VT* 24 (1974): 286–317.

Halpern, Baruch. "Levitic Participation in the Reform Cult of Jeroboam I." *JBL* 95 (1976): 38–41.

———. "The Uneasy Compromise: Israel Between League and Monarchy." Pages 59–96 in *Traditions in Transformation: Turning Points in Biblical Faith.* Edited by Baruch Halpern and Jon D. Levenson. Winona Lake, Ind.: Eisenbrauns, 1981.

Hamori, Esther J. "Gender and the Verification of Prophecy at Mari." *WO* 42 (2012): 1–22.

———. "The Prophet and the Necromancer: Women's Divination for Kings." *JBL*, forthcoming.

Haran, Menahem. *Temples and Temple-Service in Ancient Israel.* Oxford: Clarendon, 1978.

Harvey, John E. *Retelling the Torah: The Deuteronomistic Historian's Use of Tetrateuchal Narratives.* JSOTSup 403. London: T&T Clark, 2004.

Heintz, Jean-Georges. "Des textes sémitiques anciens à la Bible hébraïque: Un comparatisme légitime?" Pages 127–56 in *Le comparatisme en histoire des religions: Pur un état de la question.* Edited by F. Bœspflug and F. Dunand. Paris: Boccard, 1997.

Heller, Roy L. *Power, Politics, and Prophecy: The Character of Samuel and the Deuteronomistic Evaluation of Prophecy.* LHBOTS 440. London: T&T Clark, 2006.

Herrmann, Siegfried. *Ursprung und Funktion der Prophetie im alten Israel.* Rheinish-Westfälische Akademia der Wissenschaften 208. Opladen: Westdeutscher, 1976.

Hess, Richard S. "The Dead Sea Scrolls and Higher Criticism of the Hebrew Bible: The Case of 4QJudg^a." Pages 122–28 in *The Scrolls and the Scrip-*

tures: Qumran Fifty Years After. Edited by Stanley E. Porter and Craig A. Evans. Sheffield: Sheffield Academic Press, 1997.

Hill, Scott D. "The Local Hero in Palestine in Comparative Perspective." Pages 37-73 in *Elijah and Elisha in Socioliterary Perspective*. Edited by Robert B. Coote. Semeia Studies. Atlanta: Scholars Press, 1992.

Holloway, Steven W. *Aššur is King! Aššur is King!: Religion in the Exercise of Power in the Neo-Assyrian Empire*. CHANE 10. Leiden: Brill, 2002.

Holzinger, H. *Numeri*. KHC 4. Tübingen: Mohr Siebeck, 1903.

Hunger, Hermann. *Astrological Reports to Assyrian Kings*. SAA 8. Helsinki: Helsinki University Press, 1992.

Hutton, Jeremy M. "All the King's Men: The Families of the Priests in Cross-Cultural Perspective." Pages 117-43 in *"Seitenblicke": Literarische und historische Studien zu Nebenfiguren im zweiten Samuelbuch*. Edited by W. Dietrich. OBO 249. Freiburg: Universitätsverlag, 2011.

———. "The Levitical Diaspora (I): A Sociological Comparison with Morocco's Ahansal." Pages 223-34 in *Exploring the Longue Durée: Essays in Honor of Lawrence E. Stager*. Edited by J. David Schloen. Winona Lake, Ind.: Eisenbrauns, 2009.

———. *The Transjordanian Palimpsest: The Overwritten Texts of Personal Exile and Transformation in the Deuteronomistic History*. BZAW 396. Berlin: de Gruyter, 2009.

Japhet, Sara. *I and II Chronicles: A Commentary*. OTL. Louisville: Westminster John Knox, 1993.

———. *By The Rivers of Babylon to the Highlands of Judah: Collected Studies on the Restoration Period*. Winona Lake, Ind.: Eisenbrauns, 2006.

Jean, Cynthia. "Divination and Oracles at the Neo-Assyrian Palace." Pages 267-75 in *Divination and Interpretation of Signs in the Ancient World*. Edited by Amar Annus. OIS 6. Chicago: The Oriental Institute of the University of Chicago, 2010.

Jeffers, Ann. *Magic and Divination in Ancient Palestine and Syria*. SHCANE 8. Leiden: Brill, 1996.

Jeppesen, Knut. "Is Deuteronomy Hostile towards Prophets?" *SJOT* 8 (1994): 252-56.

Johnston, Sarah Iles. *Ancient Greek Divination*. Blackwell Ancient Religions. Chichester: Wiley-Blackwell, 2008.

Jones, Gwilym H. "The Concept of Holy War." Pages 299-321 in *The World of Ancient Israel: Sociological, Anthropological, and Political Perspectives*. Edited by Ronald E. Clements. Cambridge: Cambridge University Press, 1989.

Jong, Matthijs de. *Isaiah among the Ancient Near Eastern Prophets: A Comparative Study of the Earliest Stages of the Isaiah Tradition and the Neo-Assyrian Prophecies.* VTSup 117. Leiden: Brill, 2007.

Keinänen, Jyrki. *Traditions in Collision: A Literary and Redaction-Critical Study on the Elijah Narratives 1 Kings 17–19.* PFES 80. Helsinki: Finnish Exegetical Society, 2001.

Kittel, Rudolph. *Das Volk in Kanaan: Geschichte der Zeit bis zum babylonischen Exil.* Vol. 2 of *Geschichte des Volkes Israel.* 6th rev. ed. Gotha: Friedrich Andreas Perthes, 1925.

Klein, Lilian R. *The Triumph of Irony in the Book of Judges.* BLS 14. Sheffield: Sheffield Academic Press, 1988.

Knauf, Ernst Axel. "Does 'Deuteronomistic Historiography' (DtrH) Exist?" Pages 388–98 in *Israel Constructs Its History : Deuteronomistic Historiography in Recent Research.* Edited by Albert de Pury, Thomas Römer, and Jean-Daniel Macchi. JSOTSup 306. Sheffield: Sheffield Academic Press, 2000.

———. "Kings among the Prophets." Pages 131–49 in *The Production of Prophecy: Constructing Prophecy and Prophets in Yehud.* Edited by Diana Edelman and Ehud Ben Zvi. Bible World. London: Equinox, 2009.

Knobloch, Harald. *Die nachexilische Prophetentheorie des Jeremiabuches.* BZABR 12. Wiesbaden: Harrassowitz, 2009.

Knoppers, Gary N. "Democratizing Revelation? Prophets, Seers, and Visionaries in Chronicles." Pages 391–409 in *Prophecy and Prophets in Ancient Israel.* Edited by John Day. London: Continuum, 2010.

———. "The Deuteronomist and the Deuteronomic Law of the King: A Reexamination of a Relationship." ZAW 108 (1996): 329–46.

Koch, Klaus. "Das Prophetenschweigen des deuteronomistischen Geschichtswerks." Pages 115–28 in *Die Botschaft und die Boten.* Edited by J. Jeremias and L. Perlitt. Neukirchen-Vluyn: Neukirchener, 1981.

———. "Is There a Doctrine of Retribution in the Old Testament?" Pages 57–87 in *Theodicy in the Old Testament.* Edited by James L. Crenshaw. IRT 4. Philadelphia: Fortress, 1983.

Köckert, Matthias. "Elia: Literarische und religionsgeschichtliche Probleme in 1 Kön 17–18." Pages 111–44 in *Der Eine Gott und die Götter: Polytheismus und Monotheismus im antiken Israel.* Edited by Manfred Oeming and Konrad Schmid. ATANT 82. Zürich: Theologischer, 2003.

———. "Die Geschichte der Abrahamüberlieferung." Pages 103–28 in *Congress Volume Leiden 2004.* Edited by André Lemaire. VTSup 109. Leiden: Brill, 2006.

———. "Zum literargeschichtlichen Ort des Prophetengesetzes Dtn 18 zwischen dem Jeremiabuch und Dtn 13." Pages 80–100 in *Liebe und*

Gebot: Studien zum Deuteronomium. Edited by Reinhard G. Kratz and Hermann Spieckermann. Göttingen: Vandenhoeck & Ruprecht, 2000.
Kratz, Reinhard G. *The Composition of the Narrative Books of the Old Testament.* Translated by J. Bowden. London: T&T Clark, 2005.
———. *Die Propheten Israels.* Munich: Beck, 2003.
Kupitz, Yaakov, and Katell Berthelot. "Deborah and the Delphic Pythia: A New Interpretation of Judges 4:4–5." Pages 95–124 in *Images and Prophecy in the Ancient Eastern Mediterranean.* Edited by Martti Nissinen and Charles E. Carter. FRLANT 233. Göttingen: Vandenhoeck & Ruprecht, 2009.
Lamb, David T. *Righteous Jehu and His Evil Heirs: The Deuteronomist's Negative Perspective on Dynastic Succession.* OTM. Oxford: Oxford University Press, 2007.
Lehnart, Bernhard. *Prophet und König im Nordreich Israel: Studien zur sogenannten vorklassischen Prophetie im Nordreich Israel anhand der Samuel-, Elija- und Elischa-Überlieferungen.* VTSup 96. Leiden: Brill, 2003.
Lehnert, W. G. "The Role of Scripts in Understanding." Pages 79–95 in *Frame Conceptions and Text Understanding.* Edited by D. Metzing. Research in Text Theory 5. Berlin: de Gruyter, 1980.
Leuchter, Mark. "Eisodus as Exodus: The Song of the Sea (Exod 15) Reconsidered." *Bib* 92 (2011): 321–46.
———. *Josiah's Reform and Jeremiah's Scroll: Historical Calamity and Prophetic Response.* Sheffield: Sheffield Phoenix, 2006.
———. "A King Like All the Nations: The Composition of I Sam 8,11–18." *ZAW* 117 (2005): 543–58.
———. "The Literary Strata and Narrative Sources in Psalm xcix." *VT* 55 (2005): 30–36.
———. "The Reference to Shiloh in Psalm 78." *HUCA* 77 (2006): 1–31.
———. *Samuel and the Shaping of Tradition.* Oxford: Oxford University Press, 2013.
———. "Something Old, Something Older: Reconsidering 1 Samuel 2:27–36." Pages 533–40 in *Perspectives on Hebrew Scriptures.* Edited by Ehud Ben Zvi. Piscataway, N.J.: Gorgias, 2006.
———. "'Why Tarry the Wheels of His Chariot? (Judg 5,28)': Canaanite Chariots and Echoes of Egypt in the Song of Deborah." *Bib* 91 (2010): 256–68.
Levenson, Jon D. *Sinai and Zion: An Entry into the Jewish Bible.* Minneapolis: Winston, 1985.
———. "The Temple and the World." *JR* 64 (1984): 275–98.
Levin, Christoph. "Prophecy in the Book of Judges." Paper presented at the 2002 Annual Meeting of the Society of Biblical Literature, Toronto, November 23–26, 2002.

———. "The Yahwist and the Redactional Link Between Genesis and Exodus." Pages 131–41 in *A Farewell to the Yahwist? The Composition of the Pentateuch in Recent European Interpretation*. Edited by Thomas B. Dozeman and Konrad Schmid. SBLSymS 34. Atlanta: Society of Biblical Literature, 2006.

Levinson, Bernard M. "The Reconceptualization of Kingship in Deuteronomy and the Deuteronomistic History's Transformation of the Torah." *VT* 51 (2001): 511–34.

Lewis, Theodore J. *Cults of the Dead in Ancient Israel and Ugarit*. HSM 39. Atlanta: Scholars Press, 1989.

———. "Family, Household, and Local Religion in Late Bronze Age Ugarit." Pages 72–77 in *Household and Family Religion in Antiquity*. Edited by John Boden and Saul M. Olyan. Malden: Blackwell, 2008.

Lierman, John. *The New Testament Moses: Christian Perceptions of Moses and Israel in the Setting of the Jewish Religion*. Tübingen: Mohr Siebeck, 2004.

Lindars, Barnabas. *Judges 1–5: A New Translation and Commentary*. Edinburgh: T&T Clark, 1995.

Lion, Brigitte. "Les mentions de 'prophètes' dans la seconde moitié du IIe millénaire av. J.-C." *RA* 94 (2000): 21–32.

Loewenstamm, Samuel. "The Death of Moses." Pages 185–217 in *Studies on the Testament of Abraham*. Edited by G. W. E. Nickelsburg Jr. SBLSCS 6. Missoula: Scholars Press, 1976.

Lohfink, Norbert. "Gab es eine deuteronomistischen Bewegung?" Pages 313–82 in *Jeremiah und die "deuteronomistische Bewegung."* Edited by W. Gross. BBB 98. Weinheim: Beltz Athenäum, 1995.

Long, Burke O. "2 Kings III and Genres of Prophetic Narrative." *VT* 23 (1973): 337–48.

———. "The Effect of Divination upon Israelite Literature." *JBL* 92 (1973): 489–97.

———. "Two Question and Answer Schemata in the Prophets." *JBL* 90 (1971): 129–39.

Lübbe, John. "The Danite Invasion of Laish and the Purpose of the Book of Judges." *OTE* 23 (2010): 681–92.

Lundbom, Jack R. "Baruch, Seraiah, and Expanded Colophons in the Book of Jeremiah." *JSOT* 36 (1986): 107–8.

Madl, H. "Die Gottesbefragung mit dem Verb ša'al." Pages 37–70 in *Bausteine biblischer Theologie*. Edited by Heinz-Josef Fabry. BBB 50. Köln: Peter Hanstein, 1977.

Maier, Christl. *Jeremia als Lehrer der Tora : Soziale Gebote des Deuteronomiums in Fortschreibungen des Jeremiabuches*. FRLANT 196. Göttingen: Vandenhoeck & Ruprecht, 2002.

Malamat, Abraham. *Mari and the Bible*. SHCANE 12. Leiden: Brill, 1998.
Mayes, Andrew David Hastings. *Deuteronomy*. NCBC. London: Marshall, Morgan, & Scott, 1981.
McAlpine, Thomas H. *Sleep, Divine and Human in the Old Testament*. JSOTSup 38. Sheffield: JSOT, 1987.
McBride, Sean D. "Jeremiah and the Levitical Priests of Anatoth." Pages 179–96 in *Thus Says the Lord: Essays on the Former and Latter Prophets in Honor of Robert R. Wilson*. Edited by John J. Ahn and Stephen L. Cook. LHBOTS 502. London: T&T Clark, 2009.
McCarter, P. Kyle. *1 Samuel*. AB. Garden City: Doubleday, 1980.
McKane, William. "Prophet and Institution." *ZAW* 94 (1982): 251–66.
McKeating, Henry. "Ezekiel the 'Prophet Like Moses'?" *JSOT* 101 (1994): 97–109.
McKenzie, Stephen L. *The Trouble with Kings: The Composition of the Books of Kings in the Deuteronomistic History*. VTSup 42. Leiden: Brill, 1991.
Meeks, Wayne A. *The Prophet-King: Moses Traditions and the Johannine Christology*. NovTSup, 14. Leiden: Brill, 1967.
Melville, Sarah C. *The Role of Naqia/Zakutu in Sargonid Politics*. SAA 9. Helsinki: The Neo-Assyrian Text Corpus Project, 1999.
Mendelsohn, I. "Samuel's Denunciation of Kingship in Light of the Akkadian Documents from Ugarit." *BASOR* 143 (1956): 17–22.
Meyers, Carol. *Discovering Eve: Ancient Israelite Women in Context*. New York: Oxford University Press, 1988.
Moor, Johannes C. de, and Harry F. van Rooy, eds. *Past, Present, Future: The Deuteronomistic History and the Prophets*. OTS 44. Leiden, Brill, 2000.
Moran, William L. "New Evidence from Mari on the History of Prophecy." *Bib* 50 (1969): 15–56.
Murray, Donald F. "Narrative Structure and Technique in the Deborah-Barak Story (Judges IV 4–22)." Pages 155–87 in *Studies in the Historical Books of the Old Testament*. Edited by J. A. Emerton. VTSup 30. Leiden: Brill, 1979.
Nelson, Richard D. *The Double Redaction of the Deuteronomistic History*. Sheffield: JSOT, 1991.
Neumann, Peter H. A., ed. *Das Prophetenverständnis in der deutschsprachigen Forschung seit Heinrich Ewald*. Wege der Forschung 307. Darmstadt: Wissenschaftliche Buchgesellschaft, 1979.
Niditch, Susan. *Judges: A Commentary*. OTL. London: Westminster John Knox, 2008.
Nihan, Christophe. "Deuteronomy 18 and the Emergence of the Pentateuch as Torah." *SEÅ* 75 (2010): 21–56.
———. " 'Moses and the Prophets': Deuteronomy 18 and the Emergence of the Pentateuch as Torah." *SEÅ* 75 (2010): 21–55.

Nissinen, Martti. "Biblical Prophecy from a Near Eastern Perspective: The Cases of Kingship and Divine Possession." Pages 441–68 in *Congress Volume Ljubljana 2007*. Edited by André Lemaire. VTSup 133. Leiden: Brill, 2010.

———. "City Lofty as Heaven: Arbela and Other Cities in Neo-Assyrian Prophecy." Pages 172–209 in *"Every City Shall Be Forsaken": Urbanism and Prophecy in Ancient Israel and the Near East*. Edited by Lester L. Grabbe and Robert D. Haak. JSOTSup 330. Sheffield: Sheffield Academic Press, 2001.

———. "Comparing Prophetic Sources: Principles and a Test Case." Pages 3–24 in *Prophecy and Prophets in Ancient Israel*. Edited by John Day. London: Continuum, 2010.

———. "The Historical Dilemma of Biblical Prophetic Studies." Pages 103–20 in *Prophecy in the Book of Jeremiah*. Edited by Hans M. Barstad and Reiner G. Kratz. BZAW 388. Berlin: de Gruyter, 2009.

———. "How Prophecy Became Literature." *SJOT* 19 (2005): 153–72.

———. "Das kritische Potential in der altorientalischen Prophetie." Pages 1–32 in *Prophetie in Mari, Assyrien und Israel*. Edited by Matthias Köckert and Martti Nissinen. FRLANT 201. Göttingen: Vandenhoeck & Ruprecht, 2003.

———. "Pesharim as Divination: Qumran Exegesis, Omen Interpretation, and Literary Prophecy." Pages 43–60 in *Prophecy after the Prophets? The Contribution of the Dead Sea Scrolls to the Understanding of Biblical and Extra-Biblical Prophecy*. Edited by Kristin De Troyer and Armin Lange with the assistance of Lucas L. Schulte. CBET 52. Leuven: Peeters, 2009.

———. "Prophecy and Omen Divination: Two Sides of the Same Coin." Pages 341–51 in *Divination and Interpretation of Signs in the Ancient World*. Edited by Amar Annus. OIS 6. Chicago: The Oriental Institute of the University of Chicago, 2010.

———. "Prophecy as Construct: Ancient and Modern." Pages 11–35 in *"Thus Speaks Ishtar of Arbela": Prophecy in Israel, Assyria, and Egypt in the Neo-Assyrian Period*. Edited by Robert P. Gordon and Hans M. Barstad. Winona Lake, Ind.: Eisenbrauns, 2013.

———. "Prophetic Madness: Prophecy and Ecstasy in the Ancient Near East and in Greece." Pages 1–30 in *Raising Up a Faithful Exegete: Essays in Honor of Richard D. Nelson*. Edited by Kurt L. Noll and Brooks Schramm. Winona Lake, Ind.: Eisenbrauns, 2010.

———. "Prophets and the Divine Council." Pages 4–19 in *Kein Land für sich allein: Studien zum Kulturkontakt in Kanaan, Israel/Palästina, und Ebirnâri für Manfred Weippert zum 65. Geburtstag*. Edited by Ernst Axel Knauf and Ulrich Hübner. OBO 186. Freiburg: Universitätsverlag, 2002.

———. *References to Prophecy in Neo-Assyrian Sources*. SAA 7. Helsinki: The Neo-Assyrian Text Corpus Project, 1998.

———. "Die Relevanz der neuassyrischen Prophetie für die alttestamentliche Forschung." Pages 217–58 in *Mesopotamica-Ugaritica-Biblica*. Edited by M. Dietrich and O. Loretz. AOAT 232. Kevelaer: Butzon & Bercker, 1993.

———. "Spoken, Written, Quoted, and Invented: Orality and Writtenness in Ancient Near Eastern Prophecy." Pages 235–71 in *Writings and Speech in Israelite and Ancient Near Eastern Prophecy*. Edited by Ehud Ben Zvi and Michael H. Floyd. SBLSymS 10. Atlanta: Society of Biblical Literature, 2000.

Nissinen, Martti, with contributions by Choon-Leong Seow and Robert K. Ritner. *Prophets and Prophecy in the Ancient Near East*. SBLWAW 12. Atlanta: Society of Biblical Literature, 2003.

Nissinen, Martti, ed. *Prophecy in Its Ancient Near Eastern Context: Mesopotamian, Biblical, Arabian Perspectives*. SBLSymS 13. Atlanta: Society of Biblical Literature, 2000.

Nocquet, Dany. *Le livret noir de Baal : La polémique contre le dieu Baal dans la Bible hébraïque et dans l'ancien Israël*. Actes et Recherches. Genève: Labor et Fides, 2004.

Noll, Kurt L. "Deuteronomistic History or Deuteronomistic Debate? (A Thought Experiment)." *JSOT* 31 (2007): 311–45.

Noort, Eduard. "Joshua: The History of Reception and Hermeneutics." Pages 199–215 in *Past, Present, Future: The Deuteronomistic History and Prophets*. Edited by J. C. de Moor and H. F. van Rooy. OTS 44. Leiden: Brill, 2000.

———. *Untersuchungen zum Gottesbescheid in Mari: Die "Mari-prophetie" in der alttestamentlichen Forschung*. AOAT 202. Kevelaer: Butzon & Bercker, 1977.

Noth, Martin. *The Deuteronomistic History*. JSOTSup 15. Sheffield: Sheffield Academic Press, 1994.

———. *Überlieferungsgeschichtliche Studien: Die sammelden und bearbeitenden Geschichtswerke im Alten Testament*. Halle: Max Niemeyer, 1943.

O'Brien, Mark A. *The Deuteronomistic History Hypothesis: A Reassessment*. OBO 92. Freiburg: Universitätsverlag, 1989.

———. "The Portrayal of Prophets in 2 Kings 2." *AusBR* 46 (1998): 1–16.

O'Connell, Robert H. *The Rhetoric of the Book of Judges*. VTSup 63. Leiden: Brill, 1996.

Olyan, Saul M. "Zadok's Origins and the Tribal Politics of David." *JBL* 101 (1982): 190–93.

Oswald, Wolfgang. "Ahab als Krösus: Anmerkungen zu 1 Kön 22." *ZTK* 105 (2008): 1–14.

———. "Is There a Prohibition to Build a Temple in 2 Samuel 7?" Pages 85–89 in *Thinking towards New Horizons: Collected Communications to the 19th Congress of the International Organization for the Study of the Old Testament, Ljubljana 2007*. Edited by Matthias Augustin and Hermann Michael Niemann. BEATAJ 55. Frankfurt: Peter Lang, 2008.

———. *Nathan der Prophet: Eine Untersuchung zu 2 Samuel 7 und 12 und 1 Könige 1*. ATANT 94. Zürich: Theologischer, 2008.

Otto, Eckart. *Das Deuteronomium: Politische Theologie und Rechtsreform in Juda und Assyrien*. BZAW 284. Berlin: de Gruyter, 1999.

Otto, Susanne. "The Composition of the Elijah-Elisha Stories and the Deuteronomistic History." *JSOT* 27 (2003): 487–508.

———. *Jehu, Elia, und Elisa : Die Erzählung von der Jehu-Revolution und die Komposition der Elia-Elisa-Erzählungen*. BWANT 152. Stuttgart: Kohlhammer, 2001.

Overholt, Thomas W. *Channels of Prophecy: The Social Dynamics of Prophetic Activity*. Minneapolis: Fortress, 1989.

Parpola, Simo. *Assyrian Prophecies*. SAA 9. Helsinki: Helsinki University Press, 1997.

———. *Letters from Assyrian and Babylonian Scholars*. SAA 10. Helsinki: Helsinki University Press, 1993.

Person, Raymond F. Jr. "The Deuteronomic History and the Books of Chronicles: Contemporary Competing Historiographies." Pages 315–36 in *Reflection and Refraction: Studies in Biblical Historiography in Honour of A. Graeme Auld*. Edited by Robert Rezetko, Timothy Henry Lim, and W. Brian Aucker. VTSup 113. Leiden: Brill, 2007.

———. *The Deuteronomic History and the Book of Chronicles: Scribal Works in an Oral World*. SBLAIL 6. Atlanta: Society of Biblical Literature, 2010.

———. *The Deuteronomic School: History, Social Setting, and Literature*. SBLSBL 2. Atlanta: Society of Biblical Literature, 2002.

Petersen, David L. *Late Israelite Prophecy: Studies in Deutero-Prophetic Literature and in Chronicles*. SBLMS 23. Missoula: Scholars Press, 1977.

———. *The Roles of Israel's Prophets*. JSOTSup 17. Sheffield: JSOT, 1981.

Polak, Frank H. "David's Kingship—A Precarious Equilibrium." Pages 119–47 in *Politics and Theopolitics in the Bible and Postbiblical Literature*. Edited by H. G. Reventlow, Y. Hoffman, and B. Uffenheimer. JSOTS 171. Sheffield: Sheffield Academic Press, 1994.

Polzin, Robert. *Moses and the Deuteronomist: Deuteronomy, Joshua, Judges*. Part 1 of *A Literary Study of the Deuteronomic History*. New York: Seabury, 1980.

Pongratz-Leisten, Beate. *Herrschaftswissen in Mesopotamien: Formen der*

Kommunikation zwischen Gott und König im 2. und 1. Jahrtausend v.Chr. SAA 10. Helsinki: The Neo-Assyrian Text Corpus Project, 1999.

———. *Ina šulmi īrub: Die kulttopographische und ideologische Programmatik der akītu-Prozession in Babylonien und Assyrien im 1. Jahrtausend v.Chr.* Baghdader Forschungen 16. Mainz: Philipp von Zabern, 1994.

Porter, J. R. "Ancient Israel." Pages 191–214 in *Oracles and Divination*. Edited by Michael Loewe and Carmen Blacker. Boulder: Shambhala, 1981.

Pruin, Dagmar. *Geschichten und Geschichte: Isebel als literarische und historische Gestalt*. OBO 222. Freiburg: Universitätsverlag, 2006.

Pury, Albert de. "Pg as the Absolute Beginning." Pages 99–128 in *Les dernières rédactions du Pentateuque, de l'Hexateuque et de l'Ennéateuque*. Edited by Thomas Römer and Konrad Schmid. BETL 203. Leuven: Peeters University Press, 2007.

Pury, Albert de, Thomas Römer, and Jean-Daniel Macchi, eds. *Israel Constructs Its History: Deuteronomistic Historiography in Recent Research*. JSOTSup 306. Sheffield: Sheffield Academic Press, 2000.

Putsch, Michael. "Prophetess of Doom: Hermeneutical Reflections on the Huldah Oracle (2 Kings 22)." Pages 71–80 in *Soundings in Kings: Perspectives and Methods in Contemporary Scholarship*. Edited by Mark Leuchter and Klaus-Peter Adam. Minneapolis: Fortress, 2010.

Raabe, Paul R. *Obadiah*. AB 24D. New York: Doubleday, 1996.

Rad, Gerhard von. "Die deuteronomistische Geschichtstheologie in den Königsbüchern (1947)." Pages 189–204 in *Gesammelte Studien zum Alten Testament*. TB 8. Munich: Chr. Kaiser, 1958.

———. *Der Heilige Krieg im alten Israel*. Göttingen: Vandenhoeck & Ruprecht, 1951.

———. "The Levitical Sermon in I and II Chronicles." Pages 267–80 in *The Problem of the Hexateuch and Other Essays*. Edinburgh: Oliver & Boyd, 1966.

———. *Studies in Deuteronomy*. London: SCM, 1953.

Renaud, Bernard. "Jér 1: Structure et théologie de la rédaction." Pages 177–96 in *Le livre de Jérémie: Le prophète et son milieu: Les oracles et leur transmission*. Edited by Pierre-Maurice Bogaert. BETL 54. Leuven: Peeters, 1997.

Rendtorff, Rolf. "Samuel the Prophet: A Link Between Moses and the Kings." Pages 32–36 in *The Quest for Context and Meaning: Studies in Biblical Intertextuality in Honor of James A. Sanders*. Edited by Craig A. Evans and Shemaryahu Talmon. Leiden: Brill, 1997.

Renkema, Johan. *Obadiah*. HCOT. Leuven: Peeters, 2003.

Richter, Wolfgang. *Die Bearbeitungen des "Retterbuches" in der Deuteronomischen Epoche*. BBB 21. Bonn: Peter Hanstein, 1964.

Riesener, Ingrid. *Der Stamm* עבד *im Alten Testament: Eine Wortuntersuchung unter Berücksichtigung neuerer sprachwissenschaftlicher Methoden.* BZAW 149. Berlin: de Gruyter, 1979.

Rofé, Alexander. "Classes in the Prophetical Stories: Didactic Legenda and Parable." Pages 143–64 in *Studies on Prophecy: A Collection of Twelve Papers.* Edited by G. W. Anderson, P. A. H. de Boer, G. R. Castellino, Henry Cazelles, J. A. Emerton, W. L. Holladay, R. E. Murphy, E. Nielsen, and W. Zimmerli. VTSup 26. Leiden: Brill, 1974.

———. *The Prophetical Stories: The Narratives about the Prophets in the Hebrew Bible, Their Literary Types and History.* Translated by D. Levy et al. Jerusalem: Magnes, 1988.

Rogerson, John W. *Old Testament Criticism in the Nineteenth Century: England and Germany.* London: Society for Promoting Christian Knowledge, 1984.

Römer, Thomas. "Abraham and the Law and the Prophets." Pages 103–18 in *The Reception and Remembrance of Abraham.* Edited by Pernille Carstens and Niels Peter Lemche. PHSC 13. Piscataway, N.J.: Gorgias, 2011.

———. "The Formation of the Book of Jeremiah as a Supplement to the So-Called Deuteronomistic History." Pages 168–83 in *The Production of Prophecy: Constructing Prophecy and Prophets in Yehud.* Edited by Diana Edelman and Ehud Ben Zvi. BibleWorld. London: Equinox, 2009.

———. "How Did Jeremiah Become a Convert to Deuteronomistic Ideology?" Pages 189–99 in *Those Elusive Deuteronomists.* Edited by Steven L. McKenzie and Linda S. Schaering. JSOTSup 268. Sheffield: Sheffield Academic Press, 1999.

———. "Les interdits des pratiques magiques et divinatoires dans le livre du Deutéronome (Dt 18,9–13)." Pages 73–85 in *Magie et divination dans les cultures de l'Orient.* Edited by Jean-Marie Durand and Antoine Jacquet. Cahiers de l'IPOA 3. Paris: Jean Maisonneuve, 2010.

———. *Israels Väter: Untersuchungen zur Väterthematik im Deuteronomium und in der deuteronomistischen Tradition.* OBO 99. Freiburg: Universitätsverlag, 1990.

———. *The So-Called Deuteronomistic History: A Sociological, Historical and Literary Introduction.* London: T&T Clark, 2005.

Römer, Thomas, and Albert de Pury, "Deuteronomistic Historiography (DH): History of Research and Debated Issues." Pages 24–141 in *Israel Constructs Its History: Deuteronomistic Historiography in Recent Research.* Edited by Albert de Pury, Thomas Römer, and Jean-Daniel Macchi. JSOTSup 306. Sheffield: Sheffield Academic Press, 2000.

Roncace, Mark. "Elisha and the Woman of Shunem: 2 Kings 4:8–37 and 8:1–6." *JSOT* 91 (2000): 109–27.

———. *Jeremiah, Zedekiah, and the Fall of Jerusalem: A Study of Prophetic Narrative*. LHBOTS, 423. London: T&T Clark, 2005.

Rudnig, Thilo Alexander. "König ohne Tempel: 2 Samuel 7 in Tradition und Redaktion." *VT* 61 (2011): 426–46.

Rüterswörden, Udo. *Von der politischen Gemeinschaft zur Gemeinde: Studien zu Dt 16,18–18,22*. BBB 65. Frankfurt: Athenäum, 1987.

Šašková, Kateřina. "Esarhaddon's Accession to the Assyrian Throne." Pages 147–79 in *Shepherds of the Black-Headed People: The Royal Office vis-à-vis Godhead in Ancient Mesopotamia*. Edited by Kateřina Šašková, Lucáš Pecha, and Petr Charvát. Plzeň: Západočeská Univerzita, 2010.

Sasson, Jack M. "The Posting of Letters with Divine Messages." Pages 299–316 in *Florilegium Marianum II: Recueil d'études à la mémoire de Maurice Birot*. Edited by Dominique Charpin and Jean-Marie Durand. Mémoires de NABU 3. Paris: SEPOA, 1994.

Savran, George W. *Encountering the Divine: Theophany in Biblical Narrative*. London: Continuum, 2005.

Schäfer-Lichtenberger, Christa. *Josua und Salomo. Eine Studie zu Autorität und Legitimität des Nachfolgers im Alten Testament*. VTSup 58. Leiden: Brill, 1995.

Schaper, Joachim. "Exilic and Post-Exilic Prophecy and the Orality/Literacy Problem." *VT* 55 (2005): 324–42.

Schmid, Konrad. *Buchgestalten des Jeremiabuches: Untersuchungen zur Redaktions- und Rezeptionsgeschichte von Jer 30–33 im Kontext des Buches*. WMANT 72. Neukirchen-Vluyn: Neukirchener, 1996.

———. *Erzväter und Exodus: Untersuchungen zur doppelten Begründung der Ursprünge Israels innerhalb der Geschichtsbücher des Alten Testaments*. WMANT 81. Neukirchen-Vluyn: Neukirchener, 1999.

———. *Genesis and the Moses Story: Israel's Dual Origins in the Hebrew Bible*. Siphrut 3. Winona Lake, Ind.: Eisenbrauns, 2010.

———. "Manasse und der Untergang Judas: 'Golaorientierte' Theologie in den Königsbüchern?" *Bib* 78 (1997): 87–99.

Schmid, Konrad, and Raymond F. Person Jr., eds. *Deuteronomy in the Pentateuch, Hexateuch, and the Deuteronomistic History*. FAT. Tübingen: Mohr Siebeck, 2012.

Schmidt, Brian B. *Israel's Beneficent Dead: Ancestor Cult and Necromancy in Ancient Israelite Religion and Tradition*. FAT 11. Tübingen: Mohr Siebeck, 1994.

Schmidt, Werner H. "Jeremias Berufung: Aspekte der Erzählung Jer 1,4–9 und offene Fragen der Auslegung." Pages 183–98 in *Biblische Welten*. Edited by Wolfgang Zwickel. OBO 123. Freiburg: Universitätsverlag, 1993.

Schneider, Tammi J. *Judges*. Berit Olam. Collegeville, Minn.: Liturgical Press, 2000.

Schniedewind, William M. "Prophets and Prophecy in the Books of Chronicles." Pages 204–24 in *The Chronicler as Historian*. Edited by M. Patrick Graham, Kenneth G. Hoglund, and Steven L. McKenzie. JSOTSup 238. Sheffield: Sheffield Academic Press, 1997.

Seitz, Christopher R. "The Prophet Moses and the Canonical Shape of Jeremiah." ZAW 101 (1989): 3–27.

———. *Theology in Conflict: Reactions to the Exile in the Book of Jeremiah*. BZAW 176. Berlin: de Gruyter, 1989.

Seow, Choon-Leong. *Myth, Drama, and the Politics of David's Dance*. HSM 44. Atlanta: Scholars Press, 1989.

Sharp, Carolyn J. "The Call of Jeremiah and Diaspora Politics." *JBL* 119 (2000): 421–38.

———. *Prophecy and Ideology in Jeremiah: Struggle for Authority in the Deutero-Jeremianic Prose*. London: T&T Clark, 2003.

Shields, Mary E. "Subverting a Man of God, Elevating a Woman: Role and Power Reversals in 2 Kings 4." *JSOT* 58 (1993): 59–69.

Smend, Rudolph. *Die Entstehung des Alten Testaments*. Stuttgart: Kohlhammer, 1981.

———. "Das Gesetz und die Völker: Ein Beitrag zur Deuteronomistischen Redaktionsgeschichte." Pages 494–509 in *Probleme Biblischer Theologie*. Edited by H. W. Wolff. Munich: Chr. Kaiser, 1971.

Soggin, J. Alberto. *Judges: A Commentary*. Translated by John Bowden. OTL. Philadelphia: Westminster, 1981.

Spronk, Klaas. "Deborah, a Prophetess: The Meaning and Background of Judges 4:4–5." Pages 232–42 in *The Elusive Prophet: The Prophet as a Historical Person, Literary Character, and Anonymous Artist*. Edited by Johannes C. de Moor. OTS 45. Leiden: Brill, 2001.

Stager, Lawrence E. "The Archaeology of the Family in Ancient Israel." *BASOR* 260 (1985): 28.

Steuernagel, Carl. *Das Deuteronomium*. 2nd ed. HKAT. Göttingen: Vandenhoeck & Ruprecht, 1923.

Svärd, Saana. *Women's Roles in the Neo-Assyrian Era: Female Agency in the Empire*. Saarbrücken: VDM, 2008.

Sweeney, Marvin A. *I and II Kings: A Commentary*. OTL. Louisville: Westminster John Knox, 2007.

———. *Reading the Hebrew Bible after the Shoah: Engaging Holocaust Theology*. Minneapolis: Fortress, 2008.

———. "Samuel's Institutional Identity in the Deuteronomistic History." Pages 165–74 in *Constructs of Prophecy in the Former and Latter Prophets and Other Texts*. Edited by Lester L. Grabbe and Martti Nissinen. SBLANEM 4. Atlanta: Society of Biblical Literature, 2011.

———. "The Wilderness Traditions of the Pentateuch: A Reassessment of their Function and Intent in Relation to Exodus 32–34." Pages 291–99 in *Society of Biblical Literature 1989 Seminar Papers*. Atlanta: Scholars Press, 1989.

Tengström, Sven. "Moses and the Prophets in the Deuteronomistic History." *SJOT* 8 (1994): 257–66.

Terblanche, Marius D. "No Need for a Prophet like Jeremiah: The Absence of the Prophet Jeremiah in Kings." Edited by 306–14 in *Past, Present, Future: The Deuteronomistic History and Prophets*. Edited by J. C. de Moor and H. F. van Rooy. OTS 44. Leiden: Brill, 2000.

Thelle, Rannfrid I. *Approaches to the "Chosen Place": Accessing a Biblical Concept*. LHBOTS 564. London: T&T Clark, 2012.

———. *Ask God: Divine Consultation in the Literature of the Hebrew Bible*. BBET 30. Frankfurt: Peter Lang, 2002.

———. "The Book of Jeremiah MT: Reflections of a Discourse on Prophecy in the Persian Period." Pages 184–207 in *The Production of Prophecy: Constructing Prophets and Prophecy in Yehud*. Edited by Diana Edelman and Ehud Ben Zvi. BibleWorld. London: Equinox, 2009.

———. "דרש את־יהוה: The Prophetic Act of Consulting YHWH in Jer. 21:2 and 37:7." *SJOT* 12 (1998): 249–55.

Tigay, Jeffrey H. *Empirical Models for Biblical Criticism*. Philadelphia: University of Pennsylvania Press, 1985.

Toorn, Karel van der. "Echoes of Judean Necromancy in Isaiah 28.7–22." *ZAW* 100 (1988): 199–217.

———. *Family Religion in Babylonia, Syria, and Israel: Continuity and Change in the Forms of Religious Life*. Leiden: Brill, 1996.

———. "From the Oral to the Written: The Case of Old Babylonian Prophecy." Pages 219–34 in *Writings and Speech in Israelite and Ancient Near Eastern Prophecy*. Edited by Ehud Ben Zvi and Michael H. Floyd. SBLSymS 10. Atlanta: Society of Biblical Literature, 2000.

Trebolle Barrera, Julio C. "The Different Textual Forms of MT and LXX in Kings and the History of the Deuteronomistic Composition and Redaction of These Books." Paper presented at the annual meeting of the Society of Biblical Literature, New Orleans, November 2009.

———. "Textual Variants in 4QJudg^a and the Textual and Editorial History of the Book of Judges." *RevQ* 14 (1990): 229–45.

Van Seters, John. *In Search of History: Historiography in the Ancient World and the Origins of Biblical History.* New Haven: Yale University Press, 1983.

———. "The Patriarchs and the Exodus: Bridging the Gap between Two Origin Traditions." Pages 1–15 in *The Interpretation of Exodus.* Edited by Riemer Roukema. CBET 44. Leuven: Peeters, 2006.

Van Staalduine-Sulman, Eveline. *The Targum of Samuel.* Leiden: Brill, 2002.

Vawter, Bruce. "Were the Prophets Nabî's?" *Bib* 66 (1985): 206–20.

Veijola, Timo. "David in Keïla: Tradition und Interpretation in 1 Sam 23, 1–13." *RB* 91 (1984): 51–87.

———. *David: Gesammelte Studien zur Davidüberlieferungen des Alten Testaments.* SFEG 52. Helsinki: Finnische Exegetische Gesellschaft, 1990.

Vondergeest, Craig. "Prophecy and Divination in the Deuteronomistic History." Ph.D. diss., Union Theological Seminary and Presbyterian School of Christian Education, 2000.

Wagenaar, Jan. "Crossing the Sea of Reeds (Exod 13–14) and the Jordan (Josh 3–4): A Priestly Framework for the Wilderness Wandering Studies in the Book of Exodus." Pages 461–70 in *Studies in the Book of Exodus: Redaction, Reception, Interpretation.* Edited by M. Vervenne. BETL 126. Leuven: Peeters, 1996.

Wagner, S. "דרש." *THAT* 2:314–29.

Walsh, Jerome T. *1 Kings.* Berit Olam. Collegeville, Minn.: Liturgical Press, 1996.

Walters, Stanley D. "Hannah and Anna: The Greek and Hebrew Texts of 1 Samuel 1." *JBL* 107 (1988): 385–412.

Walton, John H. *Ancient Near Eastern Thought and the Old Testament: Introducing the Conceptual World of the Hebrew Bible.* Grand Rapids: Baker Academic, 2006.

Ward, James M. "The Eclipse of the Prophet in Contemporary Prophetic Studies." *USQR* 42 (1988): 97–104.

Watts, James W. *Psalm and Story: Inset Hymns in Hebrew Narrative.* JSOTSup 139. Sheffield: JSOT Press, 1992.

Webb, Barry G. *The Book of Judges: An Integrated Reading.* JSOTSup 46. Sheffield: JSOT, 1987.

Westermann, Claus. "Die Begriffe für Fragen und Suchen im Alten Testament." *Kerygma und Dogma* (1960): 2–30.

———. *Die Geschichtsbücher des Alten Testaments: Gab es ein deuteronomisches Geschichtswerk?* TB 87. Gütersloh: Kaiser, 1994.

———. *Grundformen der prophetischer Rede.* 4th ed. BEvT 31. Munich: Chr. Kaiser, 1971.

Wildberger, Hans. *Isaiah 28–39: A Continental Commentary.* Translated by Thomas H. Trapp. Minneapolis: Fortress, 2002.

Williamson, H. G. M. "The Messianic Texts in Isa 1–39." Pages 238–70 in *King and Messiah in Israel and the Ancient Near East: Proceedings of the Oxford Old Testament Seminar.* Edited by John Day. JSOTSup 270. Sheffield: Sheffield Academic Press, 1998.

———. "Prophetesses in the Hebrew Bible." Pages 65–80 in *Prophecy and Prophets in Ancient Israel: Proceedings of the Oxford Old Testament Seminar.* LHBOTS 531. London: T&T Clark, 2010.

Wilson, Robert R. *Prophecy and Society in Ancient Israel.* Philadelphia: Fortress, 1980.

Wray Beal, Lissa M. *The Deuteronomist's Prophet: Narrative Control of Approval and Disapproval in the Story of Jehu (2 Kings 9 and 10).* LHBOTS 478. London: T&T Clark, 2007.

Wright, Peter Matthews. "The Qur'anic David." Pages 197–206 in *Constructs of Prophecy in the Former and Latter Prophets and Other Texts.* Edited by Lester L. Grabbe and Martti Nissinen. SBLANEM 4. Atlanta: Society of Biblical Literature, 2011.

Würthwein, Ernst. "Erwägungen zum sog. Deuteronomistischen Geschichtswerk. Eine Skizze." Pages 1–11 in *Studien zum Deuteronomistischen Geschichtswerk.* Edited by Ernst Würthwein. BZAW 227. Berlin: de Gruyter, 1994.

Wyrick, Steven von. "El." *Eerdman's Dictionary of the Bible.* Edited by David Noel Freedman. Grand Rapids: Eerdmans, 2000.

Yee, Gale A. "Ideological Criticism: Judges 17–21 and the Dismembered Body." Pages 138–60 in *Judges and Method: New Approaches in Biblical Studies.* Edited by Gale A. Yee. 2nd ed. Minneapolis: Fortress, 2007.

Young, Ian M. "Israelite Literacy: Interpreting the Evidence." *VT* 48 (1998): 239–53, 408–22.

Zerubavel, Eviatar. *Social Mindscapes: An Invitation to Cognitive Sociology.* Cambridge: Harvard University Press, 1997.

———. *Time Maps: Collective Memory and the Social Shape of the Past.* Chicago: University of Chicago Press, 2003.

Contributors

Ehud Ben Zvi is Professor of History and Classics at the University of Alberta, Canada.

Diana Edelman is currently an independent scholar.

Mignon R. Jacobs is Associate Professor of Hebrew Bible/Old Testament at Fuller Theological Seminary.

Mark Leuchter is Associate Professor of Hebrew Bible and Ancient Judaism at Temple University.

Martti Nissinen is Professor of Old Testament Studies at the University of Helsinki.

Mark O'Brien is Associate Professor of Biblical Studies at Catholic Theological College, a member of the MCD University of Divinity, Melbourne, Australia.

Raymond F. Person Jr. is Professor of Religion at Ohio Northern University.

Thomas Römer is Professor of Old Testament in the Faculty of Theology at the University of Lausanne and Professor of Bible at the Collège de France.

Marvin A. Sweeney is Professor of Hebrew Bible at the Claremont School of Theology and Claremont Lincoln University and Professor of Tanak and Faculty Chair at the Academy for Jewish Religion California.

Rannfrid I. Thelle is Visiting Associate Professor of Religion at Wichita State University.

Scripture Index

Hebrew Bible/Old Testament		39	157 n. 32
Genesis		Leviticus	
15	143 n. 27	10	42
17:1	143	10:11	157 n. 32
20	143–44	10:19–20	157 n. 32
		16	42
Exodus		16:3	40
2:1–10	143	17:12–13	38 n. 6
3	129, 160		
3:4	160	Numbers	
3:5	84 n. 18	9	35
3:6	160	11	129–30
3:10–12	139	12:6	53, 67
6:2	143	12:6–8	144, 159 n. 39, 160–62
7:1	129, 144	12:7	156
14	142	12:8	163
15	154 n. 26	14	144
15:13	163	15	42
15:17	163	20:11	174
15:20	88	20:12	176
17:1–7	153 n. 21	22–24	45
19	42	24	41
19–20	131	27:12–14	176 n. 12
19:16–19	150	27:12–23	43
20:18–19	131–32	27:21	20 n. 38
21:1	61 n. 22	28–29	39
21:9	61 n. 21	29:35–38	38
21:31	61 n. 21		
24:3	61 n. 22	Deuteronomy	
32	144	1:1	81
32–34	39	1:5	56
32:26–29	153 n. 21	1:17	61 n. 21
33	141	4:1	61 n. 22
33:11	160–61	4:5	61 n. 22

Deuteronomy (cont.)

Reference	Pages
4:8	56, 61 n. 22
4:14	61 n. 22
4:44	56
4:45	61 n. 22
5	54, 55 n. 7
5:1	61 n. 22
5:4–5	148, 166 n. 58
5:22–27	141
5:31	61 n. 22
6:1	61 n. 22
6:20	61 n. 22
7	141
7:11	61 n. 22
7:12	61 n. 22
8	179
8:11	61 n. 22
10:18	61 n. 21
11:1	61 n. 22
11:32	61 n. 22
12	119
12:16	38 n. 6
12:21	177 n. 13
12:23–24	38 n. 6
12:32	179
13	56, 68, 71, 141
13:1	31, 68, 166 n. 58
13:1–5	28
13:2	68
13:2–6	53
15:23	38 n. 6
16:18–19	61 n. 21
16:21	177 n. 13
17:8–9	61 n. 21
17:8–13	56
17:11	56, 61 n. 21
17:14–20	29 n. 55, 72, 90 n. 36, 148
17:18–19	56
17:18–20	70, 154
18	28, 55–56, 67–68, 71, 129, 135, 140, 141, 144
18:1–8	167
18:3	61 n. 21
18:5–20	72 n. 46
18:9–14	27, 104
18:9–22	26, 54 n. 6, 55 n. 8, 71 n. 44
18:10–11	26, 29–31,
18:11	27 n. 53
18:14–22	86, 134
18:15	82, 179
18:15–18	148
18:15–19	56 n. 9, 64
18:15–20	70
18:15–22	27, 54, 57, 67, 130–34, 167
18:16	148
18:18	30, 82, 139, 148, 179
18:18–20	27
18:20	139
18:21–22	28
18:21	136 n. 12
19:6	61 n. 21
21:1	61 n. 22
21:17	61 n. 21
21:22	61 n. 21
24:17	61 n. 21
25:1	61 n. 21
26:12	61 n. 22
26:17	61 n. 22
27:3	56
27:8	56
27:19	61 n. 21
27:26	56
28:15	55 n. 7
28:18	55 n. 7
28:58	56
28:61	56
29:2–9	179
29:29	56
30:1	102
30:2–10	102
30:10	56
30:16	61 n. 22
31:7	85
31:9	56
31:10	85
31:11–12	56
31:14	85, 148
31:14–21	85
31:16	85
31:16–21	43

31:22	88	6:4	57
31:23	85, 148	6:6	57
31:24	56	6:8	57
31:25	85	6:9	57
31:26	56	6:12	57
31:26–29	102	6:13	57
31:30	88	6:16	57
32	88	7:14–18	105
32:4	61 n. 21	8:1	113
32:41	61 n. 21	8:18	113
32:48–52	176	8:30–31	120
33:1	83 n. 14	8:30–33	44
33:4	56	8:31–32	83
33:8–9	153	8:33	57
33:9	153	9	14 n. 21
33:10	56, 61 n. 22	9:14	19 n. 34
33:21	61 n. 22	10:8	109, 113
34	143	10:12	14 n. 21
34:5–10	84	13–21	105
34:6	141, 177	14:1	57
34:7	84	14:6	11 n. 14, 83 n. 14
34:9–10	30	17:4	57
34:10	31, 53, 82, 161	19:51	57
34:10–12	54, 129, 144, 145	20:6	57
34:11	178	21:4	57
		21:13	57
Joshua		21:19	57
1	44	21:45	85–86
1:1	85 n. 20	22:5	83
1:1–2	83, 148	22:13	57
1:6	85	22:30	57
1:8	76 n. 1, 83	22:31	57
1:9	109	23	44
3–4	142	23:3–4	86
3:3	57	23:6	83
3:6	57	23:14	85–86
3:8	57	24:1–28	44
3:14–15	57	24:2–13	86
3:17	57	24:19–20	85
4:3	57	24:25–26	87 n. 26
4:9–11	57	24:29–30	84
4:16–18	57		
5:2–9	120	Judges	
5:15	84	1	18
6:2	113	2:1–3	89

Judges (cont.)

2:8-9	84
4-5	59 n. 15, 60 n. 19
4:1	65 n. 31
4:4	57, 88, 109, 109, 119
4:4-5	88, 124, 167
4:6-7	113
4:6-9	124
5:1	88
6:2-6	89 n. 33
6:7-10	109
6:8-10	63, 86, 88, 89, 109, 149, 167
6:11-13	89 n. 33
6:16	114
7:13-15	105
8:27	154 n. 25
8:31	154 n. 25
9:8-15	89
10:11-14	86
13:6	109 n. 19
17-18	65, 66 n. 34
17:5	105
18:1-6	20 n. 37
18:11-20	105
20	18
20:26-28	19

1 Samuel

1	155
1-2	154-55, 157
1-3	151-52, 163
1-8	121 n. 60
1-12	66 n. 35
1:3	154
1:9	154
1:13-14	154
1:24-28	120
2	88 n. 31, 155
2:11	154
2:13-17	154
2:18-20	154
2:22-25	154
2:27-36	89, 90 n. 37, 109, 121, 149, 155, 162 n. 47, 167
2:29	156
2:30	90 n. 37
2:35	156, 162
3	41, 151, 158-63
3:1	62
3:6	155 n. 27
3:16	155 n. 27
3:16-18	162 n. 47
3:18	166 n. 58
3:19-21	62
3:20	62, 121
3:21	121
3:22	148
4:1	166 n. 58, 175
4:13	154
4:18	154
7	31 n. 57
7:2-12	20 n. 35
7:3-4	62
7:3-14	148
7:6	62
7:9-10	62
7:9	150
7:15-17	62
8	68, 163, 171
8:1-5	175
8:9	62
8:11	62
9	20 n. 39
9-10	106 n. 11
9:6	121
9:9	14 n. 22, 67, 110
9:10	121
9:11	121
9:12	62
9:15-17	106
9:18-19	121
9:23-24	62
10	67, 68
10:1	66, 115
10:5	121
10:8	62
10:10	115, 121
10:17-24	20 n. 38
10:17-27	148
10:20-21	105

10:20–24	106	30:7	19
10:25	62, 148, 195	30:7–8	105, 109
11:12–13	58	30:8	19
12	67, 87 n. 26, 89, 148		
12–15	67	2 Samuel	
12:3	123	2:1	20, 106, 109
12:3–5	62 n. 23	5–6	167 n. 62
12:6–25	62	5:19	19, 107, 109
12:7	62	5:22–24	19
12:8–15	86	5:23	107, 109
12:14–15	149	6	42
12:17–18	125	7	115 n. 35, 122
12:18–23	148	7:2	67
12:20–21	149	7:4	166
12:25	57 n. 11, 65 n. 30	7:12–16	115
13:5–12	20 n. 35	7:13–14	122
13:8–13	62	7:16	90 n. 37
14:18	19 n. 32	7:17	194
14:31–35	38 n. 6	9:1–13	183
14:35	154 n. 25	11:1	59
14:37	19	12:1–15	67
14:41–42	105	12:11–14	68
15:10	166	12:25	67
16:1–13	66, 148, 165	12:26–29	59
16:13	115	19:24–30	183
18:5–9	59	22	44
19	67	23:1–7	110
19:18	165	23:2	197
19:20	62, 197	24:11	67, 166, 194
19:23	197		
19:24	62	1 Kings	
21:10	20 n. 37	1	91, 116
21:11	59	1:8	194
21:13	20 n. 37	1:32–53	115
21:15	20 n. 37	2:3	69
22	154 n. 25	2:11	67 n. 35
22:5	67, 67, 113	2:26	162, 164
23:1–6	19	2:26–27	157
23:8–12	105	6	42
23:9–12	19, 109	8	42, 86
28	14. n. 22, 27 n. 53, 29–30, 108, 109, 124 n. 66	8:1–6	172
		8:18–19	172
28:3–19	29	8:46–53	86
28:6	106	8:56	86
28:15	67	8:66	84

1 Kings (cont.)

11:9–13	185
11:12	184
11:14–25	184
11:29–39	121, 190
11:31–35	86 n. 22
11:31–39	69, 185
11:34	184
11:36	183
11:37–39	112
12:15	86 n. 22, 113, 190
12:22	194, 196
12:22–24	113
12:33–13:33	70
13	17 n. 26, 31 n. 57, 68, 175, 177
13:1–2	120
13:11–32	109
13:20	166
13:32	175
14:1–18	20 n. 36, 121
14:1–20	190
14:5	14 n. 22, 17 n. 28
14:7–11	86 n. 22
14:10–11	112
14:14	112
14:18	84, 85, 86 n. 22, 134
14:22	14 n. 22
14:23	177 n. 13
15:27–29	140
15:29	84, 85, 86 n. 22
16:1–3	112
16:12	86 n. 22
16:23–2 Kgs 14:16	190
16:34	85
17	46, 141
17–19	190
17:2	166
17:7–16	125
17:8	166
17:16	85, 86 n. 22
17:17–24	124, 174
18	37–39, 33, 97, 141
18:1	166
18:18	195
18:21–40	122
18:31	69
18:36	69, 134
18:38–45	125
19	39–41, 43, 141, 171, 175
19:10	122
19:14	122
19:15–16	90 n. 38
20	172, 185 n. 30
20–22	185 n. 30
20:13	114
20:13–14	107
20:35	192
20:35–36	68
20:39–40	61
21	70, 185 n. 30, 190
21:17	166
21:19–24	172
21:20–24	113, 182
21:27–29	185
21:28	166
22:1–28	15–18, 20, 29, 89, 172, 184, 185
22:5	15
22:6	15, 107
22:7	16
22:7–28	16–17
22:10–12	17, 107
22:14	108
22:15	107
22:37–38	113
22:40	185

2 Kings

1	41–43, 14 n. 22, 109, 111
1–2	190
1:1–16	21 n. 36
2	43–44, 142, 173 n. 7, 174
2:1–18	173
2:5	192
2:7	192
2:8	142
2:14	125
2:15	192
2:19–22	125
2:23–24	141

3	44–46, 14 n. 22, 15–18, 20, 29	10:30	86 n. 22, 181
3–8	190	11:1	182
3:4–27	15	12	182
3:11	92 n. 44	13	190
3:15–16	140	13:2	181 n. 21
3:18	114	13:3–5	20 n. 35
4	140	13:14–19	141
4–8	173	13:20–21	124, 140
4:1	192	14:6	69, 76 n. 1
4:1–7	125	14:23–29	181
4:1–6:3	173 n. 7	14:25	84 n. 16, 85 n. 19, 86 n. 22, 114, 134
4:8–37	124		
4:38	192	14:25–27	97
4:38–41	125	15:12	86 n. 22
4:38–5:27	141	15:29	112
4:42–44	125	17	69
5	172	17:7	69
5:1–19	124	17:8	69
5:22	192	17:13	69, 83–84, 85 n. 19, 85 n. 19, 92, 93, 149
6:1	192		
6:1–7	125	17:13–14	134
6:8–17	125	17:14–20	182
6:8–23	20 n. 35	17:21–23	113
6:18–20	125	17:23	84 n. 16, 86 n. 22, 149
6:26	61	18–20	13, 142, 185
8	14 n. 22	18:12	84 n. 18
8:1–6	173	18:13–19:37	20 n. 35
8:7–15	20 n. 36, 106, 111	18:13–20:19	71
8:8	17 n. 28	19:1–7	121, 122 n. 61
8:18	182	19:6–7	114
8:19	180, 183	19:7	197
8:26–27	182	20:1–11	125
9–10	173 n. 7, 180	20:4	166
9:1	192	20:5–6	114
9:1–10	66 n. 36	21:3	183
9:6–10	115	21:6	105
9:7	84 n. 16, 85 n. 19, 149	21:8	69
9:9–10	113	21:10	84 n. 16, 85 n. 19, 149
9:21–26	172	21:10–15	135
9:30–37	113	22	14 n. 22, 20 n. 39, 119
9:36	84 n. 16, 86 n. 22	22–23	184, 195
10	181	22:1	77
10:10	84 n. 16, 85 n. 19, 86 n. 22	22:8	70
10:17	182	22:10	76 n. 1
10:28	172, 178	22:10–11	76 n. 1

2 Kings (cont.)

22:11	70
22:14	194, 196
22:15–20	184
22:18–22	180, 184
22:20	114
23:2	46
23:24–25	70
23:29	114
24–25	13, 139
24:2	84 n. 16, 85, 86 n. 22, 135, 149
25:27–30	93

1 Chronicles

3:16–19	183
6:13	36
6:34	84 n. 18
9:22	167
10:13–14	29, 30
16	46
16:35	86
21:9	67
21:12–13	195
25	46
25:1	88
29:29	67

2 Chronicles

1:3	84
6:15–17	84 n. 18
6:36–39	86
6:42	84 n. 18
10:15	190
12:5	196
12:15	196
17:9	76 n. 1
18	89, 184
18:7–8	17 n. 28
21:12–15	92, 190, 191
24:6	84
24:19	76
24:20	195 n. 33
34–35	195
34:14	76 n. 1
34:22	196

34:30	46
35:20–27	184, 197
36	183
36:10	183
36:15–16	89
36:22–23	183, 197

Ezra

1–3	183
2:1–2	183
3:8	183
9:11	84, 134

Nehemiah

9:6–37	86 n. 24
9:27	99
9:30	95
10:30	84 n. 18

Job

1:8	84 n. 16

Psalms

1	90 n. 36
10:13	132
18:1	84 n. 18
36:1	84 n. 18
68	44
77:21	130
78	86 n. 24
78:60–66	150, 164
99	149–50, 152 n. 16, 157, 166, 167
99:6	90, 149
99:6–7	130 n. 2
105	86 n. 24
105:25	130
106	86 n. 24
107	86 n. 24
132:10	84 n. 18
136	86 n. 24

Isaiah

2:3	101
3:2	131
6	40

8:19–22	26, 31	11	87
9:5–6	99 n. 59	11:1	159 n. 39
9:5–7	99 n. 59	11:21–23	164
11	99	15:1	90, 130, 147, 148, 149
11:1–9	99 n. 59	16:10–13	86
12	46	17:2–3	177 n. 13
19:20	60	18:18	150 n. 11
20:3	84 n. 16, 85 n. 19	20	139
30:2	19	20:1–6	147
36–39	142, 185	21:1–2	147
37:1–7	121, 122 n. 61	23:5–6	99 n. 59
37:35	84 n. 18	23:9–40	177
38–39	13	25	137
38:1–8	125	25:1	159 n. 39
39:1–8	94	25:1–7	136
40	94	25:4	84 n. 16, 95
40–66	99	26	136
41:8–9	84 n. 16	26:5	84 n. 16, 86 n. 19
42:1	84 n. 16	26:9	95
42:19	84	26:18	76
44:26	89	27:6	84 n. 16
52:13	84 n. 16	28	139
53:11	84 n. 16	29	140
56:6	84 n. 16	29:8	131
61:1	89	29:19	84 n. 16, 138
63:11–12	70 n. 41, 96	30–33	140
63:11–14	130	30:8–11	99 n. 59
65:17	99	30:10	84 n. 16
		31:31–34	99–100
Jeremiah		32:38–41	99
1	139	33:14–26	99 n. 59
1–25	147 n. 1	35	137
1:1	164	35:15	84 n. 16, 86 n. 19, 95, 137
1:4–5	148	36	195, 196
1:5–8	139	37–38	147
1:7	139	37–43	140
1:9	139, 148	37–44	186
1:13–19	159 n. 39	37:1–10	20
1:24	159 n. 39	37:17	19 n. 33
3:1	70 n. 41	38:14–18	19 n. 33
3:6–9	177 n. 13	42:1–22	20
7	137	44:4	84 n. 16, 86 n. 19, 95
7:1–2	159 n. 39	44:4–6	138
7:25	84 n. 16, 86 n. 19, 95	45	148 n. 3
7:25–26	136	48:41	60

Jeremiah (cont.)

49:22	60
50:4–5	99
50:19–20	99
50:37	60
51:30	60
52	13

Ezekiel

11:19–20	99
13	40
13:1	131
20	86
20:28	13
21:26	20 n. 37
34:23	84 n. 18
34:23–30	99 n. 59
36:25–28	99
37:1–28	99 n. 59
38:17	84, 85 n. 19, 134

Daniel

7	40
9:6	84 n. 16, 134
9:10	84 n. 16, 134
9:11	84

Hosea

1–3	185
1:1	181
1:1–2	159 n. 39
1:4	180, 181, 182
2	98
2:15	96
2:18–22	99
2:21–22	99
3:5	99 n. 59
4:1–19	159 n. 39
4:12	19 n. 34
9:9–10	96
10:9	96
12:14	96, 129
14:6–9	99
15:8–12	181

Joel

1–2	46

Amos

3–5	159 n. 39
3:7	84 n. 16, 85, 95, 134
9:11–15	99 n. 59

Obadiah

19–21	99

Micah

1	159 n. 39
3:11	131
4:2	101
5:1	99 n. 59
6:4	70 n. 41, 96, 130

Habakkuk

3	44, 46

Zephaniah

3	99

Haggai

1:13	89

Zechariah

1:4	76
1:4–6	95
1:6	83–84, 86 n. 19, 134
7:12–14	95
9:9–10	99 n. 59

Malachi

1:1	89
4:4	70 n. 41, 96–97
4:4–6	130, 142
4:5	92

APOCRYPHAL/DEUTEROCANONICAL BOOKS

Judith

5:3–23	86 n. 24

1 Maccabees
  2:50–68　　　　　　　　86 n. 24

Sirach
  44–49　　　　　　　　　79
  46:13–20　　　　　　　　168 n. 63

New Testament

Acts
  2:30　　　　　　　　　　110

Author Index

Ackerman, James S.   59 nn. 14–15, 201
Adam, Klaus-Peter   184 n. 28, 217
Ahn, John J.   147 n. 1, 213
Albertz, Rainer   86 n. 23, 203
Amit, Yairah   59 n. 15, 62 n. 20, 63, 67 n. 34, 88 n. 28 and 32, 189–93, 197–98, 201, 206
Andersen, Francis I.   181 n. 22, 201
Anderson, G. W.   54 n. 5, 218
Annus, Amar   12 n. 13, 22 n. 44, 209, 214
Augustin, Matthias   123 n. 63, 216
Auld, A. Graeme   52 n. 2, 67 n. 37, 191, 192, 194 n. 25, 201
Avioz, Michael   115 n. 35, 201
Baden, Joel S.   153 n. 21, 201
Barstad, Hans M.   10 nn. 10–11, 12 n. 14, 27 n. 50, 54 n. 4, 55 nn. 7–8, 56 n. 9, 127 n. 70, 179 n. 16, 201, 214
Barton, John   99 n. 60, 202
Beale, Lissa Wray   88 n. 27, 202
Becker, Uwe   66 n. 34, 202
Beentjes, Pancratius   189–91, 193–94, 202
Begg, Christopher   72 n. 43, 202
Bellinger, W. H.   46 n. 17, 202
Bellis, Alice Ogden   117 n. 42, 207
Ben Zvi, Ehud   1, 2 n. 2, 4, 5, 9 n. 5, 10 n. 12, 17 n. 27, 52 n. 1, 68, 71 n. 43, 76 n. 1, 80 n. 7, 81 n. 9, 82 n. 11, 87 nn. 22–23, 88 nn. 27–28, 88 n. 32, 90 n. 34, 91 n. 41, 92 nn. 42–43, 94 n. 49, 98 n. 52 and 54–55, 100 nn. 58 and 60, 126 nn. 69 and 71, 139 n. 15, 148 n. 5, 156 n. 31, 179 n. 16, 186 n. 31, 188 n. 4, 202–03, 206, 210, 211, 215, 218, 222
Ben-Dov, Jonathan   120 n. 59, 203
Bergen, Wesley J.   174 n. 9, 204
Berger, Peter L.   119 n. 57, 204
Berthelot, Katell   125 n. 66, 211
Blacker, Carmen   21 n. 42, 217
Blenkinsopp, Joseph   8 n. 5, 127 n. 75, 133 n. 7, 161 n. 45, 164 n. 52, 204
Blum, Erhard   141 n. 19, 143, 204
Boda, Mark J.   6 n. 7, 88 n. 27, 202, 204
Boden, John   154 n. 24, 212
Bodner, Keith   155 n. 27, 204
Bœspflug, F.   114 n. 34, 208
Bogaert, Pieere-Maurice   139 n. 16, 217
Boling, Robert G.   59 n. 16, 61 n. 20, 204
Bonnet, Corinne   119 n. 56, 204
Booker, Christopher   171 n. 5, 204
Brenner, Athalya   81 n. 9, 203
Breytenbach, Andries   90 n. 35, 204
Bronner, Leah L.   47 n. 20, 204
Bunnens, Guy   118 n. 52, 204
Buss, Martin J.   8 n. 2, 204
Campbell, Antony F.   169 n. 1, 176 n. 12, 178, 184 n. 28, 185 n. 29, 205
Carstens, Pernille   144 n. 27, 218
Carter, Charles E.   124 n. 66, 211
Chapman, Stephen B.   179 n. 18, 205
Charpin, Dominique   104 n. 3, 117 n. 43, 125 n. 69, 205, 206, 219
Charvát, Petr   114 n. 31, 219
Clements, Ronald E.   21 n. 40, 209
Conrad, Edgar W.   67 n. 37, 205
Cook, Stephen L.   147 n. 1, 213
Coote, Robert B.   177 n. 13, 209
Crenshaw, James L.   177 n. 14, 210
Cross, Frank M.   151 n. 13, 153 n. 21, 155 n. 28, 160 n. 43, 205

-238-

AUTHOR INDEX

Cryer, Frederick H. 10 n. 10, 21 n. 40, 24 n. 49, 46 n. 15, 205
Davies, T. Witton 24 n. 46, 205
Day, John 100 n. 57, 119 n. 58, 189 n. 5, 194, 198 n. 42, 210, 214, 223
De Troyer, Kristin 11 n. 13, 214
Dietrich, M. 10 n. 10, 215
Dietrich, Walter 70 n. 41, 103 n. 1, 121 n. 60, 127 n. 71, 141 n. 18, 152 n. 17, 205, 209
Dozeman, Thomas, B. 52 n. 2, 143 n. 24, 205, 207, 212
Duhm, Bernhard 8 n. 2, 136 n. 12, 205
Duke, William H., Jr. 139 n. 16, 205
Dumbrell, William J. 175 n. 10, 206
Dunand, F. 114 n. 34, 208
Durand, Jean-Marie 104 n. 3, 106 n. 13, 117 n. 43, 118 nn. 50–51, 125 n. 69, 131 n. 3, 206, 218, 219
Dutcher-Walls, Patricia 72 n. 45, 206
Edelman, Diana 1, 3–5, 17 n. 27, 52 n. 1, 62 n. 20, 66 n. 33, 71 n. 43, 76 n. 1, 139 n. 15, 202, 206, 210, 218, 221
Eidinow, Esther 108 n. 15, 206
Ellis, Maria deJong 114 n. 33, 206
Emerton, J. A. 60 n. 19, 213, 218
Eslinger, Lyle 159 n. 41, 2–6
Evans, Craig A. 89 n. 33, 160 n. 42, 209, 217
Fabry, Heinz-Josef 21 n. 40, 212
Fischer, Georg 136 n. 12, 206
Fishbane, Michael 170, 194, 206
Fleming, Daniel E. 116 n. 42, 206
Flint, Peter W. 110 n. 22, 207
Floyd, Michael H. 2 n. 2, 10 n. 12, 87 n. 28, 126 n. 69, 201, 203, 215, 222
Flower, Michael Attyah 110 n. 20, 207
Fohrer, Georg 23 n. 46, 36 n. 2, 207
Foley, John Miles 188 n. 3, 207
Foresti, Fabrizio 133 n. 7, 207
Freedman, David Noel 161 n. 45, 181 n. 22, 201, 223
Frolov, Serge 121 n. 60, 207
Geoghegan, Jeffrey C. 148 n. 5, 167 n. 60, 207

Gerleman, Gillis 9 n. 6, 21 n. 42, 207
Gertz, Jan Christian 126 n. 72, 127 n. 74, 143 n. 24, 207
Gnuse, Robert K. 152 nn. 14–15, 157 n. 35, 158 n. 36, 159, 207
Goffman, Erving 18 n. 29, 207
Gordon, Robert P. 126 n. 70, 214
Gosse, Bernard 138 n. 13, 207
Grabbe, Lester L. 6 n. 7, 10 n. 9, 36 n. 3, 94 n. 49, 110 n. 23, 117 nn. 42 and 48, 120 n. 59, 121 n. 60, 203, 207–08, 214, 221, 223
Graham, M. Patrick 87 n. 28, 220
Grätz, Sebastian 133 n. 7, 208
Graupner, Axel 133 n. 7, 208
Gray, John 38 n. 5, 208
Gross, W. 71 n. 43, 212
Guichard, Michaël 117 n. 43, 118 nn. 50–51, 206
Guillame, Alfred 23 n. 46, 208
Gunn, David M. 165 n. 54, 208
Haak, Robert D. 87 n. 28, 117 n. 48, 201, 214
Halpern, Baruch 152 n. 12, 165 n. 53, 208
Hamori, Esther J. 106 nn. 10 and 13, 208
Haran, Menahem 156 n. 31, 208
Harvey, John E. 64, 208
Hawkins, John David 119 n. 52, 204
Heintz, Jean-Georges 114 n. 34, 208
Heller, Roy L. 160 n. 42, 162 n. 47, 166 n. 58, 176 n. 11, 179, 208
Henze, Matthias 110 n. 22, 207
Herrmann, Sigfried 8 n. 2, 208
Hill, Scott D. 177 n. 13, 209
Hoffman, Y. 91 n. 40, 216
Hoglund, Kenneth G. 87 n. 28, 220
Holloway, S. W. 112 n. 28, 209
Holzinger, H. 129 n. 1, 209
Hübner, Ulrich 117 n. 45, 214
Hunger, Hermann 104 n. 4, 209
Hutton, Jeremy M. 149 n. 7, 150 n. 11, 152 nn. 17–19, 153 n. 21, 156 n. 29, 158 n. 33, 165 nn. 54 and 56, 166 nn. 57 and 59, 167 nn. 60 and 62, 201, 209

Jacquet, Antoine 131 n. 3, 218
Japhet, Sara 149 n. 8, 168 n. 63, 184 n. 27, 209
Jean, Cynthia 22 n. 44, 209
Jeffers, Ann 10 n. 10, 24 n. 49, 27 n. 53, 209
Jenni, Ernst ix
Jeppesen, Knut 56 n. 9, 209
Jeremias, J. 71 n. 43, 133 n. 7, 139 n. 16, 210
Joannès, Francis 104 n. 3, 205
Johnston, Sarah Iles 108 n. 15, 209
Jones, Gwilym H. 21 n. 40, 209
Jong, Matthijs de 112 n. 28, 114 n. 31, 117 n. 48, 210
Keinänen, Jyrki 127 n. 73, 210
Kelle, Brad E. 8 n. 2, 204
Kittel, Rudolph 8 n. 4, 210
Klein, Lilian R. 63, 210
Knauf, Ernst Axel 52 n. 2, 53 n. 3, 70–71, 117 n. 45, 134 n. 10, 210, 214
Knobloch, Harald 135 n. 7, 210
Knoppers, Gary N. 72 n. 45, 81 n. 9, 86 n. 23, 189–99, 202, 203, 210
Koch, Klaus 71 n. 43, 177 n. 14, 210
Köckert, Matthias 111 n. 27, 127 n. 73, 133 n. 7, 144 n. 26, 210–11, 214
Kottsieper, I. 76 n. 1, 203
Kratz, Reinhard G. 10 n. 11, 71 n. 44, 72 n. 45, 73 n. 47, 126 n. 72, 128 n. 77, 133 n. 7, 211, 214
Kupitz, Yaakov 124 n. 66, 211
Lackenbacher, Sylvie 104 n. 3, 205
Lafont, Bertrand 104 n. 3, 205
Lamb, David T. 180 n. 19, 181 n. 22, 211
Lange, Armin 12 n. 13, 214
Lehnart, Bernhard 127 n. 73, 141 n. 20, 142 n. 23, 172 n. 6, 179 n. 15, 211
Lehnert, W.G. 19 n. 29, 211
Leick, Gwendolyn 126 n. 70, 205
Leirens, Isabelle 204
Lemaire, André 22 n. 45, 80 n. 7, 143 n. 26, 202, 203, 210, 214
Lemche, Niels 144 n. 27, 218
Leuchter, Mark 4, 5, 150 n. 9, 152 n. 16, 153 n. 21, 154 nn. 24 and 26, 156 n. 31, 162 n. 47, 163 nn. 48 and 50, 164 n. 53, 167 n. 61, 185 n. 28, 201, 211, 217
Levenson, Jon D. 40, 47 n. 19, 151 n. 12, 208, 211
Levin, Christoph 88 n. 30, 143 n. 25, 211–12
Levine, Baruch 80 n. 7, 202, 203
Levinson, Bernard M. 72 n. 45, 212
Lewis, Theodore J. 27 n. 53, 154 n. 24, 212
Lierman, John 83 n. 10, 90 n. 36, 212
Lindars, Barnabas 59 n. 15, 212
Lion, Brigitte 117 n. 44, 212
Lipschits, Oded 86 n. 23, 203
Loewe, Michael 21 n. 42, 217
Loewenstamm, Samuel 141 n. 21, 212
Lohfink, Norbert 71 n. 43, 212
Long, Burke O. 12 n. 17, 21 n. 41, 212
Loretz, O. 10 n. 10, 215
Lübbe, John 66 n. 34, 212
Luckmann, Thomas 119 n. 57, 204
Lundbom, Jack R. 147 n. 1, 212
Macchi, Jean-Daniel 2 n. 3, 52 n. 2, 210, 217, 218
Madl, H. 21 nn. 40 and 42, 212
Maier, Christl 138 n. 15, 212
Malamat, Abraham 10 n. 10, 213
Mayes, A. D. H. 54 n. 6, 65 n. 32, 213
McAlpine, Thomas H. 161 n. 45, 213
McBride, Sean D. 147 n. 1, 213
McCarter, P. Kyle 159 n. 40, 213
McKane, William 9 n. 7, 213
McKeating, Henry 96 n. 51, 213
McKenzie, Stephen L. 12 n. 18, 36 n. 2, 52 n. 2, 70 n. 42, 87 n. 28, 137 n. 13, 142, 201, 213, 220
Meeks, Wayne A. 90 n. 36, 213
Melville, Sarah C. 115 n. 36, 213
Mendelsohn, I. 163 n. 50, 213
Metzing, D. 18 n. 29, 211
Meyers, Carol 163 n. 49, 213
Moor, Johannes C. de 57 n. 10, 72 n. 43, 91 n. 35, 125 n. 66, 127 n.

AUTHOR INDEX

71, 189 n. 5, 202, 204, 213, 215, 220, 221
Moore, Megan Bishop 8 n. 2, 204
Moran, William L. 10 n. 10, 213
Murray, Donald F. 60 n. 19, 213
Nelson, Richard D. 13 n. 16, 117 n. 43, 213
Neumann, P. H. A. 8 n. 2, 213
Nickelsburg, George W. E., Jr. 141 n. 21, 212
Nicklas, Tobias 121 n. 60, 205
Niditch, Susan 60, 66 n. 34, 213
Niemann, Hermann Michael 123 n. 63, 216
Nihan, Christophe 54, 55 nn. 7 and 8, 70 n. 41, 133 n. 7, 134 n. 7, 213
Nissinen, Martti 1 n. 2, 2 n. 2, 3–6, 10 nn. 10 and 11, 11, 22 n. 45, 32, 36 n. 3, 104 n. 5, 110 n. 23, 111 n. 27, 112 n. 28, 114 n. 31, 117 nn. 43 and 45 and 48, 120 n. 59, 121 n. 60, 124 n. 66, 126 n. 70, 194–95, 198, 202, 203, 207, 208, 211, 214–15, 221, 223
Nocquet, Dany 142 n. 23, 215
Noll, Kurt L. 117 n. 43, 134 n. 10, 214, 215
Noort, Eduard 10 n. 10, 24 n. 49, 56 n. 10, 215
Noth, Martin 2, 53, 66 n. 34, 71, 215
O'Brien, Mark A. 6, 12 n. 16, 66 n. 35, 169 n. 1, 177 n. 12, 184 n. 28, 185 n. 29, 205, 216
O'Connell, Robert H. 60 nn. 17 and 19, 215
Oeming, Manfred 127 n. 73, 210
Olyan, Saul M. 154 n. 24, 165 n. 55, 212, 215
Oswald, Wolfgang 109 n. 17, 122 n. 63, 124 n. 65, 215–16
Otto, Eckart 132 n. 6, 216
Otto, Susanne 70 n. 42, 127 n. 73, 142 nn. 22–23, 172 n. 6, 173 n. 7, 174 n. 9, 216
Overholt, Thomas W. 10 n. 9, 216
Pakkala, Juha 11 n. 14, 202

Parpola, Simo 104 n. 4, 114 n. 31, 117 n. 48, 119 n. 57, 128 n. 76, 216
Pecha, Lucáš 114 n. 31, 219
Perlitt, Lothar 71 n. 43, 211
Person, Raymond F., Jr. 2 n. 3, 4, 6, 53 n. 2, 73 n. 47, 148 n. 5, 187 n. 1, 188 n. 2, 190 nn. 13–14, 194 n. 29, 195 n. 32, 216, 220
Petersen, David L. 9 n. 9, 24 n. 49, 45 n. 16, 216
Polak, Frank H. 81 n. 9, 91 n. 40, 203, 216
Polzin, Robert 65 n. 31, 216
Pongratz-Leisten, Beate 108 n. 18, 122 n. 62, 216–17
Porter, J.R. 21 n. 42, 217
Porter, Stanley E. 89 n. 33, 209
Pritchard, James B. vii
Pruin, Dagmar 127 n. 73, 217
Pury, Albert de 2 n. 3, 52 n. 2, 143 n. 24, 210, 217, 218
Putsch, Michael 184 n. 28, 217
Raabe, Paul R. 99 n. 60, 217
Rad, Gerhard von 12 n. 16, 21 n. 40, 88 n. 28, 140 n. 18,
Raventós, Xavier Dupré 119 n. 56, 204
Renaud, Bernard 139 n. 16, 217
Rendtorff, Rolf 160 n. 42, 217
Renkema, Johan 99 n. 60, 217
Reventlow, H.G. 91 n. 40, 216
Rezetko, Robert 149 n. 5, 216
Ribichini, Sergio 119 n. 56, 204
Richter, Wolfgang 64 n. 29, 66 n. 34, 217
Riesener, Ingrid 134 n. 9, 218
Ristau, Kenneth A. 81 n. 9, 202
Ritner, Robert K. 10 n. 10, 215
Rofé, Alexander 12 n. 18, 54 n. 5, 70 n. 42, 142 n. 19, 174 n. 9, 218
Rogerson John W. 8 n. 2, 218
Römer, Thomas 1, 2 n. 3, 4, 5, 52 n. 2, 54 nn. 4–5, 55 nn. 6–7, 66 n. 33, 71 n. 42, 72 nn. 45–46, 118 n. 50, 126 nn. 71–72, 131 nn. 3–4, 137 n. 13, 140 n. 15, 143 nn. 24 and 27, 148 n. 5, 164 n. 52, 191 n. 15, 201, 205, 206, 210, 217, 218

Roncace, Mark   97 n. 51, 174 n. 9, 219
Rooy, H. F. van   57 n. 10, 71 n. 43, 90 n. 35, 126 n. 71, 204, 213, 215, 221
Roukema, Riemer   143 n. 25, 222
Rudnig, Thilo Alexander   123 n. 63, 219
Ruprecht, Eberhard   9 n. 6, 21 n. 42, 207
Rüterswörden, Udo   133 n. 7, 219
Šašková, Katerina   114 n. 31, 115 n. 36, 219
Sasson, Jack M.   125 n. 69, 219
Savran, George W.   157 n. 34, 159 n. 41, 219
Schearing, Linda S.   52 n. 2, 201
Schäfer-Lichtenberger, Christa   133 n. 7, 219
Schaper, Joachim   150 n. 11, 219
Schloen, David   152 n. 17, 209
Schmid, Konrad   52 n. 2, 54 n. 2, 127 n. 73, 135 n. 11, 138 n. 15, 143 n. 24, 205, 207, 210, 212, 217, 219
Schmidt, Brian B.   27 n. 53, 219
Schmidt, Werner H.   139 n. 16, 220
Schmitt, R.   76 n. 1, 203
Schneider, Tammi J.   57 n. 13, 63 n. 25, 220
Schniedewind, William M.   87 n. 28, 189, 194 n. 28, 195 n. 33, 196–98, 220
Schramm, Brooks   117 n. 43, 214
Schulte, Lucas L.   11 n. 13, 214
Seitz, Christopher R.   96 n. 51, 140 n. 17, 220
Seow, Choon-Leong   10 n. 10, 158, 161, 215, 220
Sharp, Carolyn J.   139 n. 16, 140 n. 17, 220
Shields, Mary E.   174 n. 9, 220
Smend, Rudolph   70 n. 40, 220
Soggin, J. Alberto   59 n. 14, 64 n. 29, 220
Spieckermann, Hermann   133 n. 7, 211
Spronk, Klaas   124 n. 66, 220
Stager, Lawrence E.   152 n. 17, 153 nn. 20 and 23, 156 n. 30, 221
Steuernagel, Carl   133 n. 7, 220
Svärd, Saana   115 n. 36, 117 n. 46, 220
Sweeney, Marvin A.   1, 3–4, 9 n. 5, 35 n. 1, 36 n. 3, 38 n. 4, 39 nn. 9–10, 41 n. 12, 43 n. 13, 44 n. 14, 46 n. 18, 121 n. 60, 182–83, 203, 220–21
Talmon, Shemaryahu   160 n. 42, 217
Tengström, Sven   54 n. 5, 55 n. 6, 56 n. 9, 221
Terblanche, Marius D.   71 n. 43, 221
Thelle, Rannfrid I.   1 n. 1, 3, 5, 14 n. 21, 17 n. 27, 18 n. 30, 20 n. 35, 31 n. 57, 105 n. 7, 221
Tigay, Jeffrey H.   170 n. 2, 221
Toorn, Karel van der   27 n. 53, 125 n. 69, 153 n. 20, 156 n. 30, 163, 164 n. 51, 168 n. 64, 221
Trebolle, Julio C.   89 n. 33, 190 n. 14, 221
Uffenheimer, B.   91 n. 40, 216
Van Seters, John   12 n. 18, 66 n. 34, 143 n. 25, 222
Van Staalduine-Sulman, Eveline   88 n. 31, 222
Vawter, Bruce   67 n. 37, 222
Veijola, Timo   11 n. 14, 105 n. 8, 222
Verheyden, Joseph   121 n. 60, 205
Vervenne, M.   83 n. 15, 222
Vondergeest, Craig   23 n. 46, 222
Wagenaar, Jan   83 n. 15, 222
Wagner, S.   21 n. 42, 222
Walsh, Jerome T.   92 n. 45, 222
Walters, Stanley D.   88 n. 31, 222
Walton, John H.   111 n. 26, 222
Watts, James W.   88 n. 31, 222
Webb, Barry G.   63 n. 25, 222
Westermann, Claus   ix, 9, 21 nn. 41–42, 23 n. 47, 52 n. 2, 223
Wildberger, Hans   122 n. 61, 222
Williamson, H. G. M.   99 n. 57, 119 n. 58, 223
Wilson, Robert R.   9 n. 9, 24 n. 49, 148 n. 4, 223
Wöhrle, J.   76 n. 1, 203
Wolff, H. W.   70 n. 40, 220
Wolter, Michael   133 n. 7, 2–8
Wright, Peter Matthews   110 n. 23, 223

Würthwein, Ernst	52 n. 2, 223
Wyrick, Steven von	161 n. 45, 223
Yee, Gale A.	66 nn. 33–34, 223
Young, Ian M.	165 n. 54, 223
Zamfir, Korinna	121 n. 60, 206
Zerubavel, Eviatar	79 n. 6, 223
Zwickel, Wolfgang	139 n. 16, 220

www.ingramcontent.com/pod-product-compliance
Lightning Source LLC
Chambersburg PA
CBHW030340240426
43661CB00052B/1699